It's Only
a Movie!

It's Only a Movie!

Films and Critics
in
American Culture

RAYMOND J. HABERSKI JR.

THE UNIVERSITY PRESS OF KENTUCKY

Publication of this volume was made possible in part
by a grant from the National Endowment for the Humanities.

Scholarly publisher for the Commonwealth,
serving Bellarmine University, Berea College, Centre
College of Kentucky, Eastern Kentucky University,
The Filson Club Historical Society, Georgetown College,
Kentucky Historical Society, Kentucky State University,
Morehead State University, Murray State University,
Northern Kentucky University, Transylvania University,
University of Kentucky, University of Louisville,
and Western Kentucky University.

Editorial and Sales Offices: The University Press of Kentucky
663 South Limestone Street, Lexington, Kentucky 40508-4008

05 04 03 02 01   5 4 3 2 1

Library of Congress Cataloging-in-Publication Data

Haberski, Raymond J., 1968-
    It's only a movie! : films and critics in American culture / Raymond
J. Haberski, Jr.
        p. cm.
Includes bibliographical references and index.
    ISBN 0-8131-2193-0
1. Film criticism—United States. 2. Motion pictures—social
aspects—United States. I. Title.
    PN1995 .H213 2001
    791.43'01'50973—dc21   00-012092

*This book
is dedicated with
love and gratitude
to my family.*

Contents

Acknowledgments

I borrowed the title for this book from an essay by Pauline Kael, whose style has inspired many imitators. I have also used Phillip Lopate's catchy phrase, "the heroic age of moviegoing," to introduce a time that both Lopate and Kael might agree was indeed heroic—perhaps the only thing they would agree on.

I found working on this book a pleasure mostly because of the people I had a chance to meet. Those who staff the Van Pelt Library at the University of Pennsylvania, the Chicago Historical Society's Library, Chicago's Public Library, and the New York Public Library were more than helpful and pleasant. The curators at New York's Museum of Modern Art's Film Study Center provided access to and personal assistance with the wide range of documents relating to the early years of MoMA's film preservation and distribution programs. Janet Jackson and Judith Johnson at Lincoln Center made my experience in the center's archives a satisfying and enjoyable one. Moreover, I thank the Lincoln Center for the Performing Arts, Inc., for allowing me to quote from oral histories housed in its archives.

I am also grateful to Joanne Koch who took time out of her busy schedule preparing the New York Film Festival to talk about her involvement in the city's movie scene in the 1950s and 1960s. Amos Vogel and his wife, Marcia, shared with me precious recollections of the early years of the film festival and were nice enough to do so in their home. I am especially appreciative of their hospitality.

Danny Green and Rosemary Adams, editors at *Chicago History*, gave generously of their time while working with me on an article for that journal. It appears in a different form in this book.

My new home at Marian College in Indianapolis has been the realization of a great many hopes. I thank, in particular, James Divita for his faith in my abilities as a historian.

Over the last few years I have had the good fortune to work with people who are both good scholars and teachers. Ohio University's Contemporary History Institute remains one of the best-kept secrets in academia. It was a second home for many of us who thrived on the intellectual comradeship that existed within Brown House. Instrumental to creating that atmosphere have been John Gaddis, Alonzo Hamby, Chester Pach, Steven Miner, Jeffrey Herf, and, administrative assistant extraordinaire, Kara Dunfee. Likewise, the history department, of which the institute is a part, gave me unlimited encouragement and opportunity. I was lucky enough to work with chair Bruce Steiner, and professors Katherine Jellison, Alan Booth, Lyle McGeoch, and Sam Crowl.

Three individuals deserve special mention. In my first graduate seminar in history, Kevin Shanley inspired me to pursue a life in teaching. I am grateful to him for his undying enthusiasm. David Steigerwald at Ohio State University went well above and beyond professional courtesy when he looked over earlier drafts on this work. He has been a true comrade-in-ideas. And Charles Alexander at Ohio University has served as a model of what a practicing historian should be. Charlie not only sharpened every aspect of this work, from the writing to the arguments, he also reminded me that we write to be understood not simply footnoted. While those people mentioned above have helped me get into this game, I am responsible for any mistakes in the work that follows.

My final word of thanks goes out to my friends and family. Jeff and Andrea Woods, Marc O'Reilly, Blair Foster, Jeff Coker, Steve Remy, and especially Bonnie Hagerman and Marc Selverstone helped make Athens, Ohio a home for me. I will always be grateful to them for their friendship and confidence. Jane Balbo helped put into perspective the many long hours of work on this book by removing me from my chair and my mindset. I am thankful she was there. Bob and Claudia Klein offered their home in New York City to me as they have their friendship with my family, unconditionally. My grandparents, uncles, aunts, and cousins entertained my musings with good humor and even better advice. My family, however, I thank most of all not only for making it possible for me to pursue a career in history but for being genuinely happy that I did.

Introduction

Recently something remarkable has happened to a number of America's foremost movie critics: they are in near unanimous agreement. They all believe that the movies are in a state of crisis. Not a financial crisis, but, more shockingly, a spiritual crisis. Among the leading exponents of this view are Susan Sontag, Richard Schickel, David Denby, Stanley Kauffmann, and Roger Ebert. Each has weighed in with print pieces lamenting the "decay of cinema," "the death of cinephilia," the loss of "film culture," and, in general, the waning power of critics to inspire moviegoers. The reasons these critics are concerned about the state of moviegoing and why we should care strikes at the heart of a much broader and more significant cultural malaise—the decline of cultural authority.

To understand this nearly universal lament one must remember that a little over thirty years ago these critics fell in love with movies. During the 1960s and early 1970s a movie culture took shape around universities, coffee houses, and art theaters showing foreign films. Out of endless conversations about directors and sleepless nights arguing over the latest landmark (probably foreign) film, thousands (perhaps millions) of young people contracted "cinephilia," or as Susan Sontag explains, "The love that cinema inspired." In an impassioned article for the *New York Times,* she describes this affection as "born of the conviction that cinema was an art unlike any other: quintessentially modern; distinctively accessible; poetic and mysterious and erotic and moral—all at the same time. Cinema had apostles. (It was like a religion.) Cinema was a crusade. For cinephiles, the movies encapsulated everything. Cinema was both the book of art and the book of life." In the 1960s, Sontag had developed into a very influential cultural critic because she argued that a new approach, or a "New Sensibility," was required to understand and appreciate the various dimensions of American culture. Her criticism helped rationalize the attraction that mass culture—especially movies—

had for the younger generation. Yet as Richard Schickel notes, a cinephile was a strange creature: One felt part of "a democratically self-elected elite that was in some way reshaping the culture." However, since this was the era, in Stanley Kauffmann's words, of "The Film Generation," it was possible, as David Denby suggests, for "a variety of film cultists [to turn] their obsessions into a way of life."[1]

The younger generation of the 1960s followed movies as a religion, and their chosen catechism was foreign films, primarily from France and Italy. In a piece of hyperbole, Sontag contends that "for some 15 years there were new masterpieces every month." Schickel believes that when "the intellectual balance in this country swung decisively toward the foreign film . . . it was good for foreign producers' bank accounts but even better for our souls." Schickel, a movie critic for *Life* magazine during the 1960s, describes the era as a renaissance during which the participants were acutely aware of their good fortune and unabashedly ready to talk about it. It was also an era during which the movie director came out from behind the producer and studio bosses to share top billing on marquees and in newspapers with actors.[2]

Movie critics benefited tremendously from this heightened interest in film. For the first time in American history they were respected as intellectuals. And why not? Millions of moviegoers followed them as priests who passed judgment on movies, directors, and filmmaking styles. They issued cinematic doctrine. So, not only did moviegoers have a passion for cinema, they were also passionate about what others, especially critics, said about the movies. And when movies mattered to the public, then the critics, too, seemed to matter. For a brief period both the images on the screen and the words on the printed page converged in a union of fanaticism about the movies. The assumption was that while moviegoers remained engaged with the screen, both the critics and cinema got better. It was an era of heroic progress.

So what happened? Here, too, many critics are in agreement. Since the mid-1970s a number of economic and cultural forces have joined to deflate cinephilia. First, movies became crassly commercial with every studio looking to produce the next blockbuster. Second, distribution policies changed with fewer companies willing to take chances on long shots, which meant most foreign filmmakers had slim hopes of an American run. Third, a general waning of interest among the most recent generation of moviegoers replaced the faith of their parents with a sense of apathy. Who could blame these young people, though, when everything seems like a product and nothing is authentic.

Thus, the meaning of movies has changed. The perception that they are a vital art is dead—movies no longer stand apart from that mass culture made for faceless people who are moved as much by a commercial as by a movie. As Denby explains, "Film has not died, but that ornery exasperating thing film culture has been seriously weakened. Taste as a specialized inside affair ('we' versus the eternal, undifferentiated 'them') has largely disappeared, and, as a result, moviegoing has lost its wickedness, its humor, a good part of its savor." Movies are no worse than they use to be—and there are still good movies to see—but a cynicism has seeped into and corrupted the *art* of moviegoing.[3]

Surprisingly, the critic who did the most in the 1960s to stimulate cinephilia in the United States has offered an autopsy of its death that is contrary to his fellow cinephiles. Andrew Sarris rose to great fame as the critic whose translations of a French film theory known as the "auteur theory" launched thousands of arguments over directors. In his self-effacing manner, Sarris attributes his success to saying the right things, *in the right way,* at the right time. In the early 1960s, when he championed French criticism, French critics had become directors of the New Wave, and "the English-speaking world was primed for a surge of Francophilia." For nearly the entire decade of the 1960s, every new movie out of France was seen as a major cultural event by cosmopolitan cliques around the United States—"localities," Sarris relates, "where [Alain] Resnais's *Last Year in Marienbad* could play to audiences who could pretend to understand it."[4]

When Sarris addresses the demise of foreign films, however, he does not point to the commercialization of movies but to the Europeanization of Hollywood. "No one on either side of the Atlantic—or Pacific—wants to admit it today," he suggests, "but the fashion for foreign films depended a great deal on their frankness about sex." Once Hollywood caught up and incorporated the European style, the lure of the art house vanished. Foreign films mattered because they promised glimpses into forbidden worlds. Once Hollywood abandoned traditional restraint, its superior production techniques and marketing buried foreign competition.

Nevertheless, this explanation fails to address the rise and fall of critics. Why were they so important and why are they currently so impotent? Here, Sarris is an instructive example: He made a career by intellectualizing and convincing audiences that movies were art and filmmakers were artists. But he was also preaching to an audience that already accepted film as perhaps the most important art of its time. Moviegoing came to seem heroic because it was part of a larger movement in American culture to redefine what art meant and the role movies played in American life. A sense of excitement and immediacy and even rebellion pervaded this love of movies primarily because movies challenged orthodox views on entertainment and art. The reason critics were important and spoke with authority, therefore, was because the idea of art still had relevance among the general public.

The notion of art as an idea that could be debated hit a wall in the mid-1960s. In 1985, art historian Arthur Danto famously declared an end to art. He did not believe that art had vanished. He argued that the rise of Andy Warhol and Pop had signified the dawning of the postmodern world and with it the erosion of the authority of critics. Within a decade of Warhol's soup cans, Danto explains, "you could no longer teach the meaning of art by example. It meant that as far as appearances were concerned, anything could be a work of art, and it meant that if you were going to find out what art was, you had to turn from sense experience to thought." Gone were the days when critics made declarations about how works of art must look. Critics grew increasingly incapable of discussing art in terms of boundaries, for art as a fact no longer existed—it remained only a philosophical concept, an illusion. "The true philosophical discovery," Danto suggests, "is that there is no one way art has to be: all art is equally and indifferently art. . . . Needless to say, this leaves the options of criticism open. It does not entail that all art is equal and indifferently good. It just means that goodness and badness are not matters of belonging to the right style, or falling under the right manifesto."[5] Yet an important reason for art's relevance to the public has been that critics staked claims on what was and was not art. Without grounds for such debate, there is no unifying theme joining the public, artists, and critics. Focus shifted from critics and aesthetics to theorists and theories or, worse, to politicians and public funding.

As the contentiousness of the debate over art faded, so did the vitality of the debate over movies as art. While it had once been mildly rebellious to champion movies—mass culture—as a significant cultural expression, the end of art killed that rebellion. When older cultural standards fell, the conquerors were left with little to revolt against.

Recently, widely read—and even more widely watched—film critic Roger Ebert attempted to revive the debate over movies by suggesting that they deserved Pulitzer Prize consideration. Ebert spoke of film as a "snubbed art." "Americans scarcely read a book a year, don't have the opportunity to see theater, and do not often attend serious music. People *do* go to the movies," Ebert reasoned, "[they] reach almost everywhere. No other art form mobilizes a national discussion in such a big way." While this is all true, Ebert's appeal to the idea of art fell flat mostly because a public debate over art no longer exists. Yes, one can hear name-calling over a new Mapplethorpe installation, but such arguments are a far cry from the popular discussions generated by movies. As Ebert admits, "An art form will forever be in a separate category if you can attend it while eating Twizzlers."[6]

Yet that is exactly why movies are so interesting: They challenge both critics and moviegoers to question what movies mean in American culture. But they can play such a role only if the idea of art seems relevant to the public. Indeed, affixing the label of art to movies has, judging by recent responses from some filmmakers, become a curse more than a challenge. At a symposium in 1988 sponsored by New York University's Tisch School of the Arts, a group of film students and filmmakers divided when it sought to answer the question: "Has cinema fulfilled its promise as the art of the twentieth century?" While the students could confidently analyze this question using academic theories gleaned from courses in film studies, Sidney Lumet, an accomplished director, snapped: "I call them movies. I won't even use the word film, I'm in such protest against it. And the word cinema won't pass my throat." He and other directors, including Arthur Penn, Martin Scorcese, and Chinese director Chen Kaige, surprised the younger generation by revealing their uneasiness with the title of "serious artist." Lumet lamented that "Someone decided to lay a curse on us and said, 'Here's the art form of the twentieth century; do something with it.'"[7]

The irony here lies not so much in the directors' uneasiness with the title of artist, but in the unfortunate position movies assume in American society. It seems we either accept movies as an art worthy of esoteric analysis or we consider them little more than products worth the price of a ticket. The audience has begun to divide between those who look at "films" (rather than movies) through the lens of theory, and those who attend movies to have fun. What has been lost in the transition of movies into art is that middle ground where art mixed with entertainment, where the boundaries seemed crossed but not erased. The cultural battleground where the forces of rebellion rallied against the stalwarts of tradition was an exciting place—something that interested those outside the battle as well as those fighting it. Since the beginning of the century, however, this battle has slowly been won (and lost) by the rebels.

We thus are left with a split audience watching a stale screen. One side of the audience speaks almost exclusively among itself in an intellectual dialect that seems deliberately obscure. The other side of the audience does not talk all that much, it only watches the screen hoping to get its money's worth. Conversation across the center aisle has dwindled to nothing—and with it the ageless, popular debate over the cultural significance of the movies.

The audience that once loved movies witnessed cinephilia die of an unhealthy diet: the force-feeding of cinematic ideology ended up ruining moviegoers' appetites for the cinema. People do accept movies as art, but no one cares about that distinction anymore. The twin engines of modernism—one driving art into ever more abstract and purer forms, and the other driving criticism to be more inclusive of popular forms, including those mass produced—ultimately elevated movies to art but undermined the debate that fueled that transition.

We should be concerned about the demise of cinephilia because, as many contemporary movie critics suggest, our culture seems more cynical because of it. Not incidentally, the end of art coincided with (and in a way was caused by) the intellectualization of movies. With the polarization of the debate over movies there is really no other topic to join both the experts and the rest of us in a broad-based discussion about culture. We should therefore lament the fading of Sontag's cinephilia, not because it was a sustainable affair, but because it inspired an engagement with a subject dear to so many of us. We have lost the will to debate the meaning of movies in an era that demands such discussion.

It is currently in vogue to condemn as antidemocratic the assumption that art and entertainment occupy different rungs on the cultural ladder. At the forefront of this deconstruction is historian Lawrence Levine, who persuasively argues that Americans have lived for most of the twentieth century with cultural distinctions ill suited to their era. In the latter half of the nineteenth century, an economic elite looking to solidify its position in society "removed" certain aspects of culture—such as Shakespeare's dramas, Italian and German opera, and orchestral music—from public life. This elite evidently convinced a large portion of the population that only those with specialized knowledge could truly understand high art. As a result, Levine argues, Americans have come to accept a false dichotomy: highbrow versus lowbrow culture.[8]

And yet, as artificial as these categories might seem—and they do have more legitimacy than Levine suggests—the fact that cultural distinctions existed served to inspire debates over those cultural expressions, such as movies, that occupy ambiguous positions on the cultural scale. In place of variegated culture, America seems awash in what cultural critic Dwight Macdonald called "Masscult"—a mixing of high and low culture that corrupts the integrity of both.[9] Moreover, without cultural authority against which to rebel, critics end up preaching either to the converted or to the deaf. The democratization of criticism has, ironically, undermined the national conversation over the meaning of culture in a democracy.[10]

I would like to see the cultivation of a middle ground between art and entertainment but I do not want my art as entertainment or my entertainment as art. I want something more complex, ambiguous, and vexing—something worth thought. Something that should exist in a democratic culture—a place where rules are recognized without being tyrannical, where the direction, temper, and conclusions of a conversation exist because of—rather than in spite of—those basic rules. The parameters of such a culture can coexist with the free exchange of ideas if we agree that we would prefer debate to consensus or apathy.

One only has to look at the career of Oliver Stone to realize what is missing in contemporary movie criticism and American culture. Stone is a child of the 1960s: He volunteered to fight in Vietnam, returned from the war, and enrolled in New York University's film school as an outlet for his creative energy. There he studied with Martin Scorcese, among others, and developed into an academy-award-winning screenwriter (for *Midnight Express*) and director (*Platoon* and *Born on the Fourth of July*). He is a natural successor to the generation of film school graduates such as Scorcese and Francis Ford Coppola, who embraced movies as art and in turn were embraced by a movie culture as artists. He is also the heir to the dubious legacy of using sex, violence, and vulgarity as a way to sell one's work while defending it as art.

Throughout his successful career, Stone has invoked artistic license and freedom to defend his imaginative but simpleminded dramas. He has also played the victim on a number of occasions when critics—both of Stone's cinematic and historical visions—took serious issue with his films. It is, of course, perfectly acceptable in a world of relativistic values to defend one's creations as inherently legitimate. However, because we do not live in a valueless world, we depend on critics to exercise some cultural authority, to act as buffers with which creators must contend. When called to answer criticism of movies such as *JFK* or *Natural Born Killers*, Stone cries foul. Who is to say what he can and cannot show on the screen or what he can and cannot portray as the truth in a movie? In Stone's world, critics have no more cultural authority than does the audience. If this is a fact of contemporary movie culture (and I think it is), then critics are almost useless.

What follows is a discussion through a series of case studies of the gradual inclusion of movies among the arts and what that development did to the cultural authority of critics. It is an investigation of how the perception of movies changed as the idea of art began to deconstruct and the role of critics became increasingly polarized into the twin camps of academia and irrelevance. The first part of the study looks at the boundaries that prevented movies from being accepted as art. The second part looks at how movies breached those boundaries and the implications that has had for American culture.

1

Amusement or Art?

On an evening in 1915 in Knoxville, Tennessee, a fictional little boy named Rufus took a walk with his father to see a picture show. The details of this short journey open James Agee's extraordinary narrative on loss and living entitled *A Death in the Family*. The novel won the Pulitzer Prize for Agee in 1958, three years after the author's death. The story was also made into a play and, fittingly, a movie.

Agee conveyed in much of his work the nobility of being humble and ordinary. While film scholars today attempt to fit commonplace occurrences into large methodological schemes, Agee brings us closer to the human elements of the past. His description of going to a picture show gives us a sense of the magic many Americans experienced in the early years of moviegoing:

> At supper that night, as many times before, his father said, "Well, spose we go to the picture show."
>
> "Oh, Jay!" his mother said. "That horrid little man!"
>
> "What's wrong with him?" his father asked, not because he didn't know what she would say, but so she would say it.
>
> "He's so *nasty*!" she said, as she always did. "So *vulgar*! With his nasty little cane; hooking up skirts and things, and that nasty little walk!"
>
> They walked downtown in the light of mother-of-pearl, to the Majestic, and found their way to seats by the light of the screen, in the exhilarating smell of stale tobacco, rank sweat, perfume and dirty drawers, while the piano played fast music and galloping horses raised a grandiose flag of dust. And there was William S. Hart with both guns blazing and his long, horse face and his long,

hard lip, and the great country rode away behind him as wide as the world.

Then the screen was filled with a city and with a sidewalk of a side street of a city, a long line of palms and there was Charlie; everyone laughed the minute they saw him squattily walking with his toes out and his knees wide apart, as if he were chaffed; Rufus' father laughed, and Rufus laughed too.[1]

What Rufus and his father entered was another world, the moving picture world. They sat with an audience that by 1915 resembled the millions of people who attended America's picture houses. However, as Rufus's mother said, many found this experience a vulgar thing. The humor of the shows was crass, and the stories were almost always simplistic and dependent on the viewer's fascination with the novelty of the experience. Yet children and adults alike could get lost in the grand vistas of a western, or laugh at the antics of comedians, especially Charlie Chaplin. The power of movies came in various forms. They could inject a dull day with humor or transport a person like Rufus from Knoxville to Death Valley or the jungles of some far-off land. They were the everyman's vacation from reality, and they taxed one's mind about as much as one's budget.

Movies were as young as the century. Collections of movie reviews were still forty years in the future. The first critics to deal with motion pictures groped to make sense of what millions of people seemed to accept instinctively: that movies had changed the world. Most critics believed that motion pictures occupied the uncharted cultural space that lay between fine art and mindless amusement, individual expression and mechanical reproduction. But few were able to establish their new pursuit as a serious intellectual inquiry.[2]

Yet those who attempted to investigate movies began from a simple premise: What was unique about moving pictures? The answer, it seems to me, lies in the magic that James Agee captured in his story. The picture show, unlike any other art form of the day, was popular rather than elitist. The magic of movies lay in their power to redefine how a culture understood art without necessarily making that understanding a conscious act. In a sense, movies challenged the way critics considered art by seeming to be everything that traditional art was not. As psychologist and amateur movie critic Hugo Münsterberg asked in 1916: "How can we teach the spirit of true art by a medium which is in itself the opposite of art? How can we implant the idea of harmony by that which is in itself a parody on art?"[3] Movies constituted a silent but profound rebellion against older cultural standards. Early film criticism contained ominous portents for the future relationship between mass culture and the arts, for while critics helped legitimize movies as art, the cultural authority that provided critics the power to do so began to wane.

The early critics discussed in this chapter argued that movies were unique because they were democratic. Many felt empowered by the notion that they could promote a medium that spoke to the masses rather than one that sought acceptance among traditional art critics. Movies became the art that serious critics dismissed, only to see the popularity of moving pictures threaten the meaning of culture. More than that, though, the critics described here sought to engage movies as part of the mainstream, as a medium that was both an industry and a cultural expression. Their work explored the nebulous properties and ramifications of art that had mass appeal and was mass-produced. For that reason, critics who developed aesthetic theories disconnected from the mainstream or who championed films made for distribution outside commercial theaters receive no mention. It was simply no trick to declare avant-garde films or documentaries works of art. What had the potential to be revolutionary was arguing that mainstream movies were artistically significant.

Many early critics were energized by the prospect of witnessing the birth of a new art—after all, how often was one able to claim such a thing? Movies, many believed, acted as a mirror, reflecting the dominant characteristics of their age—mechanization and democratization. Many commentators viewed movies as a combination of powerful forces. They appealed to people all over the world and could be seen in almost every town in the United States, and so were, in a sense, democratic. Motion pictures were easy to make, distribute, and exhibit and thus became financially valuable. Moreover, masses of people could be swayed by messages embedded in movies that made them seem socially relevant.

To the custodians of traditional culture, the popularity of motion pictures seemed particularly threatening to their authority to define what was good and what was vulgar. Basic concerns surfaced then and have persisted into the present day. Would movies undermine American culture? What were the implications of a democratic art form? Could art be significant even though it was vulgar? Were critics justified in praising movies simply because they served to undermine an older order? Did critics have a responsibility to uphold certain cultural standards against the assault of a new, vital, and vulgar expression? A common thread linked these various questions: Did movies force a reconsideration of the form and function of art?

The critics who addressed such questions did so within an intellectual environment ripe with change and hope. They lived in the Progressive Era—a time in which leaders in almost every field of human endeavor searched for solutions to problems that had plagued generations of Americans. One area of great creativity was the arts. An issue central to the arts at that time was changes in the triangular relationship between the artist, his or her work, and the public. To understand how movies would alter that relationship, we need first to turn to the cultural insurgency that characterized early twentieth century America.

The Modernist Cultural Insurgency and the Question of Art

In the early 1900s, the genteel tradition, the dominant artistic ethic of late-nineteenth-century America, seemed to unravel at an increasing pace as it operated in a highly industrialized and commercialized society. The emergence of mass culture, the dominant cultural description of twentieth-century America, exposed traditional values to competing definitions. The cultural elites who helped shape the genteel tradition collectively believed that a common set of ideals should guide the nation. The leaders of the cultural insurgency dismissed the old guard's worldview as stodgy and oppressive, and considered that the greatest attribute a nation possessed was its diversity of experiences. They contended that nineteenth-century ideals had prevented the United States from cultivating a modern culture. Yet as these "custodians of culture" (as historian Henry May called them) understood all too well, a pluralistic society was rich in ambiguities and hidden dilemmas for the new cultural critics.[4]

The avant-garde comprised one side of the cultural insurgency. Vanguard artists and intellectuals rejected the older generation's belief that art served a higher purpose and that "art must remain recognizable and understandable." They dismissed their obligation "to make [themselves] understood," and could therefore be "preoccupied with technique and idiosyncratic statement." The avant-gardists contributed to culture by rejecting previous standards of taste and form. In doing so, they distanced themselves from both the American elite and the American public. Although the "custodians of culture" looked down upon the people's taste, avant-gardists seemed to delight in creations that not only made a mockery of older values but also were contemptuous of the public's opinions.[5]

Cultural nationalists attacked from another angle by rejecting the old guard's limited vision of culture and championing an artistic renaissance that included every type of expression, from America's finest novels to its newest art form, the "photoplay." They wrote from an intellectual position between gentility and the avant-garde. Although they found both perspectives unduly severe in considerations of artistic form, the cultural nationalists remained closer intellectually to the avant-garde. Seeking to build a new cultural tradition for Americans that would reflect the nation's ethnic diversity, democratic institutions, and popular tastes, the cultural nationalists looked to build upon the ideals of Walt Whitman (their patron saint of democratic art) and apply them to an era of profound artistic, scientific, and commercial development. Yet infused in both sides of the modernist rebellion was a respect for some artistic standards. All cultural expressions were not equal, but they all had the potential to be significant.

For a generation of thinkers who had found gentility stuffy and oppressive, an era of opportunities had opened up. Cultural nationalists offered a way to redefine America's cultural destiny without sacrificing its cultural cohesiveness. For example, the journal *Seven Arts,* with editors James Oppenheim, Waldo Frank, and (for a time) Van Wyck Brooks, hoped to make the arts "not only the expression of national life, but a means of its enhancement."[6] Although part of the general modernist surge in America, this group did not argue, as did many in the avant-garde, for art as an end in itself. They thus made up one side of a modernist dichotomy that defined art as either part of a democratic nationalist pursuit, or as an aesthetic international club. The group wanted to explore a cultural middle ground that existed below the discriminating tastes of the genteel and avant-garde critics, and above the public's relatively simplistic tastes.[7]

Cultural nationalists understood that different tastes would compete against one another to shape artistic ideals. In a democracy, such competition seemed the only way to figure out what social and cultural values would best accommodate a diverse community of citizens. The group of movie critics featured in this chapter wrote from the perspective of cultural nationalism. Although they each had their own intellectual agenda, all hoped that movies would have a positive influence on the public and American culture.[8]

Randolph Bourne was an intellectual whose short life provided insight into the dilemma that faced many early movie critics: He was both enthusiastic and wary of popular taste and mass art. Following a trip to the movies, Bourne concluded that while he felt a "certain unholy glee at [the] wholesale rejection of what our fathers reverenced as culture," he did not "feel any glee about what is substituted for it. . . . We seem to be witnessing a lowbrow snobbery . . . as tyrannical and arrogant as the other culture of universities and millionaires and museums." Bourne proposed finding an alternative to the "stale culture of the masses" and "the stale culture of the aristocrat." "If there is—if there are mood and values in our current life which are at once native and significant—we can scarcely pursue them too avidly or express them too loudly. Such an enterprise of thought would be the democratic thing that the current popularities are emphatically not."[9]

Bourne's intellectual avenue between high art and low culture seemed to permeate the literature on movies that dealt with both their popularity as well as their technical capabilities. His desire for an art form that would both uplift and appeal to the people succinctly reflected the dominant progressive ethos of the day. Those who championed movies consistently pressed for quality over quantity and intelligent stories over sordid tales, for many found popular reaction to such vulgar amusements quite disturbing.

Yet Bourne's evaluation exposed the problem that faced critics who attempted to maintain their discriminating tastes when praising movies. He had uncovered a paradox that still exists within the criticism of popular arts: If one accepted popular taste as a legitimate standard of judgment, did one then dismiss as elitist and narrow-minded a more discriminating view such as Bourne's? The lowbrow snobbery Bourne identified persisted from these early days and may, in the end, have taken its full revenge on cultivated tastes by overwhelming and finally supplanting them. It became increasingly apparent to many cultural critics that championing movies as art broadened the definition of art but opened criticism up to challenges of elitism and stodginess. Maintaining a balance between obscure, inaccessible cultural standards and meaningless criticism would henceforth consistently befuddle movie critics.

Contours of the Debate over Movies

By 1910, motion pictures could claim to be a world of their own. As one of the nation's fastest growing businesses, they excited commentators in ways that resemble contemporary debates over the Internet. Small businessmen realized easy financial gains by setting up multiple projector stands where, for a nickel or a dime, a person could watch a short moving picture of a galloping horse or a man and woman kissing. Later, as moving picture technology advanced, exhibitors could set up screens inside vaudeville theaters to show a series of short movies. Once the industry opened large theaters to accommodate the growing popularity of moving pictures, newspapers around the United States began reporting that millions of Americans—especially recently arrived immigrants—were watching films every day. This prompted concern from a variety of quarters. Drama critics considered the photoplay the worst kind of competition for stage productions because, they argued, movies would always be less expensive to produce and exhibit and always of a lower quality than "legitimate theater." Social scientists and the custodians of culture decried the vulgarity and salaciousness of photoplay material, claiming that movies had provoked a moral crisis among the nation's youth and less educated.[10]

In November 1907, Joseph Medill Patterson contributed a long article to the popular weekly magazine *Saturday Evening Post* on the growth of movies and their worth as cultural experience. Patterson reiterated what many newspapers and other periodicals had been reporting about the rise of the motion picture industry and the type of audience pictures attracted. His particular contribution was noteworthy, though, because of the way he characterized the significance of movies. He noted that in small towns, children, the elderly, and women could be seen flocking regularly to the theaters. In urban areas the audience composition shifted to include a larger percentage of immigrants—primarily non-English-speaking citizens—and people of humble means. Thus the benefits of culture had been passed along to those normally underserved or forgotten by the custodians of culture. "Civilization," he wrote, "has been chiefly the property of the upper classes, but during the past century civilization has been permeating steadily downward." With the introduction of movies, "drama, always a big fact in the lives of the people at the top, is now becoming a big fact in the lives of the people at the bottom."[11] Since the finer arts had become distinctively upper class in the location of theaters and museums, the motion picture seemed a great bridge that would bring culture to the masses through a commercialized art form.

On August 28, 1913, an editorial appeared in the *Nation*, a relatively small but smart political weekly, that contained a note of "unholy glee" for the effect movies had on the consumption of art. The editorial writer suggested that Leo Tolstoy would have approved of the photoplay since it had "a direct and universal appeal to the elementary emotions." Attending a picture show revealed "the common predilection of the popular taste for the lurid and the fantastic." Of course it was "not a very high art, this art of the photo-play," the editorialist noted, since it was "created for the masses and largely by them." Yet that was part of the significance of movies; they were, if nothing else, accessible to the masses. "The technique of the theatre is a subject for professionals and 'highbrows.' But the crowd discusses the technique of the moving picture with as much interest as literary salons in Paris and London discuss the minutiae of the high drama." For this reason, "the number of those thus directly interested in the moving picture plays must be enormous. In a very real sense the photo-play has become a truly popular art." And "like the picture magazine," movies required "no thought and little attention."[12]

Important issues were raised in assessments such as these. Clearly, movies represented the ambiguous possibilities of an emerging mass culture. They were mass-produced and mass consumed. However, although movies catered to popular taste, they were not popular culture. They were democratic in the sense that many people liked to attend picture shows, but movies did not reflect the diversity of American culture because the masses had little real involvement in making them. What many critics found most promising about movies was the reach they had. Millions of people who rarely went to plays, the opera, symphonies, or art museums went to the movies. The motion picture had the ability, therefore, to refine popular taste. It could be used to spread the gospel of truth and beauty more effectively than any other cultural experience. The question then became: Would movies serve as an elevator, raising the level of taste in the country, or as a bulldozer, reducing all taste to one level? With the potential to be high art for the masses, popular movies could broaden rather than undermine the traditional cultural hierarchy. But if all artistic standards collapsed under the weight of mass culture, the idea that movies were significant as a cultural experience would vanish as well.

As editors came to realize the significance of the motion picture's power, a number of journals ran articles advocating a new approach to this "democratic art." Cultural authority had begun to pass from the arbiters of the old order to those who would embrace the dynamism of the modern world. In April 1914, the weekly magazine *Independent* announced the introduction of its first movie column. The editors explained that their decision reflected the significance of "the birth of a new art" that did for drama what the printing press had done for literature; it brought drama "within reach of the multitude thru a process of mechanical manifolding." Even more important, movies made "possible for the first time the unlimited reproduction of actual events." In a world of movement, the editors concluded, "no static art can adequately represent it." The motion picture camera could capture life as it really happened—in motion. The *Independent* claimed that if motion pictures continued to develop at the present pace, they would make "present pictures appear as grotesque as the reliefs carved on Egyptian tombs or the scrawls on the caverns of Altamira." In order to help movies progress, the magazine's editors offered their publication's services by providing "independent and conscientious criticism from the standpoint of the public."[13]

In other words, periodicals like the *Independent* would treat movies as they did books, paintings, and other works of art. Unlike cultural criticism of the past, however, movie criticism would by necessity consider the ability of moving picture art to shape and be shaped by popular taste.

Two critics in particular became important to this trend: Louis Reeves Harrison of the *Moving Picture World* (*MPW*) and Frank Woods of the *Dramatic Mirror* (*DM*). The *MPW* began publishing in 1909 as a trade journal for producers, distributors, and exhibitors in the movie industry. As such, it ran everything from reports and editorials on equipment and distribution techniques to opinion pieces praising movies as a popular art. It and the *DM* served as consistently positive but intelligent mouthpieces for the movie industry.

Writing a column entitled "The Spectator" for the *Dramatic Mirror*, Woods defended motion pictures as an emerging art form that deserved time to improve, and cautioned that they might possibly be harmed beyond repair by irresponsible censorship. As a former scenario writer for D. W. Griffith and a friend to many in the movie business around New York City, Woods wrote as an industry insider. He was also an astute student of the screen's possibilities, and covered much of the same intellectual terrain discussed in more systematic ways by the first movie theorists. Film historian Myron Lounsbury explains that Woods's writing "started as an apology for the film manufacturers [but] became the earliest exploration into a number of important aesthetic and social issues concerning the motion picture."[14]

Woods was convinced that movies were a democratic art form and that the public, rather than the growing army of censors, should be entitled to make decisions on what it liked and did not like. Movies should be judged, he argued, as were "other varieties of public entertainment," and should be accorded "treatment as art and dramatic productions."[15] Movies would break new dramatic ground, Woods believed, if directors explored the potential of the movie camera. His hope for movies rested on a faith in the medium's ability to refine popular taste. The motion picture industry had a special responsibility, therefore, to strive toward higher ideals because its product reached such a large, diverse audience and could communicate and inspire with a power unseen in any other art.[16]

Moving Picture World developed similar themes within its pages, emphasizing the obligation the industry had to its public. Frequent contributors such as Harrison, W. Stephen Bush, and Rev. William Henry Jackson asked producers to consider the role they could play in dispensing culture to the masses. Jackson practically screamed his hopes for motion pictures. He enthusiastically declared movies to be the greatest force in education, civic reform, and aesthetic cultivation. Bush took a different tack, blasting other critics for snubbing this new art. In a day when a majority of writing on movies offered either a simple review of plots or a quick dismissal of motion pictures as vulgar and inconsequential, Bush was among the first to justify movie criticism as a legitimate pursuit. Harrison further developed this theme by advocating a role for movie critics similar to that played by esteemed cultural commentators. He believed that movies were, in fact, vulgar for the most part, but that they had the potential to spread a gospel of beauty and refined aesthetics among the masses.

Progressive values informed many of the articles that appeared in the journals.[17] Most critics writing at that time believed the public had an undercultivated artistic taste and needed direction in developing aesthetic values. Writers for the *MPW* believed that they would be part of that process by providing constructive criticism. At times, the assumptions underlying this role revealed the critics' bigotry. For example, one article reprinted from a Los Angeles newspaper condemned American movies for making sordid tales that attracted patrons with "thick lips" and lowbrow sensibilities. In another article, W. Stephen Bush justified the need for a reform-minded elite to cultivate public taste, pointing to the success cultural leaders had had in guiding the masses away from taking pleasure in such things as public executions. Bush argued that critics such as he would lead a "crusade" in defense of "the highest aspirations of the art and its followers" against those who, he believed, "would for money stoop to any prostitution of the noble art."[18]

Nonetheless, the *MPW* became an important source for tracking the characterization of movies as an art. The journal hoped that a number of themes prominent in its pages would resonate throughout the movie industry and in journals of criticism. For one, the *MPW* repeatedly faulted photoplay producers and exhibitors for thinking that the best way to stay financially solvent was either simplistically to recycle material from the stage and novels, or make an endless succession of brief chase scenes. Of course, the movie industry operated under commercial pressures different from other "artists," but the *MPW*'s writers hoped to impress upon the photoplay community that good pictures would keep people coming back and attract new patrons. Bush contended that "the notion so prevalent among the ignorant that art cannot be served without sacrifice of profit" was fatally wrong. "Art in moving pictures pays in dollars and cents."[19]

Yet the *MPW* writers also understood that the practice of criticism had to change if critics intended to influence both the industry and the public. Various authors agreed that movies deserved a different type of evaluation because they defied traditional limits of cultural authority. Thus, writers should begin to promote the benefits of constructive criticism. A number of *MPW* editorials pleaded for critics to get to know "what the public wants or should have or should be led to accept. [Critics should] educate the public into the acceptance of the good, the artistic, and the beautiful."[20] Alan Dale, one of the most feared drama critics of the day, expanded on this theme. He contended that movies were a different medium to critique because, unlike a stage production, bad reviews had little real effect on a specific movie. One movie could "be put into the 'can' and another substituted for it much easier than a whole production of theatrical people can be disbanded and scenery sent to the storehouse and another production substituted in its place."[21] Critics needed to adapt to their new roles as facilitators rather than cultural arbiters.

Moving pictures had forced criticism into a new cultural paradigm. Reverend Jackson called it the moving picture "world," in which one need not be educated to understand what was on the screen. The motion picture had opened a "new university . . . with only the boundaries of the globe as its confines, and the inhabitants thereof as its students: seeing, reading, studying, progressing; graduating with pleasure and profit at will, only stopping short with the limitation of a satisfied ambition." It was an "instrument of worldwide value to all mankind."[22] However, because movies were a commercial enterprise, the public would have a great deal more power in controlling what types of movies they watched and how they watched them. Unlike other mediums, the moving picture responded to popular aesthetics as much as it cultivated public taste. Critics therefore could not simply pass judgment on films and expect the public to follow. As a mass art form, movies inhabited a region between cheap amusements that received little attention, and the fine arts, which were translated by an elite group of critics. The aesthetic value of movies was in their leveling of taste. Still, the question remained which direction this leveling would go—up or down.

Louis Reeves Harrison became a forceful advocate for the worth of popular motion pictures and a new type of criticism for them. He conceded that many pictures were of poor quality, but he rejected the argument that the public expected and wanted such photoplays. Both highbrows and lowbrows wanted diversion, he explained, but one could foresee a time when motion pictures would "give an entertainment for the mass that shall be comparable in quality to that now only reachable by the selfish class. The new art seems to have come into existence for that express purpose." Central to Harrison's argument was the idea that art could improve society if the masses were exposed to it. Unlike future critics who condemned the idea of cultural standards as discriminatory, Harrison acted as a cultural nationalist when he hoped that this "Coney Island attraction" could be "in reality a fine art." Movies could be both popular and uplifting if producers and exhibitors would educate their audience by creating better pictures, and if critics would provide constructive advice. The common people had appreciated fine arts since antiquity, Harrison noted, so why would they not understand good movies, as well?[23]

The editors of *Photoplay Magazine* largely concurred with Harrison's judgment. The public wanted better films, not more of them, and a larger population of people would be willing to watch movies if they did improve. Julian Johnson, the first editor of *Photoplay,* believed that a better-educated public would lead to better films, since the audience would demand it. However, in order to make this endeavor seem serious, Johnson and his successor, James Quirk, had to convince their readers that movies were indeed an art.

Photoplay began publication in 1911 and became, along with *Motion Picture Story,* one of the two most successful fan magazines. By 1918 it boasted an annual circulation of 204,434.[24] Much of the magazine's material catered to moviegoers' interest in various stars, directors, and movies in development, but the editors—Johnson from 1911 to 1917 and then Quirk—also included a section entitled "Close-Ups," in which opinion pieces would appear. The editors expressed their opinions on censorship, movie houses, audiences, and the state of the photoplay as an art form. In these pages, one can trace the recognition that the power of movies was exceeding the control of the cultural elite. Whereas older journals of opinion would run lengthy diatribes against motion pictures, the high-circulation magazines for the masses hinted at a transition in power from one group of critics to another.

For example, when Geraldine Farrar, an opera singer of great repute, crossed over into the movies, Johnson remarked that "the triumph of active photography" was complete. "Let us never hear again the snivel that photodrama is a minor art, or not an art at all." Active photography, he believed, was "destined to raise the art standard of the world by bringing every art, every land and every interpretative genius to every man's door. Broadway will come to Borneo, and Borneo will go right back to Broadway."[25]

Most early critics had few illusions about the quality of movies in general. Pictures were indeed vulgar, and the public's taste for them needed to be refined. However, those who wrote for *MPW* and *Photoplay* hoped to introduce a new type of cultural criticism through their interest in movies. Cultural arbiters had overlooked the photoplay for the very reason that these new critics picked it up: it appealed to the masses. The attraction was in the opportunity to attack the cultural arbiters who seemed smug in their appreciation of fine arts and hypocritical in their condemnation of movies. The custodians of culture were not democrats, the writers who championed movies were. Julian Johnson thus felt justified in sniping at other critics who decried the quality of movies as merely popular entertainment. They would improve, Johnson assured the skeptics, because films were reaching the stage where "they are a basic amusement, recreation, and instruction for the entire world—for the highbrow and for the fellow whose cowlick grows into his eyebrows." Moreover, they did not require the meddling of moralists whose idea of art had little room for the reality of life. "The fabric of art is the fabric of life," Johnson insisted. Art that served the public was "made from life, and from all of it; not from a prophylactic, pasteurized, denatured, eunuchized edition a la the bovine-minded censor." One had to have faith in the ability of all the people to appreciate what was good and to reject what was bad.[26]

Johnson could point to various events in the recent past to bolster his claim that movies were improving and deserving of recognition as art. He referred to 1915 as "Year I" for the movies. On March 3, 1915, D.W. Griffith had made motion picture history with the premiere in major U.S. cities of *The Birth of a Nation*. At twelve reels it extended normal screen time by sixty to eighty minutes. Audiences marveled at the movie's battle scenes and rapid-fire editing. Griffith won widespread acclaim for his technical wizardry and a measure of anger for depicting the Ku Klux Klan as night-riding heroes of the post–Civil War South. Ticket prices for admission to see Griffith's spectacle had risen to two dollars at certain New York City theaters, prompting some commentators to note that the movies could charge admission prices comparable to the stage. In a special editorial in March 1916, Johnson reflected that recent achievements in the world of movies had proven "the active photoplay" did not "have to turn anywhere for supreme artists," because "with unfailing result, it can look within its own doors." Furthermore, while it was clear that motion pictures could command highbrow prices, "the photoplay for everybody's price has fixed itself irrevocably."[27]

Even though the industry had made substantial progress since the early days when short films kept patrons entertained between vaudeville acts, Johnson believed that producers had an obligation to provide the public with pictures of increasing quality. In a number of editorials, he advanced the notion that the motion picture had to transcend its purely industrial and commercial origins in order to realize its potential. Out of the "waste, extravagance, inspiration, ambition, industry, graft, and patient experiment" of the movie industry would emerge the "world's first great art-business." However, because movies were a strange hybrid of industry and art, they should be measured by standards that coupled popular taste with artistic ideals. The audience thus had a role to play in the improvement of pictures. The remedy for the inadequate output of mainstream studios, Johnson suggested, lay "largely in the enforcement of the selective power of the audiences."[28]

In October 1916, Johnson made his appeal in the most blatant terms when he launched into a page-long tirade entitled "Aren't You Tired of Trash?" Johnson imagined he spoke for many people when he called for fewer movies but better ones, quality rather than quantity. In the same issue, Johnson criticized producers for marketing their product to exhibitors rather than the real consumer, the public. He believed that if studio output truly reflected popular taste, movies would naturally be of a higher quality, and he asked his readers to let *Photoplay* help them develop rather than dictate to them a motion picture aesthetic.[29]

In a series of editorials that praised the democratic nature of movies, James Quirk seemed to exemplify a new movie criticism. In April 1918, Quirk addressed the power of movies to undermine an older cultural authority. Quirk pointed out that the public began to feel alienated from the arts during the late nineteenth century. He contended that in the past "art scorned democracy" in the same way that a wealthy merchant class patronized the arts in order to seem aristocratic. Thus, museums were established to make the common people feel "that this was not THEIR art, that it was not made for THEM, that it was being doled out to them as a splendid philanthropy." But even though "democracy was crying in the wilderness for an art of its own . . . the artists turned a deaf ear. Then came the moving picture, and democracy clasped it to its heart. This was something for the people themselves. Not that they were blind to its defects, not that they believed it perfect from its beginning—but it was their own. It was the first art-child of democracy." And while the "aristocrats of art sneered and scoffed" at the rise of movies, there were those who "saw the moving picture as worthy of a place with its older brothers and sisters." Yet moving pictures had no pretensions to fit in among the more obscure categories of art. At their best, movies were simple and direct like other artistic masterpieces. This was what made them "an art of the people, for the people."[30]

Quirk continued to hammer this theme in another editorial in which he described the photoplay as the "fifth estate." The motion picture was "democracy's own child . . . because the vast, mute, unlettered masses, demanding a voice, has found it in the motion picture." It was the fifth estate because it lived "in the hearts and lives of the millions," and with a "magic sword of simplicity" severed all "Gordian knots" and cut into the "fundamental meaning of things." As a result, movies had come to seem idealistic rather than, as many cultural rebels had hoped, realistic or abstract. American mainstream pictures normally ended happily, frustrating those who considered themselves "students of curious psychological phenomena." But for the majority of moviegoers, for whom life itself was "sufficiently real," the happy ending was a "symbol to them of their own faith and their own desires." For this reason, Quirk stated once again, pictures were "the first form of art which is truly democratic."[31]

Three theorists writing in the early years of film history synthesized much of the prevailing opinion among intellectuals who at least accepted the potential of movies. Vachel Lindsay, Hugo Münsterberg, and Victor Freeburg approached the practice of movie criticism from different angles, but each writer also believed that his subject was significant because movies had altered how art was created and how it was defined.

Vachel Lindsay was an Illinois poet who loved movies. His influence in the creation of a motion picture aesthetic has been discussed by a number of historians.[32] Lindsay was in the artistic vanguard of his day, combining his own well-trained artistic sense with a progressive, almost religious zeal for the power of movies to uplift the masses. In Lindsay's first and most important work on movies, *The Art of the Moving Picture* (first published in 1915 and revised in 1922), he worked to convince leaders of museums and universities—as well as other artists and literary critics—that "the motion picture art is a great high art, not a process of commercial manufacture." Throughout his book, he hoped to "bring to bear the same simple standards of form, composition, mood, and motive . . . the standards which are taken for granted in art histories and schools, radical or conservative, anywhere."[33] Such rigorous but intelligent criticism would help the motion picture assume its rightful place among the other arts. Lindsay reasoned that if popular taste was to be an important new source for aesthetics, then the public had to adopt finer sensibilities. The way to ensure this process, Lindsay predicted, was to place movies in the same forums and institutions that housed other works of art.

Stanley Kauffmann has remarked that Lindsay anticipated most of the characteristics of contemporary movie culture. In fact, Lindsay predicted the process that would elevate movies to the distinction of high art. He understood that the competition between the photoplay and staged drama would cease, and the two would use each other for inspiration. Lindsay discussed movie images—what he called hieroglyphics or pasteboard scenarios—in a way that predated Sergei Eisenstein's theories of film montage. (Eisenstein's innovations were heralded in the 1920s as the greatest artistic advance in motion picture history.) Lindsay also spoke about the significance of an emerging visual culture long before Marshall McLuhan announced its arrival and its effects on society. With directors such as D.W. Griffith in mind, Lindsay predated Andrew Sarris and his auteur theory by fifty years when he argued, "an artistic photoplay . . . is not a factory-made staple article, but the product of the creative force of one soul, the flowering spirit that has the habit of perpetually renewing itself." In short, Lindsay was the first writer to treat movies seriously, but he did so as a critic who hoped that as they improved they would help create a better society.[34]

Lindsay claimed that the day was at hand when the photoplay could shape the world through the power of images. This would be possible because motion pictures created a visceral experience. Images on a screen, he observed, could enrapture an audience, for only "a crude mind would insist that these appearances are not real, that the eye does not see them when all eyes behold them." Similar to philosopher William James's concept of "The Will to Believe," Lindsay accepted that an undefined area existed between fact and faith.[35] "If the appearances are beautiful," he wrote, "they are not only facts, but assets to our lives." People would always be drawn to movies, moreover, because they offered something authentic and even primitive in lives buried under layers of superficiality and falseness. To Lindsay, motion pictures would serve a greater end rather than be an end in themselves. Unlike future generations that would find movies either an escape from mainstream culture or serious art, Lindsay applauded the mass production of movies because they brought culture to all the people—a very Whitmanesque hope.[36]

By the time the second edition of his book came out in 1922, however, Lindsay had retreated from his initial enthusiasm, finding the movie industry to be preoccupied with thoughts of money, not art and cultural uplift. In a lecture given at Columbia University's School of Journalism, Lindsay argued for the creation of an "endowed photoplay" or movies made independent of the mainstream industry. "These endowed arts," Lindsay reasoned, "will have an influence upon commercial art; they will mellow it and raise its standard." Throughout the century, many critics optimistic about the future of movies would express similar ideas—and just as many would share Lindsay's disillusionment.[37]

Hugo Münsterberg broke new ground by proposing that an older understanding of art would not effectively measure the power of movies. In *The Photoplay: A Psychological Study* (1916), Münsterberg did pioneering work on the psychological and aesthetic experience that movies provided. In an introduction to the 1970 edition of the book, Richard Griffith, at the time curator emeritus of the Film Study Center at the Museum of Modern Art, recognized Münsterberg as an underappreciated innovator. Griffith noted that Münsterberg had phrased a question much in vogue by the 1960s: "Who is the camera?" In 1915 Münsterberg understood the importance of the director's ability to manipulate not merely the movie but the audience as well. Yet Münsterberg also realized that a director was only as effective as his or her appreciation of the psychology behind the process of watching movies. Thus, the audience also imparted its own meaning to what it watched.[38]

Münsterberg was a German immigrant who came to work in Harvard University's philosophy department in 1897 at the invitation of Pres. Charles W. Eliot. William James, who pioneered in the emerging field of psychology before turning to philosophy, was instrumental in coaxing the young German to the United States. James had been very impressed with Münsterberg's research in experimental psychology, something that informed James's own work, and he helped the younger man launch his career as the nation's preeminent theorist in applied psychology. By 1916 Münsterberg had become a prominent American intellectual and had turned his talents to one of his favorite pastimes, the photoplay.

Münsterberg offered an alternative to arguments that either placed movies in the continuum of older art forms or dismissed the photoplay as a tool of mass culture. He contended that movies inspired a new category of appreciation: psychological aesthetics. The experience of creating, presenting, and watching photoplays formed a matrix of sensory elements that freed the dramatic narrative from the bounds of time and form. Movies had become (in McLuhanesque terms) nonlinear. Although his approach was unique, Münsterberg's theoretical perspective obscured as much as it revealed. It was questionable whether or not the people watching films understood the numerous variables suspended in celluloid space that operated quietly on their subconscious, and it was dubious whether or not an audience developed an aesthetic truly different from its appreciation of other arts. But if both propositions were true, as Münsterberg believed, then the effect of movies would be different than other expressions. Just how different is still hotly debated.

Münsterberg found motion pictures both an amusement and material for his own research. He watched hours of movies both with audiences and alone, and visited the Vitagraph studio in Brooklyn, New York, to observe how they were made.[39] He entered his project with a simple question in mind: What constituted "the conditions under which the works of a special art stand?" He looked at his opportunity with excitement, writing that the photoplay was "a new art ... in a world of ready-made arts ... still undeveloped and hardly understood. For the first time the psychologist can observe the starting of an entirely new esthetic development, a new form of true beauty in the turmoil of a technical age, created by its very technique and yet more than any other art destined to overcome outer nature by the free and joyful play of the mind." Unlike other early movie critics, Münsterberg had clarified the important link between film aesthetics and popular taste. His criticism was a first step in the eventual recognition that cultural authority had begun to reside with the audience.[40]

It was a "unique inner experience," Münsterberg observed, that characterized "the perception of the photoplays." He marveled at the complex environment created through a variety of techniques such as close-ups, flashbacks, dream sequences, multiple plots, and visual tricks. The photoplay illustrated how the mind created a narrative out of disparate events, associational links out of a chaotic mass of images. In the movies, "events which are far distant from one another so that we could not physically be present at all of them at the same time" would fuse in a person's "field of vision, just as they are brought together in our own consciousness."[41]

Münsterberg pursued his study not merely to satisfy his scientific interests, but as a preliminary approach to understanding what he said was "one of the strongest social energies of our time." His insights contributed to the growing (and at times unfounded) apprehensions many people had about the power of movies. After all, he observed, the popularity of picture shows was probably not based completely on their "merits and excellences."[42]

Münsterberg did not deny that the photoplay provided a "satisfaction" and "superb enjoyment" unique among the arts, but he added that if movies could take hold of an audience, "such a penetrating influence must be fraught with dangers." What he feared was that movies would undermine culture—that life would be trivialized through "steady contact," during those hours in the dark, "with things ... not worth knowing." In a sense, Münsterberg foresaw a time in which entertainment would "carnivalize" culture. Nevertheless, the future could be different, he insisted, if "an enthusiasm for the noble and uplifting, a belief in the duty and discipline of the mind, a faith in ideals and eternal values" permeated "the world of the screen." In a culture that subscribed to such principles, censorship of its entertainment would be unnecessary. Movies could portray "evil and sin" without worrying about glorifying such actions.[43]

This hope though, was predicated on the presumption that movies could assist in the cultivation of popular taste. "Hardly any teaching," Münsterberg believed, could "mean more for [a] community than the teaching of beauty where it reaches the masses." Since the motion picture was "an art in itself," he urged producers to consider that they could cultivate popular taste without the public even realizing it. "The teaching of the moving pictures," he said, "must not be forced on a more or less indifferent audience, but ought to be absorbed by those who seek entertainment and enjoyment from the films and are ready to make their little economic sacrifice." Mass art had the power to be both significant and popular; Münsterberg hoped such a role for movies would be realized in the future.[44]

On December 16, 1917, Hugo Münsterberg met an early and sudden death. Before his passing, Vachel Lindsay wrote a piece on *The Photoplay* for the *New Republic*.[45] Lindsay noted that even though many Americans differed with the German's opposition to U.S. involvement in the war in Europe, anybody concerned with serious analysis of the photoplay should turn to Münsterberg's book as a primer. The book had received enthusiastic responses initially, then suffered neglect from a public unaware of Münsterberg's name, an industry unwilling to heed his advice, and a community of intellectuals disposed to ignore him as a pioneer in cinematic theory.[46]

Victor Freeburg intended his first work on movies, *The Art of Photoplay Making*, to synthesize the theoretical works that had preceded it, but he also wanted to suggest ways to expand such theories in order to produce commercially successful, aesthetically significant art.[47] Freeburg, a professor in Columbia University's School of Journalism, was also one of the few professors in the nation to lecture on motion pictures in any serious way.

At the heart of Freeburg's work was a perceptive discussion of how movies might incorporate the requirements of art along with those of entertainment. He began with the observation that audiences responded to movies with their emotions rather than their minds. When people went to see a photoplay, they expected to be thrilled by special effects, enthralled by their favorite star, and delighted by some unexpected feature "introduced for the first time." According to Freeburg, the trick to making a good motion picture—one worthy of the term art—was to sneak significance in amongst the dazzle and thrills. "The author must design and contrive deftly, almost secretly," Freeburg explained, "to please the senses and capture the emotions and add to the intellectual possession of the audience. The results are paramount, while the ingenuity and artistry of the methods will either be ignored or unrecognized." Freeburg admitted that even a perfectly crafted photoplay would fail to reach the public if the producer relied solely on technical skill and failed to make the movie accessible. It was his hope that moviemakers would cultivate the middle ground between art for art's sake and popular art for financial reward. He believed that in order for the photoplay to realize its potential, it "must possess beneath the attractive surface, which appeals to the crowd, the permanent values of illuminating truth, universal meaning, and unfading beauty."[48]

Like his contemporaries, Freeburg would consider the photoplay as art if it could satisfy general aesthetics laws. "The author must recognize and obey the laws of the human mind, laws which have not changed since the world began. People become interested, pay attention and calm down, remember and forget in exactly the same way as when the first savage told a story or scratched the rude picture of a beast on the wall of a cave."[49] Successful photoplays, therefore, manipulated the same human responses—both emotional and intellectual—found in great art for centuries.

Movies were different only in how they generated appeal and admiration, not because they were commercial. Freeburg dismissed the argument that commercial concerns led to the corruption of art. He took Shakespeare as an example of a great artist who, in his day, created scenes of intrigue in order to attract popular attention. He commented that with Shakespeare's plays, "it is a safe wager that the spectator who came to be thrilled by a sensation will remain to be enthralled by pure art."[50] Suggesting that art could be commercial and still be beautiful gave a new twist to old aesthetics.

Walter Prichard Eaton's Objections

Walter Prichard Eaton, a widely respected drama critic for the *Boston Telegraph*, refused to take the photoplay seriously. Many of his most scathing attacks on the industry appeared in important literary journals of the day. Although Eaton has appeared to many historians as a drama critic protecting his turf against the onslaught of movies, he offered, along with Randolph Bourne, a poignant critique of motion pictures.[51]

Eaton did not begin as an enemy of motion pictures; he simply believed that movies fell far short of their artistic potential. In this failure, American producers had missed an opportunity to cultivate public taste as well as develop their own craft. Writing in *American Magazine*, Eaton contended that the French had offered a good model for comparison. Films made in France aimed at a distinctly higher artistic level than did American movies, and had found the public appreciative of this effort. "You realize," he suggested, "that unconsciously a certain standard of taste, a genuine aesthetic standard, can be set for the children and poor people who frequent canned dramas by the millions." Eaton believed that good taste did not depend on a person's income level. Anyone who had been exposed to good art could apply artistic standards. It thus was important "that ordinary canned dramas be not only free from brutality, coarseness, and suggestions to crime, but they be constructed with imagination, told with interest and coherence, and be well acted." If movies were going to be made, he seemed to ask, why not make good ones?[52]

Six years later, in January 1915, Eaton offered a more pessimistic outlook on the effect movies were having on culture. He claimed that a great divide had opened between the audience for the theater and the crowd for movies. The former received patronage from the upper classes, the latter from the proletariat. Those who had hoped, as he had, that motion pictures would cultivate the artistic taste of the masses had been mistaken. With the masses abandoning the higher-priced theater in favor of the inexpensive photoplay, American society had become divided aesthetically as well as economically. That troubled Eaton because he, like others, had hoped movies would do just the opposite. He foresaw a time when the two groups, separated by money and taste, would retreat into their separate worlds, resigned to mutual antagonism.[53]

Here, Eaton touched upon the stratification of culture in America. He observed that a man would be more likely to spend a quarter on a film ticket that entitled him to sit on the ground floor of a theater and feel a sense of class independence, than go to a staged drama and pay a higher price for seats that were only accessible through the back door. "Already the spoken drama and the silent drama are far apart," he lamented. "Each is the amusement, the pastime, of a separate and antagonistic class."[54] The movies had begun to pander as much to impoverished aesthetics as they had appealed to the lower classes. He feared a situation similar to the one Bourne had conceived, whereby the popularity of movies would divide American culture into two equally bland and hopeless halves.

In 1917, fed up with critics championing movies, Eaton trained his critical sights on the argument that movies were art. He dismissed opinions that suggested "there must a masterpiece lurking in the movies, since none has ever come out."[55] He also contested the acclaim showered on such films as Griffith's *The Birth of a Nation*. "That which entertains," Eaton quipped, "is not necessarily art." He blamed critics who "confused the actual scene with the creative process, and spoke of the beauty 'achieved' by the motion picture camera when all that has been done was to enact the pantomime in some pretty meadow by the margent of the sea."[56] In demanding so little of the photoplay, such critics had skewed the application of artistic standards.

To emphasize his point, Eaton referred to a remark made by a fellow drama authority, the formidable stage designer Gordon Craig, which "brought sudden enlightenment" to Eaton's mind. Craig had admitted to enjoying the movies, but he also believed that "the worst of the cinema is that one man's work resembles the work of all the others." Eaton claimed that Craig's observation penetrated to the heart of the matter: there was little that distinguished films or directors from one another. "The film dramas may vary in narrative interest, in speed, smoothness, and subject matter," but, Eaton asked, "can you say that the drama of one author has an original style-note which distinguishes his work, which sets it apart?"[57] To be considered aesthetically significant, a work needed a mark of originality. Writers, painters, sculptors, composers, and even architects all transcended the general outlines of their craft by imparting their artistic soul.

With this critique, Eaton had lodged the signal criticism of the pre-electronic age against the medium that would usher in the electronic future. At the core of this rebuke was Eaton's conviction that only the "living personality," best illustrated on the stage, should persuade us that the performance was authentic. Movies relied on the "interposition of a mechanical process" that broke up "the flow of nature" and ultimately reduced "all work to a level of sameness."[58] Movies were machine art and, according to critics like Eaton, lacked the imprint of a human soul. They might be lively, but they were not alive.

The criticism of Eaton and Bourne was among the most thoughtful of this early period. Both feared the corrosive influence a mass medium such as movies would have on the rich, diverse arts created across the United States. Although it was true that millions of Americans flocked to watch movies, the moving picture, they believed, remained a lifeless art. It had none of the spontaneity or fire of a live performance. It bore no marks of human handicraft. Such critics feared a time when the photoplay would replace great orators, stage performers, and other artists who practiced a craft rather than operated a machine.

Yet even critics who found the motion picture reflective of the era's mechanization and popular tastes had deep misgivings about the medium's potential effects on the audience and American culture. All agreed that the power of film lay in the significance the people invested in it. Without public attention, movies would have remained a sideshow. By 1919, Americans had clearly illustrated their fascination with the picture show. Traditional cultural authority had begun to undergo a significant change as the popular taste exerted more influence over the value and meaning of art. Hugo Münsterberg's query would haunt the moving picture world like a specter: What would happen to a society that spent hours in the dark enchanted by things not worth knowing?

2

Menace or Art?

During the late 1910s the motion picture industry began to take shape as a powerful commercial force. The first industry magnates—the Warner brothers, Marcus Loew, Samuel Goldwyn, and Louis B. Mayer—intended to expand studio operations to keep the seats filled in their newly constructed theaters. Movie budgets also swelled in order to produce more elaborate pictures and to attend to the growing stables of high-paid actors and actresses. A "star culture" flourished as the onscreen performances of Charlie Chaplin, Mary Pickford, and Douglas Fairbanks made people laugh, sigh, and swoon. But the fascination with money also kept people interested in the off-screen fortunes and lifestyles of Hollywood personalities. The influence of the movies as a business, a cultural force, and art was almost too great to comprehend. To many civic reformers, the movie industry was an entity that stood apart from the rest of society. It had an allure that seemed unholy in nature.

Early-twentieth-century civic leaders scrutinized the power of the world's newest media, the movies. They argued that the popularity and accessibility of what came to be known as "mass media" (particularly movies) threatened the health of society, especially youth. Many believed that movies were a poor substitute for more traditional forms of art and entertainment. Moreover, one needed only to pass by posters advertising such movies as *The Branded Woman, Discontented Wives,* and *Forbidden Fruit* to be suspicious of what this upstart industry was selling. However, what made the power of movies even more disturbing to civic leaders was that within the first two decades of the medium's existence, moving pictures attracted tens of millions of people every week. To many critics, this new medium seemed destined and even designed to create a world morally unhinged and aesthetically numb.

To contain this increasingly pervasive threat, civic leaders turned to censoring the movies. Unlike any other medium of expression, moving pictures became subject to prior censorship—meaning that censors cut scenes and images from what directors assumed to be finished films. In one of the most revealing confrontations over the use of censorship, the city of Chicago called for hearings to revise its laws governing the exhibition of movies. From September 1918 through May 1919, the Chicago Motion Picture Commission heard testimony from a variety of people associated with this medium—from exhibitors and producers to reviewers and censors. The commission also sponsored a survey, conducted by University of Chicago professor E.W. Burgess, in an attempt to quantify the effects of motion pictures on school children.

Although state and local censorship boards had existed for over a decade throughout the United States, Chicago's commission garnered attention because the city was the nation's second largest movie market, the commission heard a diverse array opinions regarding the role of movies in American life, and the proceedings marked the waning of civic censorship. Beginning in 1922, movie studios and producers, under the auspices of the Motion Picture Producers and Distributors of America (MPPDA), turned to Postmaster General Will H. Hays to pass judgment on their products, thereby undercutting local efforts. The hearings in Chicago therefore represented one of the last public discussions on the nature of movie power and the public's ability to control it.

From the earliest days of the nickelodeons and vaudeville movies, community leaders had waged battles against movie material. In fact, Chicago was one of the first cities to institute censorship. By 1907, the city reportedly had 116 nickelodeons, eighteen vaudeville houses, and nineteen penny arcades. The *Chicago Tribune* said that such amusements had an "influence that is wholly vicious," a remark that echoed the opinions of most community leaders.[1] To meet this threat to public welfare, the city enacted a censorship law in 1907. Chicago's City Council empowered the chief of police to issue permits for the exhibition of moving pictures. If the city's censor (usually the second deputy superintendent of the police) denied a permit to an exhibitor, the movie would either have to be cut to meet the censor's standards or removed from the theater. By 1909, both the Illinois Supreme Court and the U.S. Supreme Court upheld Chicago's right to censor movies. The city also enacted a separate permit—colored pink—to designate movies for adults over the age of twenty-one only. Both the "pink permit" and police censorship would be called into question during the hearings.

By 1909, America's largest city, New York, had enacted a censorship law of its own. Mayor George B. McClellan closed all 550 picture show establishments in the city in response to the police chief's claim that most movie material was reprehensible. Voices for and against the movie industry vied for power in a crowded city hall meeting in December 1909. McClellan decided against the industry and ordered the revocation of all operating licenses until certain conditions (the specifics of which he had not made clear) were met. Although the mayor's decision was impossible to enforce, his action reflected the growing frustration of many civic leaders struggling to regulate the rapidly growing moving picture industry.[2]

By 1915, the legal foundation for censorship had been solidified in a Supreme Court decision that classified movies as an industry rather than as a means of expression. In the landmark decision *Mutual v Ohio,* the Court rejected the Mutual Film Corporation's claim that movies deserved protection under the First Amendment right to free speech. Instead, the Court declared: "the exhibition of moving pictures is a business, pure and simple, originated and conducted for profit like other spectacles, and not to be regarded as part of the press of the country or as organs of public opinion within the meaning of freedom of speech and publication." In his opinion for the majority, Chief Justice Joseph McKenna added that while the mission of films may not be to harm the public, "they may be used for evil, and against that possibility the statute was enacted." At the center of McKenna's argument was concern about the unique power of movies to appeal to the public. Unlike newspapers or even other forms of art that many found offensive, movies "take their attraction from the general interest, eager and wholesome it may be, in their subjects, but a prurient interest may be excited and appealed to [as well]. Besides, there are some things which should not have pictorial representation in public places and to all audiences."[3] Although many agreed with McKenna's general intention, his categorization failed to proscribe an effective form of censorship.

Movie censorship was both a national and municipal concern, and should be viewed within a larger historical context of progressivism. Advocates of progressivism espoused the belief that government organizations could manage social problems, including the persistence of alcoholism, poor food, the scarcity of medicine, bad working conditions, poverty, and vice—including "dangerous" movies. Embedded in that movement was the hope of preserving traditional values as defined by the church, the family, and America's social elite. Community leaders were appalled by the apparent decline of moral standards among the public. They blamed the moving picture industry for both advancing that moral decline and for capitalizing financially on it by producing movies with salacious titles and scenarios of dubious merit. The people who sat on the board of the Chicago Motion Picture Commission sought to exert a measure of control over the movies before their effects eroded the authority civic leaders had as parents, church members, and government officials.[4]

The debate over censorship also touched upon the dwindling cultural authority wielded by traditional institutions and the growing (and as yet unformed) power of mass media over society. On one side of the debate was the belief that the public needed protection from this popular but "vulgar" medium. On the other side was the assumption that the public knew what it wanted, understood what was best for it, and had the capacity to make its own choices about movies.

Movie censorship had become such a contested issue by the 1910s in part because of the perception that movies tended to assault the moral fortitude of the nation's children. In 1921, the popular magazine *Literary Digest* ran an article bearing the ominous title, "Is the Younger Generation in Peril?"[5] "Yes!" the article emphatically declared, because children were becoming more rebellious toward their elders and were bucking older standards of behavior and taste. Near the beginning of Chicago's hearings, the *Tribune* reported that two teenage girls had caused a scandal in school by dressing like "vamps." Dorothy, one of the girls in trouble, wanted to mimic the style made infamous by movie star Theda Bara and arrived at school with her "hair blonde and fluffy and worn in our best moving picture style," according to reporter Maude Evers. "Her gown of black satin is also—well, just like Paris—low at the neck and not too long at the bottom. . . . . Fifteen year old Dorothy knows all about trimming the wild eyebrows, also."[6] As general secretary for the Big Brother Movement, an early version of organization that continues to pair up conscientious men with fatherless boys, Rowland C. Sheldon went so far as to implicate the industry in the creation of delinquency. "How I wish," he exclaimed, "that the men who write such scenarios and the men who produce them, could visit the criminals they have made!"[7] Young people, many critics argued, seemed trapped in a terrible cycle in which they patronized a business that subtly challenged their parents' values, and instead of rejecting the messages they saw, children continuously rewarded movie producers and theater operators by attending as many shows as possible. The younger generation had become both the victims and the supporters of a mass culture devoid of traditional boundaries.[8]

As important and persistent as the issue of movie censorship was, it remained a relatively minor issue in 1918. When the commission convened in September, the First World War was coming to an inglorious conclusion, and newspapers printed lists of American soldiers lost "over there" as well as those coming back home. Many states heatedly debated proposed amendments on prohibition and women's suffrage, and the single worst epidemic in American history interceded in the commissions first month of business. The influenza outbreak in the fall of 1918 took hundreds of thousands of lives, including tens of thousands of Chicago residents. The issue of movie censorship had its place, but it was not among the front-page stories of the day. There was, however, a scandal immediately preceding the hearings that directly prompted the convening of the city's censorship hearings.

On July 30, 1918, Chicago's notoriously prudish though effective chief movie censor was fired. After six years of service, Maj. M.L.C. Funkhouser lost a five-week effort to defend his performance after Police Chief John H. Alcock accused him of allowing vice to go unchecked throughout the city. The civil service commission, chaired by Charles E. Frazier, heard arguments in a case that was, according to the *Tribune*, decided before it began. "We believe," the *Tribune* editorialized, "that Maj. Funkhouser, an aggravation as a censor of any kind of artistic expression, was doing able and effective work in an endeavor which almost defies any one to do successful work. The larger idea in the police management that led to the attempt to get rid of him has not been made apparent. A low minded person might even suspect that the intent was to rid the force of an activity useful to the city but embarrassing to the police."[9] From newspaper articles and testimonies by some of the city's most respected reformers, it seems that Funkhouser had failed to play favorites with the "right" movie exhibitors and distributors and had alienated not only the moving picture industry but the police who had friends in the business. The man who ousted Funkhouser, Charles Frazier, took the major's place as the city's censor.

In addition to this controversy, Chicago had another problem with its censorship procedures. The routine of issuing pink permits for "adult" films backfired with a vengeance when movie houses used the police's distinction to promote rather than to scandalize films with salacious material. The overall ineffectiveness of the city's censorship laws had become apparent to those wishing to continue the fight against movies, especially when one could find movies such as *Home Wrecker* and *The Things Forbidden Are the Things Desired* advertised within the Loop.

On July 18, 1918, the *Tribune* criticized the means of censoring movies in Chicago and suggested that a "commission be appointed to consider all the questions that [had] arisen in connection with the exercise of the censorship authority in Chicago." A similar board had been formed in London, the paper reported, with the purpose of holding hearings and making recommendations based on its findings. In order for such a board to be respected, the paper urged the city to make the membership represent "every sincere point of view."[10]

The next day, the city council acted on the *Tribune's* suggestion. Alderman George Maypole proposed the formation of a committee with representatives from both the council and the community to determine what type of censorship the city should enforce. Maypole stated that he believed the best way to address the issue of censorship was to have an "unbiased investigating body" hear from "all persons affected and interested in censorship." If a substitute for Chicago's present laws could be found, Maypole said he would be only too glad to support it.[11] The intention of such a commission would not be to debate the merits of inspecting movies, but to arrange for a new set of laws guiding municipal censorship.[12]

On September 28, 1918, the Chicago Motion Picture Commission (CMPC) convened in meeting room D on the second floor of City Hall and began hearings that took place every Friday from September 1918 through May 1919 and were open to the public. Twenty civic and religious leaders sat on the commission, but only five were elected officials, George Maypole among them. Timothy Hurley, former chief probation officer of Cook County, was appointed chairman. Among the other members were Orrin N. Carter, a justice of the Illinois Supreme Court; Adolph Kraus, author of the city's first censorship law; Martin J. Quigley, publisher of *Exhibitor's Herald*, the most popular trade journal for the moving picture industry; and Rev. F.G. Dinneen, a powerful member of the Knights of Columbus and the Holy Name Society of Chicago

As a sign of the times, the board included an equal number of clergymen and socially active women. Among the representatives of the latter group was the formidable Florence E. Blanchard, chairwoman of the motion picture and civics department of the influential General Federation of Women's Clubs. Representing sixty-five thousand women in Illinois alone, that organization had been at the forefront of civic censorship for most of the decade. Blanchard commented: "We are convinced that the people do not demand the sensational movie. The motion picture producers have diverted the mind of the motion-picture-going public and have made profitable a type of production that never should be shown. The people never wanted the low saloon, but still the saloon flourished, and sensational movies are in the same class."[13]

As Blanchard's statement intimates, the debate over censorship ultimately can be seen in the context of a larger struggle over who was going to define national culture. If society continued to accept traditional definitions of good and evil, then traditional notions of taste would prevail against mediums such as movies. If, however, American society believed popular tastes should determine cultural standards, then elite opinions would be forced to compete with those of the masses. Such a cultural world would be significantly more ambiguous than one in which the church and women's groups held sway because the authority used to declare what should be considered dangerous and what should be dismissed as inconsequential would drift away from traditional leaders.

Quoting a similar board in London on the power of movies, the commission contended: "under wise guidance [the cinema] may be a powerful influence for good. If neglected, if its abuse is unchecked, its potentiality for evil is manifold." The commission sat bemused by moviemakers who would "deny the right of the people to prejudge a picture on the ground that such action is opposed to 'American Liberty.'" After all, the Illinois Supreme Court had once referred to moviemakers as "that class of people that are shameless and unclean, to whom nothing is defilement, and to whose point of view no picture would be considered immoral or obscene." The commission quite simply believed that the movie industry was a financial monster, not a group interested in free expression, whose power would grow out of control unless reined in by those concerned with public morality rather than profits. The motion picture had become "the most powerful force in education, and in swaying the mind of the public, greater in the minds of many than the home, the school or the church." If left unchecked, the CMPC worried that movies would cause a cultural upheaval detrimental to the stability and welfare of the public. As the commission concluded: "Wherever health has been neglected, plague follows. Wherever police regulations are weakened—where the strong are permitted to oppress the weak—revolutions may ensue. And it is surely the right of the public to protect the weak."[14]

The use of such language and metaphors might seem overblown and paternalistic, but the committee believed, as did many Progressives, that social checks were vital to a healthy society. One needed only to remember the health disaster caused by the flu epidemic or the social catastrophe unleashed by the Russian Revolution to be aware of the dangers lurking in modern society. Traditional civic leaders had seen themselves among "the best [and] the most learned minds . . . devoted to educating the youth along the lines of betterment, and protecting the weak and thoughtless from the inroads of designing exploiters." When faced with the amorphous power of movies, the custodians of culture faced a troubling prospect that could only happen in a democracy. Should they err on the side of freedom of expression, risking the decline of an older culture, or should they try to restrict a medium that was powerful because it was popular? Censorship by community boards like Chicago's usually split the difference and, therefore, failed both ways. Their logic for acting, however, remained insightful: "It cannot be that in this progressive age we should silently consent or concur in having our wives and children, our homes, our schools and our churches turned over to the entertainer in order that he may make a profit regardless of the consequence to the individual."[15]

Such sentiment raised a fundamental question: Were elitism and paternalism ever healthy in society? Many who testified endorsed the authority to oversee public welfare. The first person called to speak before the commission was George Kleine, one of Chicago's first major motion picture producers and exhibitors. Kleine, who grappled with issues raised by the power of movies, explained that he had little hope that the public might "purify itself" since most people liked to attend movies with titles that promised "salacious subjects." "While I do not believe in general interference," Kleine maintained that he did "believe that it is the business of the state to interfere in cases where salacious pictures are shown." To illustrate his sincerity, Kleine vowed, "I would not exhibit any picture that I would not show my 16-year-old girl." But he also conceded that most directors "were men of enthusiasm. They have an idea. They do not take into consideration when they are working the mixed audience before which these pictures are shown, but they go along with eyes single in their art."[16]

The newness of movies caused problems for cultural critics and censors alike because no one yet knew how movies would affect American society. Unlike books, theatrical productions, and works of art, movies allowed spectators to sit passively and absorb.[17] They seemed to possess a singular ability to affect an individual's psyche. Many witnesses who testified before the commission wondered what would become of a country that raised a generation of children to be avid moviegoers. The most eloquent spokesman for such thinking was the well-respected psychologist Hugo Münsterberg, a man George Kleine believed was important enough to quote at length in his second day of testimony.

The commission regarded Münsterberg's work so highly that it allowed Kleine to read from the psychologist's book *The Photoplay*. According to Münsterberg, "No psychologist can determine exactly how much the general spirit of righteousness, of honesty, of sexual cleanliness and modesty, may be weakened by the unbridled influence of plays of low moral standard." And he took seriously the "trivializing influence of a steady contact with things which are not worth knowing," because he believed "The larger part of the film literature of today is certainly harmful in this sense. The intellectual background of most photoplays is insipid."[18] To the nation's most respected psychologist, movies in theory posed a real danger to society. It was in practice, however, that the commission imagined moving pictures doing the greatest damage.

The commission depended on statistical information to determine the effects of moving pictures. A professor at the University of Michigan found, for example, that many more schoolchildren could identify movie stars than the figures depicted in the painting *The Last Supper*. Teachers polled by the commission observed that their students had been profoundly and dangerously moved by motion pictures. One teacher observed, "the use of a gun, no matter in what way, makes the man using it brave in the child's eyes." Another suggested that "attendance at the moving pictures creates a desire to be entertained constantly. It leads to cigarette smoking; staying up nights; premature development regarding [the] opposite sex." The commission also included a newspaper article from Osaka, Japan, detailing a case in which two boys murdered two girls prompting the police to blame "sensational" movies for inciting the suspects. Observations like these led respected figures such as Max G. Schlaff, a professor of neuropathology at the New York Post-Graduate Medical School and Hospital, to conclude, "We may not realize it, but we are rearing a race of neurotic children today, and one of the great factors is our perverse idea of youthful pleasure." Schlaff believed that allowing children to watch a steady diet of "moving-picture thrillers" would make them crave them all the more, causing damage to their "delicate nerve centers."[19]

Perhaps the most the impeccable witness was Ellis P. Oberholtzer, Pennsylvania's chief censor, who had stopped in Chicago on what appeared to be a nationwide propaganda tour for movie censorship. Oberholtzer came well prepared to provide devastating testimony against the evils of movies and in favor of the city's right to condemn and control them. In a session that extended well into the evening, Oberholtzer reminded the commission's members that they comprised an important commonwealth of civic leaders. Their duty, Oberholtzer argued, was to protect the "lazy" from the influences of the movies. If a person is too lazy to read, Oberholtzer explained, "he absorbs [the picture] anyhow, and it teaches him in spite of himself how to steal, how to murder, how to rob and how to do a number of different things." Beyond this dubious observation, Oberholtzer also cast the battle with the movie industry as an "us versus them" fight. "It is a large and rather arrogant industry," he argued. "There are many people engaged in it whose opinions do not in any way coincide with our own. The object seems to be, as we all know, to go just as near the line of impermissibility as it is possible to go." To back up his claims against the industry, Oberholtzer listed movie titles he thought illustrated the depravity of the business, including *The Sex Lure, The Littlest Magdalene, The Gutter Magdalene, Hell to Pay Austin, The Tainted, The Suicide Club, Shackled Souls,* and *It May Be Your Daughter.*[20]

Yet even with such incriminating evidence, this noted expert on censorship conceded: "It seems to me in looking at pictures you judge them instinctively. You know whether such a thing is permissible or not; you feel it somehow or other. You have no particular doubt about it, and then you look to the standard and try and find a reason for it afterwards." Although the rationale for censorship might have seemed legitimate, the practice of censorship was anything but clear-cut. Testimonies on the difficulties of applying censorship in practice illustrated how basic flaws in theories appeared when an ideal had to be translated into a reality.

For example, the week before Oberholtzer's appearance, the commission heard from Kitty Kelly and W.K. Hollander, editors on the motion picture desks at the *Chicago Examiner-Herald* and the *Chicago Daily News,* respectively. Both noted the curious results produced by censors cutting scenes from completed movies. Audiences would sit bewildered by gaps in story lines and inelegant jumps between cinematic moments. Both editors objected to the way censors assumed the audience possessed a low level of intelligence. Kelly did "not think it is fair to censor pictures entirely from the juvenile standpoint," and Hollander believed the movies operated less as a medium "for the education of the people" than as a "public place for entertainment." The type of expectations civic leaders had for movies were unrealistic and simply inappropriate, Hollander argued, because people "see pictures and judge each according to its worth, each according to its merit." Ultimately, he seemed to suggest that it mattered little what the cultural elite thought when the public determined the worth of a movie.[21]

Censorship also became so arbitrary that the arbiters of taste had to admit that the people watching the movies had as much a right to determine what was good and bad, as did the appointed censors. At a particularly curious session, L.L. Pryor, a member of the Chicago censorship board, and the infamous Major Funkhouser testified that their offices were imperfectly designed to handle an imperfect job. Pryor confessed that among the criteria that went into deciding how best to censor a picture was the amount of money spent on its production, the names and reputations of those involved in the production, and the expected popularity of the film—not exactly a system based on aesthetic or professional standards. Funkhouser fittingly revealed that not only did censors approach their job "from the attitude of a child, not from an adult," but also that relationships between censors and movie exhibitors and producers routinely corrupted the process.[22]

With such forces influencing censorship, it was no wonder that when industry personnel testified before the commission they questioned the enterprise of censorship as a whole. At the second to last session at which testimony was heard, Arthur Ryan, the man who represented the "big four" of moving pictures—Charlie Chaplin, Mary Pickford, Douglas Fairbanks, and D.W. Griffith—suggested that because of a lack of coherence among censors, the moving picture world was unfairly subjected to treatment never imposed on other arts and expressions. An exchange between Ryan and Chairman Hurley illustrated that a limit had been reached in the broader debate over censorship:

> The Chairman: Doesn't the industry realize that censorship is here, and
>   is here to stay?
> Mr. Ryan: They don't realize it in the full sense of the word from your
>   standpoint.
> The Chairman: Hadn't you better come in and be part of that move-
>   ment?

Mr. Ryan: They want a better understanding of it. The word right away
    binds up the industry.
The Chairman: We will have to change the word?
Mr. Ryan: You have got to change the word.

Ryan was a step ahead of Hurley: The industry knew that the kind of censorship practiced by Chicago and many other municipalities and states would not last. Ryan believed this not simply because he foresaw the internal measures that would be taken by the industry in the future, but because he understood that movies followed popular whims and interests (no matter how prurient) rather than elite tastes. Movies existed in a cultural realm over which cultural arbiters had little control. Cultural authority was quietly passing away from the critics and into the people's hands.[23]

The commission saved its longest and most contentious debate for last. On March 28, 1919, three hundred people crowded into the council chamber at 3 P.M. to watch leaders from the movie industry knock heads with leaders of the city in the fifteenth session of the hearings. Headlining the industry's group was William A. Brady, president of the National Association of the Motion Picture Industry (NAMPI), and Walter W. Irwin, vice president of Famous Players–Lasky and chairman of NAMPI's executive committee. Two months earlier, Brady and Irwin had organized a conference in New York City with the purpose of appointing chairmen assigned to every state to do battle with censorship boards. They approached the CMPC as men acutely aware of the animosity toward the movie industry, but also as businessmen who, like movie stars, were beginning to command more money, power, and prestige in the nation.[24]

In their testimonies, Brady and Irwin attempted to return the industry to the mainstream and counter censorship by arguing for the legitimacy of the movies.[25] Irwin made a lengthy statement in which he referred to censorship as undemocratic, intolerant, and unpopular. He claimed that movies operated best under democratic principles and that only authoritarian nations such as Germany and "old Russia" would censor creative expression. Irwin likened censors to the new rulers of Russia, suggesting that censorship boards were akin to "bolsheviki leaders" who represented the "greatest example of intolerance," since "censorship is fundamentally based on intolerance." Irwin then launched a populist attack, asking the commission that if it believed censorship laws represented the will of the people, why then did Chicago fail to "submit [that issue] to the people?" A member of the city's religious community shot back that not only did the commission possess the capacity to speak on behalf of the public, but that to suggest otherwise would be to question the authority of the entire city government.[26]

What Irwin questioned was the unique and, to him, unfair treatment accorded movies. "If we have done something wrong we are held responsible," he offered. Arguing that remedies existed other than blanket censorship, he pleaded, "You want to have us governed by the law of injunction by which we will be punished for something before we have done it." Of course, therein lay the issue that divided the commission from the industry. The former worked from an assumption that movies were generally bad for society and a force seemingly outside the control of cultural arbiters. Irwin and other industry representatives saw themselves not as criminals or even as tainted men, but as businessmen who were the producers of potentially the most successful and popular source of entertainment the world had ever known.

William Brady, speaking "as a good Catholic," attempted to return the discussion to a level where both sides saw each other as equals. He listed his significant accomplishments, among them his association with Thomas Edison, his production of Shakespearean plays, and his appointment by Pres. Woodrow Wilson to represent the moving picture industry in government service during the war. On this last point, Brady added, "I go on record now, ladies and gentlemen, in stating this one fact, which no one in this room can contradict, that throughout the war no industry in the United States rendered to its government without profit, without charge, such distinguished services as were rendered by the motion picture industry of the United States." Loud applause followed Brady's testament. Indeed, the power of movies to sway large populations toward a common goal had been witnessed in the drive to recruit men for the war and to entice civilians to buy Liberty Loans.[27]

Returning to the issue at hand, Brady admitted that there were "black sheep" in the industry producing "indecent and immoral pictures." However, he added, immoral people could be found throughout the city writing for magazines and newspapers. Why, he asked, were movies treated differently from other mediums of expression? He answered his own question by suggesting that perhaps the reason for this double standard rested on the industry's inability to earn respect through the exercise of political power.[28] Unlike the newspapers, movies "had no religion and no politics," but, Brady warned, the industry would be "going into politics" and perhaps then the civic councils would "pay a little heed to them after they got into politics."[29]

Film historian Robert Sklar has written that "there is evidence suggesting that at the time of Brady's remarks, producers were already entering into discussions with leaders of the Republican party about mutually advantageous ways of working together during the 1920 elections."[30] By 1922, such informal talk had become policy with the appointment of Will Hays as president of the MPPDA, an organization that would develop rules for the editing and distribution of movies.[31] The movie industry founded the MPPDA to counter the censorship boards and legislation in many states that had plagued the moving picture world in 1921 and 1922. The industry thought it had a tentative answer to the type of condemnation reflected in the Chicago hearings.

At its next meeting, the commission decided to compile a final report out of the testimonies, studies, and articles that had influenced its work over the previous months. Chairman Hurley also introduced a motion to create an ordinance that could be given to the city council for passage. Between May 1919 and the summer of 1920, the commission completed and published its final report (which ran over two hundred pages) and established the parameters for censorship in Chicago. As *Moving Picture World* reported, the commission voted to "give careful consideration to the protests of producers against censorship." Hurley added, "I believe these people should be met half way."[32]

The commission prefaced its findings by saying that it was "unanimously of the opinion that a department controlling motion pictures, constructive in its nature, should be created, fostered, and maintained by the City of Chicago." While not abandoning the idea that censorship was still needed, the commission wanted to take the job away from the police (who had failed as censors) and give it to an institution that did not battle crime as its primary responsibility. Such a change, the commission wrote, "would eliminate the objectionable word censor and might also take out some of the unsatisfactory limitations of the idea that goes with the word, and add others much better."[33]

The commission proposed to pay the salaries of the board members by charging a fee for reviewing movies. Pink permits were dropped from the new code, but a new censorship clause was added to deal with posters advertising movies with salacious titles. The report summarized the proposed ordinance in six parts. First, no legal or constitutional impediments existed to prevent civic censorship of movies. Second, police censorship was a completely unpopular approach and should be discontinued. Third, a new and more professional department of motion pictures should be created to issue permits for the exhibition of movies. Fourth, all posters and advertisements would fall under the department's jurisdiction. Fifth, a yearly salary of $5,000 for department heads should be requisitioned. Finally, the pink permit system should be dropped with the idea that "no picture should be exhibited that could not be shown before the father and mother in company with their children."[34] By 1922, the city had adopted the new censorship code.

To contemporary ears, a Progressive Era debate over movies may sound arcane, but the city of Chicago had at least raised a simple question, one quoted in the introduction of the commission's report and one that still echoes: "Shall we give our children, and the weak and thoughtless of the community, what they 'want' or what they 'need'?"[35]

3

Forging a Mainstream Movie Aesthetic

Among the most promising informal channels for influencing the public's relationship with movies was the National Board of Review of Motion Pictures (NBR). The NBR was founded in 1909 in New York City as a way for the movie industry to defend against prior censorship, and saw its role as being a mediator between the film industry and the public. From 1909 through the mid-1920s, the movie industry submitted thousands of films to the board for its review and approval.[1] The industry imagined that this arrangement would satisfy all concerned with movie content. The NBR believed that its policy of constructive criticism improved on censorship because it was sensitive to the nature of movies as a popular art.

In 1926, Wilton Barrett, executive secretary of the National Board of Review, explained that the NBR performed a public service by reviewing motion pictures so moviegoers, rather than censors, could make decisions about what they would watch in theaters. According to Barrett, "the Board was a kind of crystalization of a thought and a movement [against censorship], both of which had become coexistent and countrywide." Censorship, he claimed, had grown out of the fears of cultural "aristocrats" regarding the explosive financial growth of movies. Movies had begun to encroach on the "monopoly of more expensive entertainment and . . . the domain of control and enjoyment of the arts" exercised by a "jealous minority." In an effort to curb the power of the photoplay, "liberally, socially minded people, as well as narrow purists and members of the aristocracy of ignorance, prejudice and suppression clamor for some sort of regulation." But a community of people had appeared who believed in the possibilities of movies, who viewed "any ill-advised efforts to hamper [their] growth" as a tragedy for art and democracy.[2]

The NBR's relationship to the industry was, however, constantly scrutinized. Many censors found the rules by which the NBR operated to be ambiguous and ineffective. When the MPPDA took shape in 1922, the NBR lost its job as the industry's review board, but instead of disbanding, the board sought to influence the motion picture world through its publications. Film historian Garth Jowett notes that the board's ineffective response to censorship did not prevent it from making "a significant contribution to the development of a 'movie consciousness' in the American public."[3]

As early as 1916, the board had published literature on films through its Better Films National Council. Wilton Barrett explained that the council sought to gather, organize, and classify facts about movies as a way to improve both the production of films as well as appreciation of them. This approach became more sophisticated when the NBR began publishing in 1920 a journal initially entitled *Exceptional Photoplays* (*EP*), and renamed the *National Board of Review Magazine* (*NBRM*) in 1926.[4] The articles, essays, and reviews by both regular editors and commissioned experts made the NBR more than a clearinghouse for movie reviews, it became a vital source for tracing patterns in movie culture during the 1920s. Through its editorials, the NBR became a significant advocate for the recognition of movies as a new type of art that demanded a different type of criticism.

The NBR's two journals made a serious attempt to understand and criticize movies without necessarily hoping that they would perform some moral or aesthetic magic on the public. In a world in which aesthetic judgment seemed progressively less important, the NBR had decided to consider popular taste within its cultural criticism. Such an approach would enable the board to deal with the movie industry and the public on their own terms without Progressive Era expectations.

At the same time, the editors of *EP* and *NBRM* sought to bridge the gap between the art film and the popular movie. The board wanted to explore the possibilities of a movie aesthetic for both popular as well as artistic pictures. Its editors would consider the popularity of a picture as well as its contribution to the technical development of the film. Ultimately, such an approach would make it easier to redefine movies as art and redefine art within mass culture.

The NBR reviewed a great number of mainstream productions

because that would be of interest to readers trying to decide what to see at their local theaters. Although the tone of most commentary was devoid of aesthetic theory, the editors argued that since movies were part of a growing, unwieldy industry that combined, for example, the star-driven, audacious pictures of Hollywood and the sparse, reflective films of Germany, mainstream productions could learn a great deal from the cinematic avant-garde. They also believed their readers would benefit from discussions on how to distinguish among movies based on a set of standards.

An editorial appearing in the first issue of *EP* illustrates the difference between the NBR's approach to criticism and that of the censor. Motion pictures, the editorialist argued, needed freedom in order to realize their potential as a popular art. Censorship "deprives the screen of the sympathy and full enjoyment of its audiences. Without their support the photoplay's chances of becoming a great popular art would be nil."[5] Mass appeal had to be a factor in determining a movie's quality, but it was not the only factor: "a high artistic finish is demanded, such indeed as may be said to place [movies] at the very front as vehicles of fine and worthy popular entertainment."[6] Still, if people stopped going to the pictures, movie magic would be inconsequential. It was the mixing of popular taste and artistic qualities that made motion pictures and criticism of them unique.

Alfred B. Kuttner, chairman of the board's Committee on Critique, looked for producers to have vision—to help the public discover what it wanted rather than pander to its base interests. His idea of leadership was to remain in touch with the people, but always with the intention of helping them realize higher ideals. Kuttner believed that "following the path of least resistance has proven to be a boomerang for the producer." The producer had "made the mistake of failing to lift the public gradually to a higher level of taste," even though he may have given the public what he thought it wanted.[7]

It was also possible to err by trying to please critics and aesthetes. Filmmakers could sin "aesthetically," offending "those standards of taste that make for healthy, vigorous art." In "groping to be artistic (spelled with a capital)," they made movies that "failed to be truthful and therefore beautiful."[8] Kuttner contended that "the superior ability of the motion picture to interpret our culture comes from the fact that the very processes of modern life can be used as the materials of motion picture art."[9] Adopting methods and techniques for other mediums such as the stage or the novel violated a basic premise of movie aesthetics.

An editorial entitled "Is It Art?" suggested that over time movies had proven to be a healthy art form. "For a long time the motion picture, considered merely a toy, floundered along innocent of its social significance and of its artistic possibilities." However, with the introduction of longer movies, more advanced scenarios, and better directors, "the question of whether the motion picture was really an art could no longer be put off." At first, those "nursed in the traditions of the older arts rose in denunciation," but soon "voices of authority ... were gradually raised in ... defense" of motion pictures. The creation and application of a movie aesthetic had begun to seem reasonable to those who initially doubted the worth of film. "Certain aesthetic effects had to be granted as belonging uniquely to the art of motion pictures." Not least was the power of movies to absorb "the pleasure and recreational instincts of millions of people, while the other arts were either withering or standing still." In a follow-up piece, the editors agreed "that in this machine age art was apparently a rapidly diminishing function ... the great masses of the people were no longer interested in the traditional arts."[10]

In a luncheon address at the NBR's thirteenth annual conference, dramatist Max Reinhardt spoke to the power movies had to make the notion of art as popular as it once had been. "I do not believe that the motion picture, whose greatest virtue is its power to speak to all ... should be made for the few," he argued. Turning to a device used consistently by early champions of movies, Reinhardt pointed out that while Shakespeare had "created an entire world ... he also created it for the entire world." In recent times, Reinhardt believed the theater had become inaccessible to most people and that the movies had "democratized the auditorium, extending to every spectator the equal privilege of the eye."[11]

James O. Spearing, a well-respected *New York Times* movie critic, also played up similarities to the work of Elizabethan bards. Speaking at the NBR's fourth annual conference, Spearing contended that many of history's greatest artists were quite conscious about pleasing their audience. For example, Molière used to read his comedies to his cook: If she laughed, "they were good. If she didn't laugh, they were bad." Likewise, Shakespeare "gave the people the things they loved. [But] he molded the common clay of popular taste into great works of genuine art." Thus, the trick remained not to "go looking for art on the screen," but "to make the whole motivation of ... photoplays intelligent and intelligible" so as "to let treatment of the elements be in the eloquent, imaginative language of kinetic photography."[12]

In order to make the movie industry, especially Hollywood, understand the potential of the art it created, the NBR throughout the 1920s consistently underscored the idea of a Little Cinema movement.[13] Drama critic Ralph Block was most likely the first champion of this idea. Based on his impression of the New York Theatre Guild, he wrote that small movie companies, independent of the industry and of the general public, could "find at once a potential audience which the professional movie-producer and distributor has never touched." Ultimately, their advocates hoped, Little Cinemas would influence the commercial producer by illustrating how to achieve "beauty at a low cost."[14]

The Little Cinema movement was the clearest manifestation of the NBR mission: to encourage the improvement of popular taste. In his *Times* column, "Screen," Spearing praised the board for performing "a unique service ... a service for which it, and no other existing institution, is equipped." The board, he said, had the ability to "establish an experimental theatre of the screen."[15] The board vowed to help exhibit pictures that failed to attract commercial attention and to cultivate the public's awareness of such films. Moreover, if such screenings became popular with audiences, the editors hoped they would inspire the industry to support the production of better pictures.[16] The goal thus remained to attract big producers so that the "photoplay at its fullest present and future reach" would be realized by mainstream companies rather than merely among small independent operations.[17] For the time being then, the Little Cinema movement would rely on independent producers, independent theaters, and an independent audience, serving as sources for exceptional photoplays as well as a reflection of the movie industry's failings.[18]

Frances Taylor Patterson, a member of the NBR editorial board, reported on the progress of this movement. A sign of its success, she believed, was the production of pictures bearing the mark of a single influential force. "One-man" pictures by documentarians such as Robert Flaherty, Robert Bruce, and Charles Brabin, as well as the more mainstream comedic talents of Mack Sennett and Charlie Chaplin, had produced pictures "stamped indelibly with the personality of the maker."[19] Unlike most Hollywood movies that bore only the "imprint of the machine" and therefore lacked artistic soul, the personal film had the capacity to be artistic as well as commercial. Such artists proved that movies could be made outside mainstream formulas.

Alfred Kuttner pointed to the German film industry as an example of creative efficiency. "With insufficient funds, inferior equipment and a less advanced stage of technique than ours," he wrote, "the directors proceeded to make the best pictures they knew how on the theory that a picture well done will find its proper audience, and without any silly notion that it was necessary to write down to a group of defective adults at the nine-year old level." *The Cabinet of Dr. Caligari*—a pioneering expressionist film from Germany—had illustrated that inexpensive films could also be popular. In December 1926, *Caligari* had played to "packed houses for over four weeks" at Manhattan's Fifth Avenue Playhouse, a member of the Little Cinema movement. Audience response, Kuttner believed, proved that "a sufficiently large part of the American public appreciates the best if given a chance to see it."[20]

While supporters of the Little Cinema movement might have encouraged filmmaking outside of Hollywood, they also hoped alternative movies would influence mainstream producing. Kuttner thought that Little Cinemas had "had a most stimulating influence upon the commercial theatre, and [have] done much to correct the besetting fallacy of play and picture magnates alike—the underestimating of the intelligence and receptivity of the public."[21] He noted that the success enjoyed by the International Film Guild at the Cameo Theatre and the Fifth Avenue Playhouse in New York City had inspired groups in Rutherford, New Jersey; Jacksonville, Florida; and Atlanta, Georgia, to begin special screenings of "notable" pictures.[22]

Symon Gould, director of New York City's Film Arts Guild, confirmed that his programs of independent and foreign films had drawn consistently large audiences at Manhattan's Cameo Theatre. The "film-art movement" he believed, would continue to grow because "its propelling principles are evolutionary and not revolutionary."[23] Eric T. Clark, general manager of the massive Eastman Theatre in Rochester, New York, seemed to agree, explaining that alternative theaters could help develop alternative tastes among moviegoers. He suggested that while large theaters would never cater "to the tastes of the few while the many stay away," there was a place in America's movie culture for "special houses . . . showing pictures of limited appeal." Indeed, he observed, many people might find it refreshing to see a picture made "in disregard for the box office." Kuttner imagined that Little Cinemas might find favor among the nation's cultural elite—"that part of the public still unreached" by movies.[24]

By 1927, the NBR reported that Little Cinemas had taken hold in urban areas throughout the country, including Cleveland, Brooklyn,

Chicago, East Orange, and the nation's capital.[25] Bettina Gunczy, an *NBRM* editor, witnessed the opening of Washington's Little Theatre of the Motion Picture Guild on April 7, 1927. Gunczy reported that this Little Cinema might show "unusual" pictures, but by necessity it had become, physically, a big theater. On opening night, the crowd had filled the theater's lounge to "overflowing." Nathan Machat, a movie exhibitor, and John Milligan, a reporter, had experimented with the idea of showing "art-films" in a theater of the Wardman Park Hotel in one of Washington's more posh residential districts. The success of that venture led them to open a new theater in the capital's downtown. Fittingly, they opened with Sergei Eisenstein's *The Battleship Potemkin*, a favorite among intellectuals who liked movies.[26]

Little Cinemas had illustrated that movies could attract audiences with discriminating tastes, and pictures made by such figures as Robert Flaherty could stamp a film with the authenticity of an individual creator. The NBR had thus proved that film could be art under the proper conditions.[27] But what were popular movies then? Were they popular art? Did they serve the public as perhaps other popular entertainment had in the past? In other words, was a Shakespeare to be born to Hollywood?

H.L. Mencken, a fiercely acerbic critic and editor of *Mercury,* not surprisingly answered with an emphatic, "NO!" He contended that money in Hollywood had spoiled any possibility for a true artist to emerge. The industry had "built their business upon a foundation of morons, and now they are paying for it." It seemed that making a popular picture required "pouring tons of money" into it, and once it was finished, the producers either had "to sell it to the immense audiences of half-wits, or go broke." Mencken concluded that the movies were "too rich to have any room for genuine artists." He asked if anyone could imagine Beethoven making $100,000 a year, or Bach owning nine automobiles, as did some movie stars. Artists had to be "damned fools" and "romantics," not businessmen.[28]

The 1920s, however, revealed that Mencken might have been wrong. Artists had begun to enjoy fame and some prosperity as talented musicians and writers. In a sense, an older and perhaps more European grounded ideal of the artist was beginning to give way to a Yankee version that was both commercially as well as culturally significant—one that could satisfy different levels of taste. The remarks of Max Reinhardt and James Spearing had hinted at the secret behind movies as popular gems: genius could in fact be forged in service to popular appeal.

In a brief, illuminating glimpse of early moviegoing, journalist Celia Harris captured the sense that perhaps movies possessed a genuine artistic spark.[29] She wrote about a small-town movie theater in rural Wisconsin that had an "arched white-and-gold entrance," and a girl who sold tickets at twenty cents apiece to people who waited in line in front of "tri-colored posters" announcing the daily bill. To Harris, the enthusiasm of the crowds who flocked weekly to this theater was reminiscent of Elizabethan England. Theatergoers of that period had also "worried the literary critics and social reformers" with their "apparent enthusiasm ... for cheap melodramas, low comedies, and plays with unclean dialogue and situations." Like movies, sixteenth-century stage productions required commercial backing and used contemporary scandals to attract "the whole of London for an audience crowd." Harris observed that "such an audience" seemed to create "a demand for playwrights"—particularly popular ones such as Shakespeare, Christopher Marlowe, Robert Greene, Thomas Kyd, and George Peele. While her understanding of Elizabethan England was a bit too rosy, Harris did accurately predict that at a similar rate of progress, "the movies would have until 1936 to produce their first scenario writers of significance and until 1941 to launch a fully representative genius."[30]

Harris was reasonably prescient. By 1936, an army of gifted writers had descended upon Hollywood, including William Faulkner, F. Scott Fitzgerald, Ben Hecht, and Preston Sturges. And by 1941, Orson Welles, the boy genius, had launched a career and a movie that would land him atop lists of great directors.

Comparing movies to Shakespearean stage plays seemed credible to intellectuals who had an affection for movies but had not yet begun to champion the industry that produced them. Such critics navigated between the cultural conservatives who rejected movies outright and the movie enthusiasts who were unconcerned with their cultural value. Thus, a "third way" seemed near at hand, marrying artistic as well as popular aspects within movie criticism. This approach also allowed intellectuals to continue their mild rebellion against the artistic standards of conservatives without sliding into the aestheticism of cultural radicals.

A young Dwight Macdonald expressed this type of enthusiasm for movies. In 1929, he and a group of his Yale comrades began publishing a "little magazine" entitled *Miscellany*. In the second article he published on movies, Macdonald also compared motion pictures and filmmakers to their Elizabethan counterparts. What impressed him even more, however, was the creation of a new aesthetic based partly on the variety of tastes represented in a movie audience. At "a cheap movie house," Macdonald recalled watching both a Tom Mix western—"one of the most vapid and infantile forms of art ever conceived even by the brain of a Hollywood movie producer"—and the *Lash of the Czar*, "a Russian film of the greatest subtlety and sophistication." This "incongruous" combination illustrated to Macdonald that even though the public did not bother with "aesthetic distinctions," the movie artist seemed "to draw strength from contact with his fellow men as Antaeus was refreshed by touching his mother earth." Unlike other arts, such as painting, that seemed targeted for a "small, narrow, specialized" audience, movies communicated to a "broad and inclusive" public. That was possible, Macdonald thought, because critics had yet to catalog, formally, what made a movie good or bad. He viewed that as "a great source of strength for the movies," since the best filmmakers could create for the masses without the burden of trying to impress the cultural elite.[31]

Gilbert Seldes, the most influential critic of the popular arts during the 1920s, also engaged the problem that apparently faced many intellectuals who appreciated both popular as well as fine arts. To answer the charge that the "lively arts" (the expression used to describe such things as movies) were inconsequential or, worse, debasing to the fine arts, he developed a criticism that depended on respecting different cultural spheres—a person could legitimately praise both Picasso and Charlie Chaplin without betraying rigorous standards of taste. Seldes did not advocate leveling cultural distinctions so that all expressions were treated with equal reverence or, as the case may be, irreverence. Rather, he made the somewhat revolutionary proposition that critics could incorporate things that entertained the masses within a vision of culture that embraced things that bewildered them.

In 1924, Seldes finished *The Seven Lively Arts*, his first book on culture in America. He was only thirty-two years old and had written his manuscript while on a year's leave from his duties as a cultural critic for *Vanity Fair*, which was among the first magazines to devote serious attention to the popular arts. Seldes wrote the book to point out the creativity and significance of Mack Sennett slapstick comedies, the *Krazy Kat* comic strips of George Herriman, the performance of Al Jolson, the energy of Alexander's Ragtime Band, and other forms of entertainment that rarely received anything other than derision. In doing so, Seldes's criticism became not merely an alternative to the genteel tradition, but a bridge between an era when great art was popular and a later period when mass culture was great art. Moreover, Seldes did not merely embrace mass culture, he criticized it—and by doing so he afforded it a semblance of legitimacy. There were, in other words, standards one could apply to the lively arts—not simply to make them seem more legitimate, but to put them in some perspective.

Like Randolph Bourne, Seldes believed that middle-class taste had corrupted cultural criticism. As a result, America had become awash in expressions that were pretentious rather than authentic. For example, the "It" girl movies of the 1920s and Cecil B. de Mille's costume epics looked sophisticated but had hollow artistic cores. Seldes scoffed: "They are 'art.' They are genteel. They offend nothing—except the intelligence." He had no patience for unauthentic art: that which pretended to be serious but failed to "fathom the secret sources ... [or] understand the secret obligations, of art." To him, it was possible to appreciate both the popular and the fine arts at once and accept that they could be mutually exclusive. But popular arts should remain popular and endearing, he argued, and fine arts should strive to be serious and enduring. "Slap-stick," for example, "never pretended to be anything but itself and could be disgusting or tasteless or dull, but it could not be vulgar." It was not, in his words, bogus.[32]

The best popular arts, Seldes pointed out, were timely expressions of life rather than timeless works. "We require arts which specifically refer to our moment," Seldes wrote, "which create the image of our lives. We must have arts which, we feel, are for ourselves alone, which no one before us could have cared for so much, which no one after us will wholly understand." Those "fully civilized" could recognize the high seriousness of fine art and also be able to "appreciate the high levity of the minor arts."[33] Seldes had legitimized the criticism of popular arts because they informed a part of life that was significant: the need for enjoyment.

Seldes also wondered if "praise of the minor arts isn't, at bottom, treachery to the great. I had always believed," he explained, "that there exists no such hostility between the two divisions of the arts which are honest—that the real opposition is between them, allied, and the polished fake." He made a fairly involved argument that the reason society had difficulty accepting spheres of art was that a middle-class sensibility had made it imperative that one recognize cultural significance in the "right" places. He characterized such people as "those who invariably are ill at ease in the presence of great art until it has been approved by authority." Furthermore, since the lively arts would cease being lively if subjected to such treatment, Seldes advised not expecting "art" to arise from such expressions as the movies. At base, Seldes identified an irony that would follow the lively arts throughout the century: "It is only because the place of the common arts in decent society is always being called into question that the answer needs to be given."[34]

Indeed, the treatment of movies was a good example of the strange place occupied by the lively arts. During the 1920s, Seldes would establish himself as the preeminent movie reviewer in the United States by making it acceptable for intellectuals to appreciate movies. His essays appeared in important journals of opinion such as *Harper's,* the *Atlantic,* the *New Republic,* and the *Nation,* and in popular magazines such as the *Saturday Evening Post.* He took the position that movies not only represented a significant new art form but that a new criticism—including a new aesthetic—was needed to address it.

Seldes, like so many other people, loved the slapstick comedies of Mack Sennett and his primary muse, Charlie Chaplin. He believed that Sennett and Chaplin had explored the dimensions of moving pictures better than any other team in the silent film era. It was movement, rather than dialogue, that propelled the action of slapstick comedies and that created the greatest reactions among the audiences. It was a great trick, Seldes seemed to say, to get people in the audience to forget themselves and their surroundings and laugh out loud at the antics of shadows. The art of movies, if one could claim to have found one, was the ability to entertain thousands of people simultaneously without them realizing what a dazzling feat that was.[35]

Seldes remained skeptical of those critics who advanced the art of the motion picture, such as the Little Cinemas. To Seldes, film art usually meant "good interior decoration ... [and] it suggests a great infusion of 'artiness'; the whole attitude of movies for the few is arrogant and patronizing." In a letter to the International Film Art Guild published in the *New Republic,* he offered advice to Little Cinemas. He commended the attempts made by such theaters to show "exceptional photoplays," but he reminded their operators that he could not "think of the movie except as a popular art or form of entertainment." There was a need, he admitted, to educate a popular audience to appreciate good films. Although Little Cinemas looked to encourage "an audience for new and unpopular things," he hoped that they would also "try to create ones also for the old and the popular. Keep all the movies alive," he implored.[36]

While Seldes was not the first critic to introduce a separate movie aesthetic or the first to argue that movies were significant because they were popular, he was the most important early critic to explore the implications of movies as a popular art form. "The artistic elements can exist in a film," he argued, "without for a moment touching upon the subject in such a way that the spectator is made uncomfortably aware of them." Filmmakers and critics illustrated their talent not by announcing their devotion to the arts but by rejoicing in the joy that moving pictures can do what no other art is capable of: projecting the illusion of reality before thousands of people while they simultaneously react to what they see. Movies were art because it took creativity to compose believable and entertaining illusions.

In a new preface for the 1957 edition of *The Seven Lively Arts*, Seldes wrote revealingly, "as a piece of propaganda, my work did not sufficiently identify the enemy." Seldes believed that in overemphasizing his enthusiasm for the lively arts, he had failed to draw a sharp enough distinction between the "great arts" and the "bogus arts." Considering the era in which he wrote the first edition, that is not surprising. Seldes composed his ideas at a time when a majority of critics dismissed most popular arts as inconsequential. It was, after all, daring for a critic to treat movies seriously. What he seemed to regret, though, was his inability to foresee the trajectory that popular arts would take in American culture. Rather than become the high art of mass culture (and flourish within their own sphere of appeal), popular arts would slowly become indistinguishable from fine arts. Once that happened, cultural criticism gradually lost its relevance and critics grew increasingly powerless to distinguish art and artists from bogus products and hucksters. Thus, while Seldes had made a forceful argument for recognizing the cultural value of entertainment, his criticism ultimately became most useful as a signpost on the road to cultural relativism. The worth of Seldes's aesthetics would make no sense in a world in which movie directors can hide behind both the title of artist and the power of the box office.[37]

Two years after Seldes first published *The Seven Lively Arts* and an ocean away, Iris Barry began a career that would place her among the most significant figures in the creation of a modern movie aesthetic. Barry was a poet turned movie critic who wrote for two of London's largest daily newspapers. She was also the founder of the London Film Society—the first of its kind in England's largest city. In 1926, Barry's *Let's Go to the Pictures* introduced readers to the author's characteristically unpretentious approach to movies. She wrote neither as a member of the cinematic or literary avant-garde nor as a member of the self-anointed cultural elite. Both groups had dismissed popular movies as more rubbish for public consumption. Rather, Barry fell into the tradition of Vachel Lindsay and alongside Seldes—two critics she included in a very brief bibliography.

Her enthusiasm for movies reflected a belief in their inherent virtues as a popular art form and as a medium that had challenged the distinctions between highbrow and lowbrow culture. She hoped to convince England's cultural elite—the audience reading her book—that movies possessed special qualities that made them difficult to characterize and worthy of serious attention. "At the moment we are a little ashamed of ourselves," she claimed. "Critics and connoisseurs demonstrate their deep sense by damning the film in every key. So those of us who go to the pictures every week, or everyday keep it rather quiet, or allude to it as being cheap, or restful." She concluded sharply: "Going to the pictures is nothing to be ashamed of."[38]

Much like Seldes, Barry fought a lonely battle in her attempt to win respect for movies. And also like her American contemporary, Barry believed that the implicit value of movies lay in their ability to entertain the masses. In other words, she argued, "art should be intelligible to the simplest people." Yet the reason movies failed to earn the imprimatur of art (and respectability) was because critics had failed to do their job. She called for critics to "invent terms, lay down canons, derive from your categories; heap up nonsense with sense and, when you have done, the cinemas will still be open and we can all flock in as proudly as we do now to the theatre and the opera." Barry did not dispute the terms used to pronounce artistic merit, but she did insist that one could speak about movies intelligently. For Barry, the magic of movies made them as important as any other art form.[39]

In an early chapter, Barry addressed the concerns of critics such as Walter Prichard Eaton who viewed the cinema as a poor substitute for the theater. In an impassioned statement, she urged critics to consider why moving pictures drew millions of people. "It is no mere accident that films are so well adapted to treat fantasy and dream," she began, "the art of the cinema offers the world that escape from everyday life, that rationalization of conflicts which lifts the audience so completely out of themselves to a region that other ages found to lie somewhere about an altar, but which we, with our wise freedom from superstitions, our cheap agnosticism and common sense are denied. . . . The cinema provides us with the safe dreams we want: and if our dreams are often not worth having, it is because we demand no better." To Barry, movies had become a new secular religion. While not suggesting that celebrities and film-makers had created a new catechism, she argued that people living in an industrial, civilized society still needed an escape from the reality of their lives, something a mysticism of earlier times had provided. There was indeed a magic to moviegoing. It tapped into a primal desire to move beyond oneself without necessarily going anywhere physically. That such magic came from a flickering, fleeting experience did not, in Barry's eyes, diminish the significance of the impulse that drove millions of people to darkened halls and before the silver screen.

Barry thus made a somewhat rebellious argument: Perhaps the conditions on which the quality of cultural expressions were based could incorporate popular as well as elite taste. Cultural arbiters (whether of the elite or the avant-garde) need not "find" the material for it to be "good" or "artistic"—perhaps that discovery could be made (and was being made) by millions of people every week. To correct the obvious oversight of those who dismissed popular taste, Barry wanted to charge critics with a new mission. They would no longer simply pass judgment on works, but would help shape the relationship between the industry that produced movies and the audience that supported the industry. Much like the National Board of Review, Barry wanted critics to assume a new attitude toward movies in the hope that the public would begin to take moviegoing a bit more seriously and thus prompt the industry to produce better movies. She also believed that her crusade would help overcome the resistance of "professional classes" to the cinema. Such an attitude, she maintained, "is only now slowly breaking down because persons in this category have been forced to recognize the hold which the cinema has over the minds of the people, and the extreme importance of the role which film plays in a nation's social life." Once movies breached traditional barriers, Barry believed the medium would assume its rightful place among the other arts. As she wrote in the concluding chapter of her book, "It would be better said that beauty is the same in all of [the arts], but that each expresses beauty in aspects peculiar to itself."[40]

With a touch of humor, Barry mused about the peculiar role she was asking fellow intellectuals to play. She described a man telling his children about a strange encounter during his day. "I saw a very curious thing in the Strand to-day. I saw what do you think? I saw a Film Critic!" The eldest of the clan looked up at the father, crying, "What is a filmcritic, Daddy? What does it do?" In the years ahead such questions (and the intent behind them) would evolve into less of a joke as film critics grew more important and the difference between movies and art collapsed. In the late 1920s, however, a film critic's role was as undefined as the cultural position of movies. Nonetheless, steps had been taken that made both movies and their critics almost respectable. Other barriers still lay in the way before Barry's hopes were realized. Her part in this intellectual and cultural fight had just begun.[41]

4

Dreiser versus Hollywood

In 1941, at the end of the Great Depression, Preston Sturges made a movie entitled *Sullivan's Travels.* The picture was ostensibly a romantic comedy staring Joel McCrea and Veronica Lake. McCrea plays a wealthy and popular movie director named Sullivan who is wracked with guilt because he makes seemingly inconsequential Hollywood pictures. While the rest of the nation contends with the harsh reality of the depression, Sullivan pumps out box office hits filled with fantasy and humor. Having failed to address the great dilemma of the day, Sullivan decides to become socially conscious.

In order to empathize with the desperate many, the director dresses like a hobo and sets out to collect information for a movie that will be both socially responsible and artistically serious. His experiment succeeds all too well. First, though, he gets a gentle dose of humility when he meets a beautiful but failed actress, played by Lake. She is a person equally envious of Sullivan's success and contemptuous of his desire to understand poverty. However, Lake's character also makes Sullivan realize that he has come close to mocking the downtrodden with his misguided sympathy.

The story takes a darker turn in the last third of movie when Sullivan is wrongly accused and convicted of murder. Unable to convince the authorities that he is a famous director—another hobo has lifted his wallet—Sullivan is sentenced to hard time in a work prison in the Deep South. Once there, he meets men who represent the class of people he wants to understand but can never know. Sullivan's fellow prisoners turn out to be less than the saints he imagined, and he gets little sympathy for his frantic desire to break out. In the movie's pivotal scene, the prisoners, including a very somber Sullivan, shuffle, feet shackled, into an all-black church to watch a movie with the congregation. On a white sheet hung above the church altar, the pastor shows a series of cartoons and a silly Hollywood comedy. The entire audience, much to Sullivan's surprise and then joy, erupts into laughter scene after scene. At that moment he realizes the great entertainment value of movies.

Sturges was clearly poking fun at other artists who produced socially realistic (and serious) commentaries on American life. Had they, he seemed to ask, taken themselves too seriously and in the process come dangerously close to creating a false sense of sympathy for the poor? In addition to taking a satirical jab at the film industry, Sturges also posed important questions: Should entertainment be an end in itself? Did Hollywood have a responsibility to some higher moral and social concerns?

Sturges enjoyed enormous success as both a writer and director. Although *Sullivan's Travels* was only his third directorial project, he had written some twenty-four movies, most during the 1930s. His career, as well as this specific movie were, however, laced with a paradox: Writers who went to Hollywood during the depression benefited financially from their employment in movie studios but the craft of writing tended to suffer under that system. Perhaps the same could be said about American culture: Movies entertained millions of people, cheering up their bleak lives, but the culture as a whole suffered under the barrage of senseless pictures.

There is a case that illustrated the multiple issues involved in the rise of movies to prominence. Theodore Dreiser, a writer who made his reputation by criticizing American materialism and made money selling his stories to Hollywood, argued before the New York Supreme Court that the movie industry had an obligation to artists and the American people. By doing so, Dreiser hoped to make the movie industry more socially conscious and hoped that it would amend a maxim that the movies entertain people, and no one should expect them to do any more. From the beginning, Dreiser's legal case against Hollywood was a losing proposition, yet his challenge illustrated a troubling trend: The movies had not only begun to overwhelm the other arts, they were gradually changing the definition of art itself. The broader implications of Dreiser's criticisms spoke to the role that movies play in shaping American culture.

During the 1930s, Hollywood attracted a large number of talented writers and directors from the theaters, newspapers, and publishing houses of the East Coast. As a result, movie studios assembled perhaps the greatest generation of literary talent in the history of motion pictures. Of course, many contemporaries of these people were not so easily impressed. George Jean Nathan, the era's greatest drama critic, did a great deal, as one historian has written, to "popularize the notion that most playwrights who went to Hollywood prostituted their talents and turned their backs on the American theater." Nathan believed that the silent film had already managed to siphon popular interest away from traditional arts such as the stage, and the "talkie" seemed destined to do even more damage. Hollywood was not merely dumbing down culture, he argued, it was also destroying the scores of talented writers lured west by promises of money. While this assessment was a bit exaggerated, the profession of writing did experience a profound change. In fact, artists in general had to redefine their positions in relation to the expanding cultural marketplace. In the movie industry, this change was fed by the conversion from silent films to talking pictures.[1]

In a humorous take on the "pursuit of [the] elusive story which shall become the Great American Picture and make millions of dollars," theater critic Leda Bauer contributed a piece to Nathan's and H.L. Mencken's *American Mercury* about the movie industry's treatment of literature. Bauer covered territory familiar to those who, like Nathan and Mencken, viewed Hollywood as a machine that consumed story material as if it were present-day fast food—it was good as long as it satisfied popular tastes. There was, she said, a secret formula for success. Movie ideas had to come from either a best-selling novel or a long-running play and then fit a particular genre, create a cinematic spectacle for which producers could charge a high price, and serve as a vehicle for a star. After an idea found tacit acceptance, the story itself went through a process intended, she said, "to prevent it from resembling the idea the producer bought." A story would be completely rewritten until there was "no longer any connection with the story on which the screen play was based." Once completed, the scenario was "pronounced perfect, the title ... changed to something short, spicy, and entirely inapplicable, and the original story re-sold to another picture company to go through the same process."[2]

With studios offering steady paychecks to a generation of writers used to living on freelance diets, this brave new lucrative world seemed attractive, even if at times frustrating. Writers had grown accustomed to literary editors they usually knew personally. In Hollywood, writing became a communal, vaguely mechanical process in which producers and their staffs contributed to the creation of a story. Although the financial rewards surpassed those offered by any other field, writers and directors had to swallow the notion that motion pictures were still considered an illegitimate art form. A writer who felt that paradox acutely was Theodore Dreiser. He complained that writing for Hollywood was "a debauching process" that worked "harm to the mind of the entire world. . . . For the debauching of any good piece of literature is what?" he asked. "Criminal? Ignorant? Or both?"[3]

Dreiser had come to pride himself on his realistic portrayals of life in the United States. Alfred Kazin has written that "naturalism was Dreiser's instinctive response to life; it linked him with the great primitive novelists of the modern era . . . who found in the boundless freedom and unparalleled range of naturalism the only approximation of a life that is essentially brutal and disorderly."[4] Hollywood's excesses fed Dreiser's view that life under capitalism promised little more than economic servitude and moral compromise. A person was lured into a vast underclass of people on the make, looking for a way to possess more goods and willing to sell their souls to satisfy their cravings. Yet Hollywood also tempted Dreiser's desire for the fortune and fame that went with being a celebrity in a world increasingly dominated by mass-mediated creations.

Dreiser had long had an antagonistic relationship with the movie industry. In 1915 he made an attempt to direct scenario development for Mirror Films, but the deal came undone when producer Jesse Lasky bought the company and declined material Dreiser either brought to him or wrote himself. This initial contact with movies contributed to Dreiser's somewhat mordant attitude toward the industry. This clearly was yet another example of the wealthy and hollow rejecting the poor but brilliant. In a series of articles about making it in the movies, Dreiser told tales of aspiring actresses providing sexual favors to heartless studio executives and then returning to their Midwest homes as broken women. In many ways, Hollywood was the perfect illustration of place and medium for Dreiser's cynical but salacious worldview.[5]

Within such cynicism, though, was a shrewd commentary on the cultural effects of the movie industry. In January 1929, Dreiser wrote a short, condemnatory piece on Hollywood for Symon Gould's Film Arts Guild. Gould's organization ran Dreiser's remarks as part of an advertisement in the Communist Party's literary magazine, the *New Masses.*

Dreiser contended somewhat prophetically that "each of the arts in America has been reduced rapidly to a money-making level, and there is no better example of the enormity of this degradation than the cinema." Worse still, he continued, "the influence of the movies on the American public has been greater than any other force." The introduction of sound would only inspire Hollywood to do more damage by reproducing the works from other mediums for commercial gain. The Film Arts Guild could counter such influence by promoting the principles of film—"the artistic use of light, shadow and movement"—through its exhibition of Soviet films. Both liberal and radical critics had praised the work of Soviet directors for advancing the craft of filmmaking. Yet in the ideologically charged 1930s, Soviet films took on a greater political importance. By screening such films, Gould's group would introduce Americans to true film art that challenged the "meretricious and ignorant entertainment" produced by the amoral capitalists of Hollywood. In the dialectical terms that were much in vogue during the 1930s, Dreiser maintained that Soviet cinema represented the antithesis to the Hollywood thesis both aesthetically and politically.[6]

This attack was but a preview of Dreiser's most sustained and involved critique of Hollywood. A real battle broke out over Dreiser's most famous and blunt indictment of American materialism, *An American Tragedy.*

When Dreiser's novel *An American Tragedy* was first published in 1926, Boston censors banned the book from libraries and stores because it dealt with illicit affairs, discussions of abortion, and the drowning of a young pregnant woman. Such elements, however, made the story attractive to thousands of readers as well as to Hollywood. Dreiser had used the details of a turn-of-the-century murder trial in upstate New York to construct an allegory linking the crimes of one person with the sins of an entire nation. His main character, Clyde Griffiths, is a young man who emerges from a humble religious family with dreams of materialistic success and social importance. Griffiths's journey allows Dreiser to scrutinize many aspects of American life, including organized religion, capitalism, the law, wealth, and free will. In the book's pivotal section, the young man is indicted for the drowning death of the young woman he had gotten pregnant. The murder case itself served as a vehicle for Dreiser's larger intention: to indict American society for creating killers and sinners out of young men like his fictional character Clyde Griffiths.

Dreiser sold the silent screen rights for *An American Tragedy* to the Paramount Publix Corporation in 1926. The $90,000 paid for the novel was, at the time, one of the highest sums offered for a work of fiction. Yet studio executive Jesse Lasky and his associates let the book sit dormant at Paramount from 1926 through 1930. Dreiser suspected that the producers feared battles with censors and prudish civic groups. In 1929, Dreiser let his impatience show in an article he wrote regarding censorship laws. He argued that artists everywhere in the United States were "faced with one of the most fanatical and dangerous forms of censorship that ever existed because the effect of all such activity is to reduce all human intelligence to one level . . . that of a low-grade (not even high grade) moron!"[7] Seemingly undeterred by hostile conditions, Dreiser pressed to have a movie version of his book made. In 1930 he threatened to sue Paramount if it failed to act on his contract. He also demanded additional money for the sound rights, whereupon Lasky offered Dreiser another $55,000 for rights to make a sound picture out of *An American Tragedy.* Since "talkies" had become the rage in Hollywood, it was vital that Lasky secure Dreiser's consent. This brought the total sum paid to Dreiser for the screen rights to his already popular novel to $145,000, of which he kept all but $10,000.[8]

At the same time that Lasky and Dreiser negotiated a new contract for *An American Tragedy,* Sergei Eisenstein, the Soviet director of *The Battleship Potemkin* and *Ten Days that Shook the World,* was offered the chance to develop Dreiser's novel for the screen. Eisenstein had become a celebrity in the film world, particularly among radical critics. Not surprisingly, he accepted this chance eagerly and set to work on a long screenplay with Ivor Montagu, an English film critic and cofounder of the London Film Society.

In a letter to Dreiser, the director explained his approach to translating the story. Paramount had told Eisenstein that it wanted a "realistic plain police-story . . . a murder story." The director, however, wanted to focus on the "leit-motif of destroying the psychology and ruining step by step the character of the boy by the surrounding social conditions." Ivor Montagu added that both he and the director had received "repeated assurance from [Paramount's executives] that the treatment we desired for the film comprise the theme and incidents of the book unaltered, that this had been approved by the Hayes organization, and the uncertainty which we several times expressed . . . was quite groundless and unnecessary." Afterward, both men wondered if Lasky and others at Paramount had actually read Dreiser's book before they offered Eisenstein the chance to adapt it to the screen.[9]

Eisenstein's draft, which he expected to cut by as much as one-third, met with a mixed response at Paramount.[10] Those who read it, including Lasky, B.P. Schulberg, and David O. Selznick, considered Eisenstein's script a masterfully wrought depiction of Dreiser's novel, but they had serious doubts about its commercial value. In October 1930, Selznick wrote to Schulberg that Eisenstein's work was "the most moving script I have ever read . . . positively torturing. When I finished it, I was so depressed I wanted to reach for the bourbon bottle." But "as entertainment," he added, "I don't think it has one chance in a hundred." Selznick doubted "that Paramount could risk so radical an interpretation in so important a project." The executive argued that "the advancement of the art" in cinema was "not the business of this organization," nor was offering "a most miserable two hours to millions of happy-minded young Americans." Abruptly, Lasky pulled the project away from Eisenstein and gave it to a safer employee, Josef von Sternberg.[11]

Von Sternberg had become a well-known and well-respected director, mostly for making German actress Marlene Dietrich into a Hollywood star. He and a Broadway playwright named Samuel Hoffenstein finished a script in a little over five weeks. Rather than concentrate on the first volume of Dreiser's novel (the part that detailed a poor young man's struggle to rise above his humble origins), they used the natural drama and rapid pace of the second volume as their foundation. They thus highlighted the novel's exciting courtroom scenes, in which the district attorney launches a zealous effort to convict Clyde Griffiths for the murder of his girlfriend.

Dreiser received a copy of the script in February and rejected it. In a letter to Jesse Lasky, Dreiser explained, "I want this picture to be a success, as much as you and your company do, but it must be obvious to anyone who knows pictures that Sternberg and Hoffenstein have 'botched' my novel." Dreiser claimed that the script writers had made the novel's main character into an "unsympathetic, scheming, sex-starved 'drug-store cowboy,'" rather than a "creature of circumstances" who was compelled to act as he did. The present script lacked the romance, complexity, and ideas that drove the novel, which Dreiser called a "progressive drama." Dreiser seemed to place most of the blame on von Sternberg, who, he said, lacked "sympathy for my writing and for the script generally." To remedy the situation, Dreiser told Lasky he wanted four weeks to prepare a new script with the help of screenwriter Hy S. Kraft, and he also requested a new director. "I should also like to have Chester Eskin engaged to direct the picture and Kraft to work with him on the script and the direction, with my cooperation and supervision." Dreiser was "sure it would be a happy and successful association for everyone concerned." It needed to be, he explained, since a movie of his novel could be "a great picture," one for which the studio had already spent a large sum of money to own and publicize.[12]

Lasky remained steadfast regarding the production of the movie. Paramount owned the rights to Dreiser's novel, he explained, and that gave the studio the authority to decide who would write, direct, and act in it. Lasky told Dreiser that his offer of a new shooting script arrived too late to receive serious consideration, and that it was the author's fault rather than the studio's, because Dreiser had made it nearly impossible to reach him any earlier. "I am stating this at length," Lasky wrote, "not in the spirit of controversy but to remind you of the facts so that you will see that it is far too late to accept your suggestions as to the treatment, writer, and director to be selected for the work, without even referring to the qualifications of the gentlemen suggested."[13] At the beginning of March 1931, von Sternberg began shooting the movie.

Dreiser then threatened legal action if Paramount and von Sternberg refused to include the revisions Dreiser demanded. His letter established a number of issues important to the subsequent legal entanglement. First, Dreiser invoked a clause of the agreement he had signed in early January with Paramount that required the studio to "use its best endeavors to accept such advice, suggestions, and criticisms that the Seller may make in so far as it may be, in the judgment of the Purchaser, consistent to do so."[14] Second, Dreiser conveyed his frustration that the studio had rejected the Eisenstein-Montagu script, which, the author understood, had received very favorable responses from readers. The second script was so far inferior in its interpretation of the "spirit" of the novel that Dreiser felt he "was left [with] no recourse but to dismiss it and him [von Sternberg] entirely." Third, Dreiser was exasperated by the fact that von Sternberg, a man with obvious personal hostility toward him, had been allowed to take over the project. Finally, and perhaps most importantly, Dreiser feared that "the talking version" would give "the impression to millions of people throughout the world" that the novel was "nothing short of a cheap, tawdry confession story," and would thus lack "the scope, emotion, action and psychology of the book involved." His artistic integrity as well as his interest in his property seemed threatened by this simplistic adaptation. As *Commonweal,* a progressive Catholic journal of opinion, noted around that time, Hollywood had "slapped Mr. Dreiser; not on the cheek [a reference to Dreiser's recent slapping of Sinclair Lewis at a Manhattan dinner party] but on the aesthetic sensibilities—the seat, one gathers, of much deeper pain."[15]

Paramount evidently found it reasonable to attempt to placate the writer. On March 22, 1931—three days after the "slap heard round the world"—Dreiser and writer Hy Kraft flew out to Hollywood. They worked on additions to the von Sternberg–Hoffenstein script by adding to Clyde Griffiths's psychological profile. This meant including material at the beginning and end of the movie to introduce ambiguity into the character's guilt—a vital element in the novel.

Schulberg wrote to Dreiser, telling him in carefully crafted statements that the studio wished "to have your unqualified approval of the picture when it is finished, and this sincere desire should assure you that we wish to accept and incorporate every suggestion made by you which may appear to be to the best advantage of the completed picture." But, the production chief said, the studio ultimately had "no legal obligation . . . to you or Mr. Kraft . . . and . . . we are free to use these scenes or eliminate them later, as may be later decided."[16] Shortly after Dresier read Schulberg's letter, he fired off a telegram to MPPDA president Will Hays in New York that amounted to a declaration of war against Paramount.[17] Dreiser complained that his trip to Hollywood, prompted by Hays's "talk with Lasky," was a bust, a "total loss of time and money." There was "no grasp of significance of my contentions no genuine desire for cooperation." Only when von Sternberg had completed the film would he be shown it and his "suggestions considered." Outraged, he concluded: "This is sheer bunk an official fake am determined film shall not issue this way unless cooperation immediately secured propose to attack in press here and elsewhere and to sue in New York if you have influence wire Schulberg at once for square deal."[18] Upon his return to New York on April 11, Dreiser made good on his promise to Hays. In a published interview he referred to the movie capital as "Hooeyland" and said that Paramount had not adapted his novel but "traduced" it, creating a *"A Mexican Comedy,"* rather than *"An American Tragedy."*[19]

Later that month, Dreiser began preparations for his case against Paramount. He sent letters to figures in New York's literary community whom he considered prospective jurors to review Paramount's version of *An American Tragedy*. In one such letter, Dreiser presented his case to Harrison Smith, a partner in a New York publishing house. He assumed (incorrectly) that his handpicked posse would be able to influence the outcome of both his legal battle and, consequently, of the finished movie. At base, Dreiser questioned whether the studio had the right to take his book and produce something that did not resemble his perspective. Of course, the studio's production mattered much more than all the stage versions that had been produced because movies attracted the masses. The danger of Paramount's mistreatment was not merely the corruption of Dreiser's ideas, but that, as he said, "the millions and millions who have never read the book and who may or may not have heard of me will . . . be offered a distorted as well as a belittling interpretation of a work which is entitled, on its face, to a far more intelligible and broadening conception of the inscrutable ways of life and chance." Dreiser's concern extended beyond authorial control; his fight was against the power of movies—the dumbing down of culture by mass media. Dreiser hoped that his jury could save "not only my character and powers as a novelist, but my mental and artistic approach to life itself."[20]

Dreiser biographer W.A. Swanberg has suggested somewhat sarcastically that Dreiser's reaction to the adaptation of his novel "involved a comparatively new principle in the conception of motion pictures. Dreiser shocked Hollywood with the idea that the studios had an obligation to interpret serious work with integrity and intelligence."[21] That was apparently the frame of mind of the critics who gathered on June 15, 1931, to preview Paramount's version of *An American Tragedy*. Dreiser had assembled a panel totaling thirty-eight people. None of them, especially the eighteen who comprised the primary "jury," had any connection to the movie industry or mass entertainments in general. Besides being Dreiser's friends, they were critics and artists whose interests directly conflicted with those of the promoters and practitioners of mass culture. In letters to Dreiser written immediately following the screening, the critics concluded that Paramount had failed to adapt the novel successfully. Opinions differed mostly over why this had happened and how best to rectify the situation.

Each "juror" seemed to understand the potential for damage done to one's work if it were translated into a popular medium. As drama critic Barrett H. Clark wrote to Dreiser, "unless you had a real genius as director and an exceedingly clever film writer, almost any picture made from *An American Tragedy* would remain essentially an aesthetic libel."

Because of the way motion pictures were normally produced, any version of Dreiser's novel "would seriously damage your reputation as an artist and a thinker." Movies focused on action; Dreiser's novel was largely psychological. "In *An American Tragedy*," Barrett concluded, "the violent action is relatively unimportant; in the film it is practically all-important. Herein lies the aesthetic libel."[22]

An abstract of comments like Barrett's was included in a letter to Paramount from Dreiser's attorneys, Arthur Garfield Hays and Arthur C. Hume. Hays and Hume argued that the expert testimony of Dreiser's "jury" exposed Paramount's failure to present "the novel in its ideology, psychology, in its essential problem and final resolution." If the studio continued to dismiss their client's demands, the lawyers threatened that they would take legal action.[23]

In a twenty-page letter drafted by Dreiser that apparently became the basis for his attorneys' official statement to Paramount, the author provided significant insight into his frustration. At the heart of the dispute was Dreiser's belief that the film version "completely misrepresents the ideology and psychology of the novel—its essential problem and its final resolution." Yet the reasons why Dreiser believed this had happened did not fall within the legal realm alone. He accused director Josef von Sternberg of intentionally seeking to undermine his story "to avenge himself for some fancied grievance or other against me personally." Dreiser had recalled von Sternberg making a statement to reporters in which he suggested that George Bernard Shaw and Theodore Dreiser, both Hollywood critics, were "antiquated and old fashioned" in their ideas about movies. Reporters were at a loss to explain von Sternberg's specific inclusion of Dreiser—they had failed to note that the director had begun filming the already irascible author's book that day.[24]

Dreiser also mentioned a deal brewing in 1929 between Will Hays, Dreiser, and Lasky, whereby Hays "suggested that he and myself go about the filming of the thing together—that it was really a stupendous matter, one of international film import, and that he was greatly concerned to see it done in the large and inspired way in which it deserved to be done."[25] That plan apparently failed when negotiations over the sound rights took precedence over completing a silent version. Since Paramount decided not to include Dreiser directly in the adaptation of his novel and had, moreover, assigned the hostile von Sternberg to cowrite and direct the picture, the author seemed primed to object not merely to the finished film but to the entire process.

What was Dreiser doing taking a film studio to court? What did he hope to accomplish by placing the movies on trial? In the short term, Dreiser had raised the issue of authorial control, but in the long run he seemed to want to impress on the industry the need to get serious. If the movies were ever to be treated with respect, they needed to serve the purpose of art rather than the other way around. Intellectuals like Dreiser held tight to the notion that commerce corrupted art. Therefore, what Paramount was doing to his work was a cultural scandal rather than simply a legal conflict. At the same time, however, he was asking a court of law to force the movies to be something they were not. Movies existed between the worlds of art and entertainment; they had never fit exclusively into either category. Ultimately, Dreiser's stand against the movies mattered as one of the last efforts to force movies to conform to a formal understanding of culture. Modernist writers might have reinvented the way the novel looked, but their rebellion was one of form—the movies were changing the way culture functioned.

The case went before Judge Graham Witschief of New York's Supreme Court in White Plains on July 22, 1931. Besides Dreiser's occasional dramatics—the court reprimanded him a couple of times for his outbursts—the proceedings were decidedly anticlimactic. The defense presented its own panel of experts who testified that Paramount had done a fine job translating a massive, "pedantic" novel into an entertaining picture. Playwright Owen Johnson claimed that in his experience "no author's reputation could be hurt or helped by either a theatrical dramatization of his book or by a motion picture production." He concluded that, "In common with authors generally, I regard a motion picture presentation as a by-product." The defense also argued that Paramount had entertained and used suggestions made by Dreiser, adding hundreds of feet to the film.[26]

On August 2, Judge Witschief handed down his decision in the case pending between the famous writer and Paramount Publix Corporation. The judge rejected Dreiser's charge that Paramount had violated his artistic rights—his "intellectual property"—by poorly translating his massive tome. The defendant had had a tall order to fill, Witschief reasoned, in adapting the two-volume work of more than 336,000 words into a ten-reel motion picture that ran two hours.

Witschief did not share the novelist's "indictment of our social system" and, more importantly, the judge rejected the notion that there was only one accurate interpretation of Dreiser's novel. It depended, he wrote, on one's point of view. When it came to the movies, Witschief seemed to suggest that everyone was a critic of equal worth. Dreiser therefore had no legal grounds to claim that Paramount had misused his material or harmed his reputation as an author. Moreover, the court had failed to recognize Dreiser and his literary cohorts as cultural authorities. Thus, not only did Witschief oppose the novel's social message, he also believed that reflecting the public's taste, rather than the artist's, was a defensible approach when one translated material from a personal medium, like a novel, into a popular medium, such as the movies. Denied an injunction against Paramount, Dreiser's legal attack against the studio ended.[27]

Dreiser was enraged. He wrote to a friend that he found the judge's comments "priceless."[28] Dreiser believed Witschief's deference to popular taste established a frightening precedent in a society wracked by an economic depression and stupefied by mindless amusements. A year later, in the consummately bourgeois magazine *Liberty,* the author quipped that the judge's ruling spelled "the end of art." Dreiser believed that movies offered "great possibilities as a medium of art," but that Hollywood made little attempt to nurture the creative process and was for the most part unsympathetic, even destructive, to creativity. Such problems, he believed, stemmed from the fact that producers were not artists but capitalists. "Of course, there would be less cause for complaint on this score if these business men allowed the writers, directors, and players whom they employ and control to exercise freely their artistic perceptions and capabilities." Such an arrangement, however, was unimaginable in an exploitative system that prized selling products more than creating art.[29]

Dreiser also took the case as a personal affront to his authority as an author. "The basis of my attack," he wrote, "is that the picture corporations, with their monopoly, owe a certain percentage of their enormous profits to the artistic development of the film." Dreiser insisted that producers had a responsibility to make a "genuine effort . . . now and then to portray a masterpiece of literature, or present a gifted actor or actress in some such fashion as to widen the appeal of masterpiece or artists, or both." This effort should be made in order to raise "the general standard" of the motion picture rather that leave it where it was, or lower. By refusing to consider broader social concerns, the industry had committed a "great sin."[30]

Dreiser's case revealed many of the frustrations of 1930s radicalism. He embodied the conflicting notions of social responsibility and cultural elitism. He had pity for the masses he wrote about or, as biographer Richard Lingeman phrased it, "a burning sense of injustice and unfairness and deep sympathy for the poor dumbbells who really could not do anything but work themselves to death with illness and privation." Although Dreiser wanted to help those he saw as less fortunate, he also made a small fortune doing so. Like many other radicals, Dreiser could loathe those institutions that gave the masses pleasure even while he championed the masses as a cause. He also wanted people to remember that his struggle was not merely for his own benefit; it was against the force of a mass medium that simplified everything it touched.[31]

Dreiser's case received a lively response in the press, especially since it involved a character of Dreiser's magnitude and temperament, but it also attracted attention because of the questions Dreiser had raised about the responsibility the motion picture industry had to America. Commentary on the case illustrated the strange place movies continued to occupy in culture. For those who saw movies as senseless entertainment, Dreiser's fight was nonsensical—it was only a movie, many writers exclaimed. For those who believed that movies had a tremendous capacity to sway the masses, Dreiser's case was another example of money corrupting what could have been a great cultural enterprise. Not a few reports, though, mocked Dreiser's posturing. For example, the *New Republic* and *Commonweal* ran editorials suggesting that Dreiser's attack had a basic flaw. Editorially, the *New Republic* reminded readers that most authors voluntarily worked under the conditions in Hollywood. In fact, most writers were "more concerned about the money they will get from the movies than about the possible damage to their reputation." *Commonweal* said much the same thing, but with a bit of humor, observing that an "author who sells for $150,000 must know that he is selling not so much his work as his name."[32]

Frank Dennis of the *Kansas City Star,* a friend of Arthur Garfield Hays, called the case "one of the most interesting and important law suits attending the motion picture industry," adding that "one of the worst faults of many motion picture producers is their willingness to ruin a great piece of literature for the sake of a few extra dollars." If Dreiser had won, his victory would have helped protect "the public in the future in respect to other pictures." The *Chicago Tribune* argued that Paramount never should have purchased Dreiser's story. "For fifty cents the pictures do not indict society, nor will they do it for two dollars." Hollywood liked villains and exploited sex but would never allow society itself

to be characterized as a "stupid, brutal, ravenous beast." Society was, after all, "composed of the very fifty cent pieces which makes the gross on
a picture."[33]

Novelist John Fort, writing in the *Chattanooga News*, treated Dreiser
not as an artist battling the darker forces of Hollywood but as a demented
Don Quixote tilting at Hollywood's windmills. Fort scolded Dreiser for
thinking that the public would want to hear his "materialist and mechanist" views and praised Paramount for giving Clyde Griffiths "the Christian soul of a free spirit. . . . Clyde was not swept into villainies by the
social system." Fort quipped that if Dreiser "wanted to preach his materialistic doctrine he might just as well have hired a hall and limited his
congregation to admission by ticket." William Soskin, literary critic for
the New York *Evening Post*, wondered "what Mr. Dreiser would have done
himself if the Paramount people gave him a free hand to produce his
840-page novel on the screen." Soskin found Hoffenstein's translation
"both dignified and powerful." Charles Hanson Towne, in the *New York
American*, argued that Dreiser had exaggerated the harm the movies would
do to an artist's image. "If anything," Towne contended, "this austere rendering of 'An American Tragedy' will add to rather than subtract from
Mr. Dreiser's reputation as a writer. After all, the movies are but a byproduct. . . . His standing as a supreme artist remains unchanged; for it is
through his book, and through his book alone, that we judge him."[34]

A different sentiment echoed among leftist writers. Matthew Josephson in the *New Republic* found von Sternberg's attempt mediocre
and lacking in the moral lessons. "But," Josephson asked, "what could
Mr. Dreiser have expected of our movies? It would have been a miracle if
an artistic and dignified tragedy had been created out of his novel."
Alexander Bakshy offered a clearer indictment of Hollywood's shortcomings: "if there is anything tragic about the film version of 'An American
Tragedy,' it is the pathetic spectacle of its producers trying to crash the
gate of artistic heaven with the yellow ticket of their profligate trade."
Edmund Wilson found Dreiser's struggle significant for what it said about
the power of Hollywood to corrupt profound ideas. Dreiser had called
on writers to fight for their authorial power over work appropriated by
Hollywood. Wilson believed that Dreiser "reminded them that the imagination of the Americans got most of its food from the movies; and that
at a time when the country was in a crisis which peculiarly demanded
realistic understanding the movies were still bemusing them systematically with sentimental lies about their own lives and lies about life in

general." The movies had clearly encouraged a serious response, but had yet to earn enough respect to be treated as serious art.[35]

Harry Alan Potamkin, writing in *Close Up*, the first English-language journal devoted to film aesthetics, offered perhaps the most significant commentary on Dreiser's lost cause because he believed so emphatically that even movies had to meet rigid artistic standards. Potamkin insisted that Dreiser's fight was not merely about his right as an author, but a "struggle against the debasing of the intellectual and social level of an experience."[36] Every piece of work, every artistic creation, had larger social implications because, Potamkin suggested, art hit with a moral force. Such idealism was a product of the communist ideology on which Potamkin built his criticism, and it was mass culture's ability to soften that ideology that enraged radical critics.

Not surprisingly, Potamkin had helped the journal *Experimental Cinema* (*EC*) transform itself from an avant-garde publication into a mouthpiece for communist movie criticism. He had begun writing about movies as part of the avant-garde but became the most important Communist film critic of the late 1920s and early 1930s.[37] What unified the journal's leftism and avant-gardism was disdain for popular taste. Potamkin attacked Hollywood as a corrupter of art as well as "a medium of middle-class society" that catered to the "cultural minimum—a maximum of illusions or evasions to assume a minimum of dissent."[38] Dreiser had lost his case, Potamkin argued, because neither Hollywood nor Judge Witschief wanted to see a movie critical of American society. Yet both Dreiser and Potamkin were at a loss to determine which was worse: Witschief's dislike of Dreiser's leftist politics or Hollywood's blind pursuit of wealth. At least the judge posed a political challenge; the movie industry was simply too vacuous to fight.[39]

Potamkin found Paramount's *An American Tragedy* lacking in any semblance of thought. It was a simple courtroom drama, not an artistic experience informed by ideology. Director von Sternberg had reduced Dreiser's ideographic plan to "makeshift 'equivalents' for the process" of the novel, but lacked any "constantly informing theme." Potamkin snipped: "The picture has been called 'lively'. . . . We do not ask that a monument bounce like a rubber-ball. But the film is lacking in all resilience. It is not leavened by an idea, it is dismal, tedious, aimless."[40]

While Dreiser's and Potamkin's hopes revealed the paradoxical idealism of the American left in the 1930s, they also illustrated that a central organizing principle in Hollywood was the almost universal avoidance of ideas. How could any critic take movies seriously? To the radical mind there was nothing to challenge: Hollywood was all fantasy and fluff.[41]

Thus, the assumption that Hollywood only gave people what they wanted was, in a way, the central problem. Unlike studio bosses, Dreiser did not claim to know what the people wanted, only what they needed. For that reason, the author was on firm ground when he condemned the studios for advancing mindless entertainment under the aegis of popular art. The transition of An American Tragedy from novel to screen illustrated a basic difference between art for the public and art that is popular. The former addresses the mind in an attempt to move the heart; the latter aims for the heart with little concern for the mind. Dreiser thought a screen version of his novel would successfully join these two propositions.[42]

Dreiser's accusation that Hollywood was parasitic and exploitative was a lament common to both sides of the political spectrum—a feat made possible because movies operated in a no-man's-land of culture. Filmmaking was an art that existed between the inconsequential and the serious; it was a medium with seemingly omnipresent force that served as a purveyor of basically senseless entertainment. As long as the definition of art and culture remained embedded in concerns for public morality, movies would continue to be disreputable.

It thus should not be surprising, though perhaps ironic, that Dreiser and motion picture censors paralleled one another in their attitudes toward Hollywood. Both believed movies had the potential to shape mass consciousness. Moreover, because the industry had consistently disappointed, both parties advocated some kind of regulation in order to protect the public. Dreiser sought to awaken Americans to the sins of their nation, whereas censors hoped to prevent Americans from making their society sinful, but neither had the cultural authority to control the movies.

The world in which literary figures and civic leaders once spoke with voices that, even though they conflicted attracted the attention of the people, was evolving in an increasingly mass-mediated universe. Thus, the relevance of standards in art and culture had less to do with what was "right" or "good," and more to do with what was popular. One could not consider movies in terms traditionally reserved for other arts, and one could not expect the movie industry, as Dreiser had, to advance unpopular ideas. Movies did not abide by rules that governed more respectable cultural expressions. Since the audience did not expect movies to act like art, moviemakers chose not to treat their employees like artists or the audience like adults. Episodes such as Dreiser's battle with Hollywood made it clear that the movies themselves did not have to change as much as the perception of what movies meant in American culture. In coming years that was exactly what would happen.

5

Movies into Art

Museums tell us what art is, right? The paintings, sculpture, and exhibits inside large, ornate, imposing buildings help us identify what is significant to our culture. Facilitating that process are the experts who choose pieces for museums, place each piece in the history of art, and, through such work, create a set of standards that we can apply to other cultural expressions. Through the early 1930s, most people understood why a painting by Rembrandt was high art and a Charlie Chaplin movie was popular culture. The painting was a significant landmark in Western culture; the movie was an important source of enjoyment in our lives. An implicit value judgment informed such distinctions: some expressions were simply better and more vital to our culture than others.[1]

By the early 1930s, museums in Boston, New York, Chicago, and Washington remained centers of intellectual activity, but they also had to compete for the public's attention with other attractions such as world's fairs, department stores, sporting events, and the movies.[2] To succeed in a rapidly transforming cultural marketplace necessitated recognizing that contemporary objects such as movies were significant to the public and that exhibitions of art could, and perhaps should, entice people, not simply promise to educate them.

A good example of the contrast between the old sensibility and a newer one could be seen in New York City. When it was founded in 1870, the Metropolitan Museum of Art (the "Met") began, as cultural critic Russell Lynes once explained, "as a touchstone of taste for all Americans, an emblem of America's cultural coming of age." By the 1920s, the Met still had its nineteenth-century genteel attitude, becoming "largely a curators' and collectors' preserve, to which the public was invited but by no means welcomed." On the other hand was the Museum of Modern Art (MoMA), an upstart that opened in 1929 near the heart of midtown

Manhattan and that surveyed a different cultural landscape. Lynes recorded that "all the visual arts were . . . [its] province . . . architecture, industrial design, films, photography, decorative design—all of which [were] envisioned as pertinent to the modern movement." MoMA attracted its audience by appealing to the one thing other museums had scorned: contemporary expressions. Without set limits on what or how it could exhibit the arts, MoMA enjoyed much greater latitude than older museums such as the Met.[3]

In 1933, a slight, thirty-seven-year-old female movie critic from England made a most significant contribution to MoMA's evolving personality. Her name was Iris Barry, and by a relatively lucky encounter she became a member of MoMA's inner circle. Barry had been in the United States for a little over a year and had, through the kindness of friends, entered New York's artistic community. At a cocktail party, Barry met Alfred Barr, his college buddy and MoMA colleague Jere Abbott, and MoMA's architect, Philip Johnson. The latter was so impressed by Barry that he insisted she interview for a job at MoMA. Barry arrived the next day and was immediately hired as the museum's librarian.[4]

Barry's past experiences, however, determined a different future for her at MoMA. She had come to New York by way of Birmingham and London. She had published poetry in one of London's little magazines and subsequently became associated with the city's literary modernists. In 1925 one of those acquaintances, John Strachey, got Barry a job reviewing books and plays for a London weekly called the *Spectator*. Once there, Barry also began reviewing films. This position placed her among England's first movie critics writing for a major newspaper. Impressed with her work, the *Daily Mail* stole her away, keeping her as their movie critic until 1930. Barry had also become friends with a number of movie enthusiasts, and with them founded the London Film Society in 1925.[5]

By the time Barry landed in New York in 1932, she had achieved some notable firsts as the first film critic on a major London newspaper and as a cofounder of England's first film society. She had also written a well-received book entitled *Let's Go to the Pictures,* in which she appeared more enthusiast than theorist, grasping, as few others had at the time, that movies possessed cultural significance. Yet Barry added a twist to the approach of her fellow British critics who wrote for self-proclaimed "serious" film journals such as *Close Up, Sight and Sound,* and *Cinema Quarterly.* Barry actually liked American movies and believed that Hollywood had earned its place at the center of film history. She not only appreciated movies as *modern* art but as works of hybrid culture: they were *popular* art.[6]

Barry's perspective echoed at least the general sensibility of MoMA director Alfred Barr. As early as 1929, Barr had considered the motion picture part of his original scheme for the museum. In an early report, Barr made his most serious attempt to expand its departments to include both motion pictures and architecture. He lamented that "Little Cinemas" built to show films of "high artistic quality" had rarely been financially solvent. "As a result very few films of artistic value have had proper presentation in America, and a great many such films have never been seen at all." Since the type of film societies that had thrived in London and Paris never really lasted in New York City, Barr hoped to serve that part of society that would appreciate and support good films. He assumed that people knowledgeable of great artists in painting and literature had little real understanding of comparable figures in film. "It may be said without exaggeration," Barr claimed, "that the only great art peculiar to the twentieth century is practically unknown to the American public most capable of appreciating it."[7] Barr imagined that his museum would help cultured Americans respect filmmakers as they did great painters, writers, and playwrights.[8]

It fell to Iris Barry to expand upon the basic, though radical, idea that movies were important to cultured Americans. By doing so, she would not only establish the first permanent collection of movies in a museum, but also contribute to the general redefining of art that had begun in the United States earlier in the century. If a remarkable feature of the modernist movement was the revitalization of American arts, then Barry made a significant contribution to it by championing movies as the most vital art of the day. Ironically, however, by doing so she altered an idea central to the modernist definition of art: that art shared nothing in common with mass culture. By suggesting that aspects of mass culture such as movies could be art, Barry introduced the notion that popular taste could help shape artistic standards. Such a notion also further eroded the cultural authority that had been used to dismiss and condemn the cultural significance of movies. Moreover, Barry did all of this in a museum founded with money from New York City's ruling elite and under the guidance of Barr, one of Manhattan's most important modernists.

Barry's first concern, though, was preserving those films that still existed. In order to consider the cultural significance of movies, the raw material for such a study needed to be made available. By the mid-1930s, only thirty-five years after the making of the first motion picture, that prospect was gloomy.

From the early days of film in the late 1890s through the 1930s, movie companies used film stock known as nitrate (nitrocellulose). Eastman Kodak invented it and producers used it because of the rich black and white images it produced. But nitrate had two drawbacks: The film was highly flammable, and if not stored under proper conditions—correct temperature and moisture—it would deteriorate into a soapy chemical and then into dust. By 1934, 50 to 75 percent of all movies shot in the previous three decades had most likely been lost.[9] Film archives with the money to preserve old stock were desperately needed. To Barry and others who had come to enjoy watching old films, the realization that at some point this past would be lost forever pushed them to act. However, it took one of the wealthiest and youngest of the museum's trustees to make Barry's dream of a film collection become a reality.

In 1927, when Payne Whitney died, his son John Hay "Jock" Whitney inherited $179 million, making him one of the richest twenty-four year olds in history. In 1935, Whitney was both a MoMA trustee and an investor in the motion picture industry. Joining his two interests, he sponsored a report prepared by Barry and John E. Abbott on the feasibility of creating a film library at the Museum. Barry and Abbott, who were married by 1935, submitted the report to the Rockefeller Foundation to secure a grant. Since MoMA was generally cash poor during its early years, the trustees were hesitant to endorse a separate department for film. Barry and Abbott needed to find outside funding in order to buy, protect, and exhibit a part of U.S. history that was rapidly deteriorating.

The task facing the two grant seekers when they set to work in February 1935 was to convince the Rockefeller trustees that there were valid reasons to preserve what many considered to be nothing more than an amusement. Barry and Abbott decided to illustrate the relevance of their project by appealing to the audience they hoped to attract. They sent out a questionnaire to educational institutions, museums, art galleries, and film societies inquiring whether or not there would be any interest in a series of films chronicling movie history. When tallied, the responses proved very encouraging. Out of about two hundred replies, 84.3 percent "expressed a desire to exhibit" movie programs. The two writers concluded, "it is clear from the response to the Museum's preliminary enquiry that there does exist a widespread demand for programs of films and other material for the serious study and proper appreciation of the motion picture."[10] Such findings enabled the authors to boast that their project was not a trivial exercise but a useful service to the educational and arts community. The exhibition of films might ultimately help MoMA become more accessible to the public and more in line with an important aspect of its mission.[11]

The authors then turned to the specific work of a film library. At the top of the list was preservation. As Barry explained it: "There is no body of reference available, no 'sources' to inspire, no heritage other than the most accidental and fragmentary. Makers of films and audiences alike should be enabled to formulate a constructively critical point of view, and to discriminate between what is valid and what is shoddy and corrupt." By salvaging what was left of the motion picture's past, a film library would be a positive influence on both sides of the screen. "A comprehensive film library or any library of films at all must become invaluable historically," she added, " and of major importance in raising both the level of production and appreciation. Unless the better films of the past are preserved no standards are possible."[12]

Barry and Abbott understood that the Rockefeller trustees expected a museum to speak with some authority about its exhibits, whether they be of modern paintings or of movies. The authors needed to assure the trustees that a film library would not become a glorified penny arcade. Films chosen for preservation and, more importantly, presentation would need to meet critical standards. Clearly not every movie Hollywood produced was worthy of preservation. By collecting the great masters of the cinema, as one would do in painting, the museum could help establish aesthetic and historical standards for motion pictures. Barry's scope, however, was as wide as it was deep.

Her judgment incorporated popular taste as much as contemporary film aesthetics, and her standards were flexible, incorporating and equating a great number of films that had yet to be considered significant. When Barry and Abbott wrote that the film library would "trace, catalog, assemble, preserve, exhibit and circulate . . . all types of films," they meant every conceivable genre of film known at the time, including "narrative, documentary, spectacular, Western, slapstick, comedy-drama, musical, animated cartoon, abstract, scientific, educational, dramatic, and news-reel."[13] However, this approach came dangerously close to equating social relevance with artistic significance. Had Barry turned a museum devoted to art into a museum devoted to social history?

In short, it seemed that the film library would be the first and most important organization designed solely for the historic preservation and exhibition of the art of motion pictures. Considering that an estimated 100 million people attended movies weekly in the United States, to say nothing of global attendance, it was not difficult to argue the social significance of movies. But Barry believed that movies were a "lively art"—one that reflected the modern age—and to overlook even seemingly mundane movies would be akin to destroying all paintings and novels a year after they were produced.[14] Did anyone, she asked, really know what parts of culture would be considered significant in the future?

With mass culture becoming increasingly important to American life, preserving movies in a museum required constantly balancing the popular and the significant—since many people figured the two were mutually exclusive. Iris Barry's greatest and most dubious achievement, it seems to me, was to join these two points: some cultural expressions were significant because they were popular. Yet if such logic prevailed, who could stop museum curators or critics from praising work that was popular but of fleeting significance?

Nonetheless, Barry and Abbott convinced the board that their logic was sound. On April 17, 1935, they submitted their final report, and one month later the Rockefeller Foundation approved a $100,000 grant for the purpose of establishing a film library at MoMA. Jock Whitney also managed to arrange an additional $60,000 from private contributions (mostly his own) to create the Film Library as a separate corporation, with all stock held by the museum. The quick decision on the proposal was no doubt aided by those sympathetic to the experiment, including trustees Nelson Rockefeller, Edward M.M. Warburg, and Jock Whitney. Whitney became president of the corporation, Alfred Barr's former Harvard University classmate Jere Abbott was the vice president, and Warburg the treasurer. Barry's husband, John Abbott, who was no stranger to finances having worked on Wall Street, agreed to be the library's director and handle its administration. This arrangement would allow Barry to focus on the duties of curator. With a staff of five employees, she set about amassing a collection that in time would be seen as priceless.

John Reddington, writing for the *Brooklyn Eagle,* understood MoMA's interest in film: "the curiosity of the whole project is the realization that a product manufactured with the essential objective of being profitable to its sponsors has, nevertheless, managed to retain sufficient contact with the realities of its time to make its presentation worthwhile." Indeed, Barry later said, "It was . . . the advent of the talkies and—by that time—their prevalence which had slowly made us realize what we lacked or had lost." The need for a film library, once founded, became almost self-evident. What would have been missed, Barry mused, if people could "never again experience the same pleasure that *Intolerance, Moana,* or *Greed* had given with their combination of eloquent silence, visual excitement, and that hallucinatory 'real' music from 'real' orchestras in the movie theaters which buoyed them up and drifted us with them into bliss."[15]

By 1935, moviegoers had enjoyed thirty years of silent films and then five or six years of rapidly improving talking pictures. The ascendancy of the sound movie made it clear that an entire epoch in film history would soon be a faint memory. To understand the gravity of this situation, one needed only to reflect on the millions of hours people had spent watching silent pictures flicker across screens in every corner of the United States. Even if a person still considered early movies simple amusements, he or she could also appreciate that the movies had a rich history that was directly relevant to many people's lives. The Film Library would help preserve that history as part of the public's legacy—rescuing their art from time and chemistry. Frank Nugent wrote in the *New York Times* that "a museum for cinematic art is full vindication for those true prophets of the screen who, for years, have been chanting their litany against a mocking chorus of blatant agnosticism and arrogant heresy."[16] Iris Barry had infused a new element into appreciation of the arts by making the movies part of them. In turn, she had bestowed a legitimacy on the movie industry that seemed so much a break from the past that even Hollywood questioned the relevance of MoMA's new venture.

Almost immediately after founding the Film Library, Barry and Abbott began the substantial tasks of locating films and convincing their owners to donate them. Barry understood the problems her new project would entail. Many movies had already been lost; others were housed in people's attics, basements, and old factories. However, the bulk of the movies Barry sought lay in one place: Hollywood. In August 1935, she and Abbott traveled to meet the industry. Jock Whitney had supplied the duo with letters of introduction to many of Hollywood's top producers and studio heads. The warmest reception came from silent picture queen Mary Pickford, who agreed to hold a dinner at Pickfair, her Los Angeles estate. On the evening of August 25, 1935, Barry and Abbott had a chance to make their pitch to some of Hollywood's luminaries.

Before that occasion, few in the movie industry had given much time to the East Coast visitors. As Barry remembered, "We soon realized that, perhaps understandably, no one there cared a button about 'old' films, not even his own last-but-one, but was solely concerned with his new film now in prospect." The atmosphere at Pickfair was different, however. By hosting the dinner, Pickford had given her tacit endorsement to the Film Library. That was of some consequence since she controlled many of her most famous films and was highly regarded by many in the industry. The trick remained to convince other Hollywood notables to do the same.[17]

"That evening," Barry recalled, "pioneers of the industry like Mack Sennett met newcomers like Walt Disney for the first time, old acquaintances were renewed and new ones made. For once the exponents of this new art-industry who normally live for the immediate future and the work in hand, stopped the clock briefly to consider the past." The scene could not have been scripted better. Barry and Abbott had hoped to impress upon Hollywood the importance of preserving the industry's past. There before all of them were living examples of the silent film era. The Film Library would secure that era's place in history.[18]

Abbott spoke briefly, first thanking Pickford for her generosity and acceptance of a position on the Film Library advisory board. Then he turned to what he believed would be the industry's misgivings about his proposal: "You will be thinking here: but films *have* been preserved, we have them in our vaults. True, but are they remembered as they deserve, and what do they mean to the rising generation who have never seen them?" Although Abbott conceded that many people believed that movies had no place in a museum—that westerns and early biographs were not art—he contended that such people were shortsighted. "They seem to believe that art is something apart from life, already consecrated in museums and—above all—something which the common man cannot enjoy." Such thinking was nonsense, he claimed. Hundreds of students in universities, art schools, and other educational institutions had expressed a genuine interest in the "masterpieces" made by the "masters of film" about whom they had heard but had never seen. "To the students themselves," he added, "the motion picture is—to say the least—as significant and exciting as the Punic wars." Hollywood might see itself as an industry only, but many others, Abbott assured his audience, viewed movies as something culturally important. He beseeched his audience to help preserve the record of hard work done by hundreds of people throughout the last thirty-five years. "Let us save the outstanding films of past and present from turning, in the end, as they must unless something of this is done, into a handful of dust—and memories."[19]

After Abbott's speech, Barry ran a short program of five films, intending to take the guests on a short trip to the past. "This glimpse of the birth and growth of an art which was peculiarly their own," Barry wrote, "both surprised and moved this unique audience." Some of those gathered gave audible gasps and sighs when an old departed friend appeared on the screen or when a younger Mary Pickford flashed her beautiful eyes toward the camera. That evening, Harold Lloyd, Mary Pickford, and Samuel Goldwyn promised films to the Film Library. Other industry people also came forward to offer gifts, including Walt Disney.[20]

In an article for MoMA's *Bulletin,* Barry recounted the trip to Hollywood as a triumphal conclusion to the founding of the museum's Film Library. "It is commonly granted," she explained, "that the motion picture is important not only for its pervasive social effect but because it is one of the two most lively contemporary arts and the only new art-form of modern times." Like literature and paintings, movies should be made available for study and analysis. The museum would preserve and collect "outstanding motion pictures of all types," so students could enjoy "for the first time a considered study of the film as art."[21]

Barry also announced recent acquisitions for the Film Library's collection, including Edward S. Porter's *The Great Train Robbery* (1903), recognized as among the first narrative films ever shown. Among the holdings were other prints, such as *A Fool There Was* with Theda Bara, which, Barry noted, "in 1914 introduced the new word, 'vamp,'" as well as the Irene and Vernon Castle film *The Whirl of Life,* also made in 1914, "which was in considerable measure responsible for the popularity of bobbed hair, jazz bands and the dancing craze."[22] Barry hoped that her audience would recognize that these films were more than just movies: they were artifacts with social and artistic value.

She also promised that the museum would soon be offering two programs, the first entitled "The Development of Narrative" and a second on "The Rise of the American Film." Each program offered members a visual history of the motion picture. Never before had anyone created a movie retrospective through the medium itself. Barry explained that her purpose was "above all . . . to create a consciousness of tradition and history within the new art of the film." She hoped that through her film programs, students would form "for the first time an accurate perspective of the history and aesthetic development of the motion picture since 1894." Unlike shows at "Little Cinemas," however, the Film Library would embrace popular and domestic movies as well as artistic and foreign. It was important to Barry that she illustrate the strong influence American movies had had on European films. She agreed with Gilbert Seldes that the motion picture tradition was American.[23]

Yet Barry also appreciated and wanted to recognize the international nature of the motion picture. In an article for the British film periodical *Sight and Sound,* she announced that she and her husband would soon be "setting out on a tour of the principal European film-producing centres" in the hope of acquiring "representative films of all countries for our future years' work." It was no small task, Barry admitted, constructing a "first-hand record of the birth of a new art." But she found their search for films "most encouraging and most helpful," because "far from being solitary workers—we represent only the American wing of a spontaneous and universal movement to preserve a record of the birth and development of the art of the cinema."[24] Indeed, film archives had emerged during the mid-1930s in all major European centers of moviemaking. With a network of curators and preservationists to call on, Barry's job became much easier and her idea of expanding the fine arts to include their popular relatives gained transatlantic validation.[25]

In speeches throughout the first years of the Film Library's existence, John Abbott reinforced Barry's contention.[26] For example, addressing the National Board of Review at its annual luncheon in the late winter of 1935, Abbott made a typical pitch. He praised the board for its own work, particularly fighting the intellectual prejudice against motion pictures, since "neither the public at large nor the leaders of opinion have been accustomed to take the film really seriously." The Film Library, Abbott assured his audience, would "lend that authority which is now lacking, to the work of the great film makers." He continued that although MoMA was a young institution, it was the appropriate place for the motion picture because both were of the twentieth century. Moreover, MoMA had not sought to inflate the power of movies or compromise their basic qualities by characterizing them as an elite art. "That the motion picture is a popular art is one of its greatest assets," Abbott said. "It lacks authority, but it is living and lively, it is of our time, it speaks in terms we can all understand." Many art patrons had accepted other contemporary arts with difficulty, and Abbott thought movies would be no different. But "the motion picture nevertheless has traditions and tendencies which are proper material for study. Its very influence on modern life and thought entitle it to a serious examination, while its inherent aesthetic qualities entitle it to a place with the arts."[27]

The National Board of Review had covered similar intellectual territory throughout the 1920s. Yet the "Little Cinemas," which the NBR had championed a decade earlier, had fed people a steady diet of European films and very few American movies. That had made "younger filmgoers . . . unaware that the film is a markedly American expression." Consequently, Abbott explained, the Film Library intended to place movie history in a broader context, with American productions at the center of the narrative and foreign pictures influenced by and influencing the American mainstream. The response from universities and art museums to MoMA's film programs justified Abbott's contention that there was wide academic interest in popular movies.[28]

Barry and Abbott continued pressing their case, stumping for movies before audiences of museum folk. Convincing MoMA's trustees that movies were an art had taxed the talents of Alfred Barr and his dedicated duo, but addressing audiences in traditional museums remained one of the greatest intellectual challenges that Barry and Abbott would face. Abbott tackled the issue of "The Film as a Museum Piece" for members of the American Association of Museums, while Barry ventured out to the Albright Gallery in Buffalo, New York. Taken together, the two speeches represented the clearest and most forceful explanation they had for treating movies—all movies—as art.

Abbott conceded that motion pictures were unlike any other "museum piece"—they were not to be displayed as quaint relics. The motion picture, he declared, was "an art not only with a past," but a lively art, "with a large, popular and alas, only too articulate present." Abbott contended that if his present audience continued to snub movies, it would be underestimating the greatest popular art since Shakespearean theater. He advised people to read Allardyce Nicoll, a well-respected theater critic, who had recently published a book entitled *Theatre and Film* that compared the popular theater of Elizabethan England to the best motion pictures. Moreover, MoMA was the first institution to do something to protect and promote "the historic or the aesthetic significance of American films."[29]

When Iris Barry spoke at the Albright Gallery in April 1936, the tone of her address belied one of her most characteristic features: She did not suffer art snobs gladly.[30] After a smart anecdote in which Barry illustrated how something seemingly inconsequential could have cultural value, she sized-up her audience: "I am assuming for the moment that none of you here *values* the film particularly, or allows it the rank of an art. But in regarding it merely as popular entertainment, a means whereby the many can distract themselves inexpensively for an evening, one is apt to overlook this extremely important function which it fulfills—that of holding up, all consciously, a mirror to contemporary life." Both the experience of going to the movies and the movies themselves were important. If people could appreciate paintings from the past as a reflection of their time and as a representation of a certain period in the stream of history, it should follow that movies served a similar purpose. "While it is possible for us today to get a glimmering of the mentality, of the profound human nature of the unknown artists of the Middle Ages," Barry contended, "it is possible, in exactly the same way, to see in the motion pictures of our own era a searching and profound reflection of the mentality, of the soul of our own time."[31]

Although Barry had discussed such issues before, she had yet to refine her ideas on motion pictures as art. In previous statements she had reported rather than reflected on the details of her work. Now she had a chance to explore the intellectual side of her job and thus more fully establish a mission for the Film Library. Barry was, after all, speaking about something that few "cultured" people respected. She wanted to protect herself from charges that her ideas merely inflated the importance of movies to serve a selfish end. She had chosen to be a historian of movies because she not only found them significant as social commentary—on the styles, tastes, and entertainment of an era—but because movies had their own masters, masterpieces, and unique character. The motion picture, she emphasized, "is an independent medium, and the less it resembles any other medium, the better, the purer it is." Moreover, motion pictures were improving. Unlike other arts, their greatness lay in the future rather than in the past. By preserving the origins of the movies, Barry ensured that future generations of historians would have a record of what she believed to be the world's most powerful art form.[32]

By 1939, MoMA had spent a decade establishing itself as a serious museum. Yet it had done so by merging the more traditional functions of a museum with newer, more expansive ideas about what constituted culture. On the opening night of MoMA's new building (and present-day home), Pres. Franklin D. Roosevelt made a brief radio address from the White House, praising the museum's traveling exhibits for the opportunities they afforded people all over the country and soon all over the world to see modern art. "Most important of all," the president continued, "the standards of American taste will inevitably be raised by this bringing into far-flung communities results of the latest and finest achievements in all the arts."[33]

In 1953, Dwight Macdonald reflected on MoMA's unique character. First, the museum had attracted financial support and the public's patronage "just as the wave of American interest in modern art was building up." Macdonald added that MoMA was resourceful enough to push "the wave higher." It also helped that the museum's board of trustees included the Rockefeller, Whitney, and Bliss families—some of the nation's wealthiest and most respected art collectors. As Macdonald noted, "few Americans care to argue with a hundred million dollars." Ironically, because MoMA's endowment was considerably less than most other museums, particularly the Met, it also had to operate on a budget that forced administrators to raise money. The difference was significant, Macdonald contended: "The Met is thus in the position of a rentier, living on income from capital, while MoMA is an entrepreneur, dependent on its own exertions." While the Met could remain aloof, as its original charter suggested, Alfred Barr and his colleagues had to operate on the premise that the public expected to be directly engaged.[34]

Macdonald compared MoMA's operation to a "nine ring circus" that had revolutionized museum work by having "something to say—or rather to show—about practically every visual aspect of American life." It did so, moreover, by treating its exhibitions as "shows" that were "staged" on "sets" easily manipulated and arranged, in the way department stores and the 1939 World's Fair presented their attractions. The public responded in kind with admissions rising from 120,000 in 1938 to 585,000 in 1939.[35]

The Film Library had clearly contributed to MoMA's astonishing popularity, even though 1939 marked the first time the Film Library ran a series open to the public. Frank Nugent of the *New York Times* wrote approvingly: "the Film Library—which has been criticized in the past for withholding its programs from John J. Citizen—now is indicating a willingness to meet him more than half-way, not simply financially (for the museum, queer thing, is forbidden to profit from these showings) but by removing the attendance restrictions. And this, of course, is eminently desirable." During the special summer series entitled "A Cycle of 70 Films, 1895–1935," the public came en masse to the new Fifty-third Street building. Barry had created the "hottest show in town," even in competition with the World's Fair out in Queens, a borough of New York City. The metaphor of heat was apt, the *New York Times* reported, since "it appears that the more unbearable the heat over weekends, the larger are the crowds which flock to the museum." The museum frequently had to turn away large crowds of people because the Film Library's 498-seat auditorium was full.[36]

Late in 1939, two popular programs carried the Film Library's message to the masses—an audience that had helped MoMA reconfigure the role art played in society by being part of the museum's patronage. The widely seen weekly newsreel program *The March of Time* featured the Film Library in a program entitled "The Movies March On." The program covered the preservation and presentation of movie history made possible by Barry and her staff. It also spliced together a series of film clips from the Film Library's archives to create a seamless visual history of motion pictures from the late nineteenth century to the present. Echoing the core of Iris Barry's message, narrator Westbrook Van Vorhees explained that motion pictures had been originally conceived as an industry, but grew into an art that was also entertaining. Movies, he said, had their own masters, masterpieces, innovators, and history. But unlike other arts, motion pictures had a unique group of critics. "For 250 million moviegoers," Van Vorhees intoned, "each week pass final judgment on the most powerful medium of expression that the world had ever known, an art form as great as any in man's history."[37] Indeed, here was an art that appealed to and had to satisfy the tastes of the masses. How could one continue to claim art, by its very nature, existed apart from mass culture?

The unique dynamics of MoMA's experiment was well illustrated in a radio skit about the Film Library. On Saturday evenings in December 1939, residents of the New York metropolitan area could listen between 6:30 and 6:45 P.M. to a program entitled "What's Art to Me?"[38] It was a show sponsored by MoMA for CBS radio. On one December evening, listeners heard a man ask: "What did you do this afternoon, dear?"

> Woman: Went to the movies.
> Man: That so?—what did you see?
> Woman: Oh, they had *The New York Hat,* directed by D.W. Griffith, with Mary Pickford.
> Man: *What?*

Woman: Yes, that's right—and also a cowboy picture, with William S.
    Hart, and then one of those slapstick comedies, with the keystone
    cops....
Man: Wait a minute, dear—Is this 1939, or is it 1914? Where are we?
Woman: It's 1939 all right, dear—and we're on the Columbia program.[39]

Holger Cahill, the host of the show, entered the mock discussion to explain the evening's topic. At the time, Cahill was the director of the Federal Arts Project, a venture begun under the New Deal's Works Progress Administration to help visual artists who were hit hard by the depression.

Man:What have a lot of old movies got to do with modern art?
Cahill:The question is a good one: what have a lot of old movies to do
    with modern art?

The purpose of the program was to explain how MoMA could justify showing motion pictures as part of American social and cultural history. Anticipating their audience's response, the writers asked how popular movies could be considered art. To that question, Cahill replied:

Yes, they were just nickel movies—but they were also milestones
in the advance of the liveliest, most popular, and most influential
art of the twentieth century. Of course, the movie qualifies as an
art. It is one of the most powerful means of expression open to
creative talent—it has won a place with painting and sculpture,
music and literature, as a medium capable of capturing our
imagination, and stirring our emotions. And it is the only new
means of expression developed by modern man.[40]

Still skeptical, the "man" wanted to know at what point a movie stopped being "just a good show" and turned into "a work of art." Enter Iris Barry. Barry explained that because movies were both popular and important they deserved preservation and presentation. It was her responsibility to popularize the notion that movies could be both art and entertainment.

Barry proceeded to survey the major periods of film history. She spoke of pictures, directors, actors, and actresses whom her audience would most likely remember but had not considered within a historical context. She kept her narrative lively and used analysis only to explain transitions from one period to another. For example, she mentioned that movies had gained a measure of credibility in the early 1910s when stage personalities crossed over to the screen. But that development had actually slowed the progress of motion pictures because they began to resemble filmed stage productions. Then innovators entered the scene and pushed movie history in a different and ultimately more popular direction.

Barry continued her quick journey through the teens and into the twenties, speaking about such people as Theda Bara, Mary Pickford, Rudolph Valentino, and Charlie Chaplin, and films such as *The New York Hat, The Four Horsemen of the Apocalypse,* and *The Birth of a Nation.* She discussed the introduction of talking pictures and the seemingly effortless leap made by Walt Disney in his 1937 color, talking, animated feature *Snow White.*[41]

The show concluded by returning to the skeptical man. He explained that while some experts might find movies worthy of real study, for him they were just good entertainment and he didn't expect much more. Barry added to that last claim a fitting afterthought: Sure moviegoers might simply sit back and enjoy the pictures without the mental gymnastics required of critics or curators, but she believed that that while it was true that "the average moviegoer doesn't appear to make heavy demands on the movie-makers ... the public is not satisfied with the films that do not at least reflect [some] advance. After Griffith, it was not possible for directors to go back to earlier methods. After Charlie and Pickford, all acting had to grow subtle. After the imaginative acts and camerawork of the twenties, all productions must reach a higher level. Actually, the public has a keen instinctive sense about the real advances. And why not?—for to make movies with deeper interest and pleasure for the audience is the one objective of the artists of the film."[42] What made movies any different from all other arts cataloged and subjected to historical treatment? What made them different was the sense that the people, rather than the museum, made movies matter. That aspect also made Barry a unique curator of modern art.

The approach taken by Barry and the museum offered a new twist on the dilemma that had plagued other critics who claimed films were art. Rather than expect movies to carry forth the genteel gospel of truth and beauty (as had film theorists in the Progressive Era), or to corrupt the masses (as had both conservative and politically radical critics), Barry accepted that movies were important because they were entertaining, but calling them art forced a reconsideration of the definition of art. The Museum of Modern Art's inclusion of movies suggested that popular taste contributed to the creation of artistic value. Movies could represent noteworthy cultural achievements both because of the way they were made and because of the number of people who watched them. The decline of an older cultural authority had allowed an institution such as MoMA to help shape a new, more expansive set of cultural standards. But what would inclusion in a museum do to the movies?[43]

Barry helped set an agenda for film study by selecting films for preservation and exhibition.[44] Yet her power had to be tempered by the need to remain sensitive to a general audience; she could not afford to alienate moviegoers. If people rejected MoMA's project, then the purpose for having movies in the museum would disappear and an important function of the Film Library would become irrelevant. The clearest illustration of such concerns could be found in a confidential report prepared by British journalist Alistair Cooke. Cooke had been associated with MoMA as part of its informal group of advisers whom the Film Library used to promote and legitimize its activities. Early in 1940 he spent three months observing the library, discussing its operations with the staff, and considering its future course.

The bulk of Cooke's comments centered on the approach the Film Library might take toward exhibiting the movies it collected. Ideally, he hoped the Film Library would catalog all films from each period that were popular, critically acclaimed, and technically innovative. However, Cooke knew that the museum had neither the money nor the influence to wrangle all the films it needed from an industry spread around the world. He also knew that "younger assistants on the staff . . . flushed as a rule with superior knowledge of the movies, believe that we should decide for ourselves what is the best and worst in any year and make a note for future filing." While he respected expert opinion, he also understood how little relevance it had to popular taste.[45]

To press his point, Cooke spoke about the transience of artistic standards and the fallacies of criticism that treated art politically rather than culturally. A nation, he explained, could come to admire and cherish certain artists, but such acquired distinctions were culturally bounded rather than universal. Cooke cautioned Barry against making sweeping aesthetic and historical pronouncements in film notes she compiled for programs. "We . . . cannot guess what later generations, with different perspective, will consider significant or good," he argued. "We must consequently be at great pains not to falsify or prejudice the record." Cooke reasoned that to characterize an era properly, the Film Library must feature both the "best" movies as well as the most popular—including "B" pictures. Such an approach would earn the trust of the public and was simply good history. In order to prevent the inaccurate classification of movies, Cooke proposed that the library keep three lists on file. One list would be of the top ten movies at the box office, the second list would track what critics considered to be the ten best movies, and a third list would include those pictures the staff found especially compelling.[46]

Cooke was relatively satisfied with the existing programs. "If there is a fault," he told Barry, "it is one which I know you are well aware of— namely the apparent preponderance of European over American film."[47] Even though the Film Library had triple the number of American films, its programs had consistently featured European pictures. For example, in eight consecutive exhibitions held at the American Museum of Natural History, there had not been a single American production. Although attendance was quite good, Cooke's impressions were confirmed. In a revealing comment, Cooke showed that he understood the logic behind such presentations: "for it helps silence the belligerent art-cynics who are always ready to say we truckle to the trade but deliberately ignore the great achievements of the Prenez-Garde film in Corsica." His point was that the Film Library had to contend with movie snobs as well as art snobs as it went about educating people about movie history. Cooke advised Barry to intersperse American films with exhibitions of foreign movies in order to make "a deliberate play for general public interest, or the interest of a special group." At base, Cooke was sensitive, perhaps more so than Barry, to the public's perception of both MoMA and its Film Library.[48]

The Film Library had to remember that movies were not the province of aesthetes or scholars but of the people who watched them under less austere circumstances. In his conclusion, Cooke made clear that "in general I should say we go a little too far in aligning ourselves (not by intention but by implication) with the people who want to make the movies an esoteric art. We are primarily historians of a popular art, and we must not shrink from any connotation of the word 'popular.' We should especially remember that many thousand students will be conditioned in their view of the movies by our notes and our programs and we have an alert obligation here to anticipate cultural snobbery, to prevent American college students from developing, from proximity with us, bad cases of cultural superiority. Consequently we must learn how to cultivate the public, not for our own publicity, but because the movies is their art."[49]

Barry and the Film Library were in a difficult position. Just as modern art had split museum patrons and critics over art's form and function, the debate over movies had at least two sides to it. On one side was the argument that movies were entertainment, no more. The other side found the creation of motion pictures a perfectible process and therefore despised Hollywood. There was the danger that elevating movies to the level of other art forms would do an injustice to both motion pictures and the fine arts. Yet one also had to admit that the criteria for judging art had changed. Barry walked a fine line between deflating fatuous artistic standards and inflating equally fatuous artistic pretensions.

At times an irony inherent in the modernist rebellion against cultural standards appeared: Some modernists chose to advance a new cinematic language in order to bolster both the seriousness of studying films and their own superiority over the masses—the group that had made movies significant in the first place. B.G. Braver-Mann, a former editor of the avant-garde-turned-communist journal *Experimental Cinema,* castigated the Film Library for "serving as an instrument for the perpetuation not of a genuine film culture based on a serious approach to the medium but merely of the nickelodeon and show-business 'culture,' which all still operates as the fundamental and sole motivating force behind the streamlined façade of modern Hollywood." A few months later, Kirk Bond, another film critic, questioned the Film Library's selection of movies for exhibition. "In four and a half years," he contended, "it has shown at the most fifteen or twenty picture of real filmic importance." Both critics believed that the Film Library had struck nefarious deals with the Hollywood establishment.[50]

What their comments revealed, of course, was their displeasure with Barry's approach to movies. Quite simply, she had not been sufficiently elitist. The Film Library had exhibited all types of movies to a wide audience and even allowed people to laugh during the screenings. In other words, Barry had treated art as if it were an amusement rather than a relic. She had not only broken with the museum crowd who rejected movies as art, but those who took movies as serious culture. In an article for MoMA's *Bulletin,* Barry conceded that the Film Library had problems pleasing everyone, that accommodating the experts while pleasing the general audience was impossible. Still, she admitted, "Individuals violently protest against the spectacle of films which for any reason displease them: custom seems to have entailed upon the showing of films a peculiar moral responsibility."[51]

Nonetheless, by 1941 the Film Library had at least introduced a new way to consider movies by challenging the way people understood art. The Film Library had circulated ninety-one programs to 476 museums, colleges, and other noncommercial and educational institutions. It held a total of 16 million feet of film for preservation and exhibition. Both the public and MoMA's members had strongly supported it. The Film Library had become a great disseminator of movie history. William Troy, a well-respected film critic for the *Nation,* thought that "Future Ph.D.s making a study of the early twentieth-century cinema from the standpoint either of its technical evolution or of its sometimes bewildering reflection of our culture, will be grateful for the spirit of devoted foresight which has prompted its founding."[52] Indeed, much of later movie literature would be based on the Film Library's vast holdings of periodicals, books, stills, and movies. In November 1938, MoMA had helped found the International Federation of Film Archives, perhaps the crowning achievement in the early period of film preservation and restoration. The agreement joined the Film Library with domestic and international partners: Britain's National Film Archive, the French Cinémathèque Française, and Germany's Reichfilmarchiv.

Barry had often remarked that her approach to movies had been greatly influenced by the art historian Erwin Panofsky.[53] Panofsky had served on the Film Library's board of advisers as an expert in art history and criticism—a role made weightier by being a member of Princeton's Institute for Advanced Study. He gave an address to MoMA's members in 1937 on the unique qualities of movies, pointing out that early filmmakers had been inspired to create by "the sheer delight in the fact that things move" rather than out of a desire to create art.[54] In the process of making films, pioneers such as D.W. Griffith and Mack Sennett had developed the essentials of an important, evolving medium—a visual narrative propelled by movement.

Yet technical innovation revealed only half of the power of movies. Panofsky declared that "the movies, and only the movies, have established a dynamic contact between art production and art consumption so that not only do the works of art develop according to the leanings of a public comprising 60% of the population of the earth, but also mould in turn the spirit, the language, the dress, the behavior and even the physical appearance of the public." Movies were lively, timely, vital, and popular, mass-produced, consumed, and critiqued. After listening to Panofsky, Barry remarked with characteristic wit, "what snob could venture now to doubt that films *were* art?"[55]

Edward M.M. Warburg, a MoMA trustee and treasurer of the Film Library, wrote that Barry "gave the Film and even Hollywood a new respectability. That wasn't her primary object, but she found this, in any case, very amusing. This glorious sense of fun, this making something worthwhile out of the broken 'found objects' of iconoclasm—this was, I think, her talent."[56] Warburg hit upon how Barry accomplished her tasks. She had a sense that movies could reflect an era, a generation, an evening out, but they should not be treated like a religious object. The motion picture could be magical but it was not transcendental. Barry had given movies a tangible and appropriate legacy.

By necessity, Barry had to justify labeling movies "modern art." Unlike other arts that had been tucked away as museum pieces, motion pictures were anything but inaccessible. To study them as one would a painting or a statue almost seemed to threaten the essence of moviegoing. But Barry had accomplished a neat trick of classification: She had couched her description of movies in terms familiar to art historians. She had identified key figures, different schools of thought, and even masterpieces that marked significant junctures in film history, and she had emphasized the point that movies were a modern art with relevance to people's lives. Thus, she suggested a rather radical proposal: Motion pictures were a significant modern art because they reflected and incorporated the tastes of those people most interested in seeing them preserved—the public. Movies were everyone's art because everyone had helped make them important. Iris Barry had helped popularize the arts by making people aware of the treasures that filled their afternoons and evenings in dark theaters across the United States.

6

A Certain Tendency in Film Criticism

In 1932, Norman Wilson, founder of a new film journal called *Cinema Quarterly,* insisted "there is an intelligent cinema audience sufficiently large to support films of the highest artistic standard if they are given the benefit of the commercial resources that are placed behind any other type of picture." His journal spoke to moviegoers who "have come to realise the potentialities of the cinema as a medium of expression with greater range and depth than any of the other arts." A significant faction of that audience also generally despised Hollywood. "In the fullness of life," Wilson argued, "there is abundance of material for the director to dramatise; only poverty of intellect or an inherent dread of facing the tough facts of existence can be responsible for the creation of an artificial world where everything is possible and nothing is of consequence."[1]

Although *Cinema Quarterly* failed and Hollywood continued to thrive through the 1930s and 1940s, Wilson's ideals persisted. In the post–World War II era, the notion that movies were not only serious business but also serious art started to take hold. A movie culture evolved during the 1940s and 1950s in which moviegoers expected more than simply entertainment from films. Helping to advance the taste of audiences was a new breed of critics—a generation raised in a "filmic" rather than a solely literate culture. A certain tendency in criticism appeared that reconceived movies as serious cultural experiences. This tendency came in the forms of manifestos, theories, and feuds. It also helped to unhinge the cultural authority of traditional critics, enabling the reevaluation of mass culture to have a real effect on artistic standards. Reflecting that wave of interest were film journals.

Three journals dominated the postwar era, and collectively they altered the parameters of movie criticism. England's *Sight and Sound,* France's *Cahiers du Cinema,* and America's *Hollywood Quarterly* operated as mouthpieces for critics determined to raise the level of discourse over movies high above what one typically found in mainstream publications. Such elevation, these critics believed, bestowed a legitimacy on movie criticism and helped to refine the art of moviegoing. Yet a vibrant and at times comic debate broke out between these critics over the editorial positions of their journals.

Sight and Sound began publishing in 1932 to provide British educators with information about movies for their classrooms. It became the in-house organ of the British Film Institute (BFI) and a stalwart in support of the social significance of movies and the role critics played in advancing political agendas. *Cahiers du Cinema* released its first issue in 1951 with essays by French cinephiles who, as members of the Cinémathèque Française, created a furor by declaring the director king of the moving picture world. These critics met their British counterparts head-on over the primacy of form and content. Both groups ultimately turned to filmmaking, thereby putting their words into action. In the United States, a journal emerged that established a middle position in the war over criticism. Founded in 1945, *Hollywood Quarterly* took a more serious look at the center of the motion picture world than had any other journal before it. By doing so, it helped advance the art of movies without either snubbing Hollywood or adopting a political agenda. It also became the first American publication to survey trends both inside and outside mainstream movie culture.

The fact that all three journals not merely existed but thrived during the postwar period announced the emergence of moviegoers who were much more serious about their entertainment. That seriousness revealed the expectations of moviegoers who wanted criticism to go beyond plot synopses and brief declarations of like or dislike. Thus, as popular opinion shifted to accept movies as art, film journals acted as a bridge between intellectuals who had for years taken movies seriously and a growing population of moviegoers who read and approved of their criticism. Film journals would also play an important role in launching the movement to reconsider mass culture as something other than the artistic opposite of high culture.

A number of trends converged during the early postwar era that helped significantly alter perceptions of movies as a cultural force. First, by the late 1940s, art and art criticism had thrown off the yoke of public relevance adopted during depression and war. Art moved toward greater abstraction and art criticism became more specialized with less concern for relating broad themes to popular audiences. Into this expanding cultural vacuum, mass culture began to replace the fine arts as the most relevant and significant cultural paradigm of the day, prompting an unprecedented outpouring of critiques from intellectuals. Movies, in fact, became a worthy substitute for high art among some of the artistic vanguard.[2]

Second, from the late 1940s through the 1960s, Hollywood seemed unusually vulnerable to foreign competition. Robert Sklar notes that "by the early 1950s, interest in British and foreign-language films was strong enough to support the first significant innovation in audience segmentation since the arrival of talking pictures—the rise of 'art houses' devoted exclusively to non-Hollywood movies."[3] Indeed, beginning immediately after the Second World War, foreign films entered the American market offering reality in place of Hollywood fantasy. Italian filmmakers Vittorio de Sica and Roberto Rossellini led the procession of new films—also dubbed, art films—with *The Bicycle Thief* and *Open City*. In both productions, the directors had used actual locations rather than studio sets to provide backdrops for their sobering tales.

De Sica's film provided a perfect contrast to Hollywood movies. The characters in *The Bicycle Thief* are poor urban workers who suffer through the chaos of life in postwar Italy wearing a single set of clothing. The movie's central premise is the absolute importance of a bicycle to the livelihood and survival of a poor Italian family—a concept completely foreign to American audiences used to watching actors and actresses devour consumer items as if they grew on trees. The ending of de Sica's movie was a stark illustration of the potential power of realistic films: After attempting to steal a bicycle in order to replace the one stolen from him, the protagonist is caught and humiliated in front of his son, set free by the owner of the bicycle, and closes the film weeping and still without a bicycle. No Hollywood producer would have dared left the audience with such a final image.

Surprisingly, de Sica's film was a minor commercial hit with Americans. Its success helped open the American market for a wave of movies from foreign filmmakers such as Ingmar Bergman of Sweden, Carol Reed of Great Britain, Akira Kurosawa of Japan, Satyajit Ray of India, and France's Jean Cocteau. The reception of these filmmakers and the many others who followed them in the late 1950s through the 1960s, gave film critics cause to hope that movies were beginning to mature and there-fore would need a more advanced form of criticism. Yet even without the invasion of foreign films, Hollywood had cause to get serious.

A third reason movie culture seemed to change was that audiences craved more complex aesthetic experiences. In 1945, *New York Times* movie critic Bosley Crowther reported on a study conducted by George Gallup for the Audience Research Institute. Gallup's polls had revealed a surprising trend: Movies had become the entertainment of choice for educated and prosperous people rather than, as had always been assumed, for the undereducated and poor. If Hollywood truly wanted to maintain its audience base, it needed to appeal to a group whose expectations de-manded something more than traditional formulaic movies.[4]

As recently as 1946, Hollywood had boasted its single greatest year on record: 90 million people a week attended movies out of a possible 38 million households. That same year, the industry took in $1.7 billion from admissions, accounting for 82 percent of the public's total expen-diture on amusements. The industry had first studied its audience dur-ing the mid-1940s, finding, much to its pleasure, that it had already captured three-quarters of its "potential" audience. Audience patronage would never be that good again. By 1950, attendance would drop by half.[5]

Hollywood's declining fortunes paralleled the rise of television. Although the technology to produce televisions had been available since the late 1930s, the machine itself had remained impractical to purchase on a normal income. Moreover, a limited number of stations and sparse programming made it a poor alternative to the movies and radio. In 1946, when only eight thousand families owned a television set and there were only six stations nationwide, movie attendance reached its zenith. Within four years the number of families owning televisions had sky-rocketed to almost 4 million, the number of stations had increased to ninety-seven, and motion picture attendance had dropped to 60 million. The irony of this challenge was that while motion pictures had begun as entertainment for immigrants, by earning respectability among the edu-cated and the affluent, they had lost out to television as the most popular mass medium.[6]

Periodicals such as the enormously popular weekly *Life* noticed the impending crisis. In 1949, America's most popular magazine ran a long article entitled: "What's with the Movies?" The magazine organized four panels—made up of critics, scholars, exhibitors, and consumers—to dis-cuss this question. Novelist Eric Hodgins moderated the exchange, suggesting in his introductory remarks that the crisis Hollywood seemed to be in was "less a financial crisis than a crisis of motives, direction, reasons-for-being."[7]

The critics recommended that Hollywood find a middle way between the elite few and the passive many. Since television would absorb those viewers looking for a distraction, the movies needed to satisfy an audience seeking tales that engaged their intelligence. Academics on the panel concluded that Hollywood would kill itself if it continued to aim low in an effort to capture a wide audience with every film. The studios, they argued, had to think of their audience as a heterogeneous group of people rather than as a homogeneous mass. Movie exhibitors, who were especially sensitive to economic considerations, believed that pictures could be separated into two categories, "art" and "commercial," with two types of audiences. The former attracted an increasingly dedicated though small number of people; the latter played to those looking for entertainment and a snack. One exhibitor remarked: "God help us all if the American people start hating popcorn." A group of "consumers" from Bryan, Ohio, criticized the false advertising and phoniness of the movies and the regularity of simpleminded themes. As the other panelists had predicted, they asked for pictures with story lines that were both more believable and more enjoyable.[8]

One could trace the evolution of postwar movie culture in the pages of film journals. For example, *Hollywood Quarterly* ran a study of American film literature by Arthur Rosenheimer (later Arthur Knight) that reported on the diversity of movie periodicals. On a typical newsstand one could find information on everything from Cary Grant's latest romantic tryst and the best place to rent 16-mm projectors to the aesthetics of documentaries and the lost art of D.W. Griffith.[9]

Lewis Jacobs first published his landmark research on experimental films in the United States for *Hollywood Quarterly.* Early in its history, the experimental film movement in the United States had been overwhelmed by mainstream productions and largely ignored by critics. Such treatment, Jacobs explained, tended to make experimental filmmakers "cliquey and in-bred, often ignorant of the work of others with similar aims." Yet following the war, the movement gained new life through MoMA's circulating exhibitions on the history of films and the strength of the documentary movement.[10]

Two centers of creative, independent filmmaking also emerged in the early postwar years—one at the San Francisco Museum of Art, under the guidance of Frank Stauffacher and Richard Foster, and another in New York City's largest film society, Cinema 16, managed by Amos Vogel. In both institutions, audiences watched and listened to pioneers of avant-garde filmmaking such as Maya Deren, Jean Cocteau, Kenneth Anger, Curtis Harrington, Man Ray, Hans Richter, and Stan Brakhage. Amos Vogel used the pages of *Hollywood Quarterly* to declare that "New Yorkers no longer have to be school children, 'shut-ins,' or club members in order to see documentary films. Cinema 16, at first an ambitious dream to create a permanent showcase for 16-mm. documentary and experimental films, has today become very much a reality." Begun in October 1947, Cinema 16 would grow by the late 1950s into the largest film society in the world. The community of movie enthusiasts it attracted viewed movies not merely as art but as personal and ideological statements. Vogel wrote that his film society "hails a film that is a work of art, but will not hesitate to present a film that is important only because of its subject matter. Its avant-garde films comment on the tensions and psychological insecurity of modern existence or are significant expressions of modern art." Another enthusiast thought the audience for Cinema 16 was "almost fanatically enthusiastic. It likes to talk of 'technique of appreciation,' and to consider appreciation itself as an art. It likes to meditate on what it can legitimately accept as intrinsically filmic."[11]

Such commentary expressed a recurring theme that made both film journals and film societies important to postwar movie culture. A community of movie enthusiasts had begun to gather that thought and spoke about movies in a manner distinct from the rest of the movie audience. Yet unlike previous generations, this group had journals and institutions that bound disparate segments together. As more people attended film societies such as Cinema 16 and read journals such as *Hollywood Quarterly*, a new epistemology of movies took shape.[12]

European film critics took the lead in debates over movie criticism, however. Peter Noble, a leading British film authority remarked, "It is safe to say that Europe and more specifically Britain, has shown during the past twenty years a far greater interest in an examination of the aesthetics of cinema than has the United States." As evidence, Nobel listed a number of serious British film journals, including *Sight and Sound;* the *Penguin Film Review,* edited by Roger Manvell; *Cinema, Stage and Screen; Film Forum,* edited by Norman Wilson (the former editor of *Cinema Quarterly*); and *Sequence,* edited by a trio of young, sharp Oxford undergraduates, Penelope Houston, Lindsay Anderson, and Peter Ericsson.[13]

Among the leaders of the new criticism, a measure of elitism was expected. Ernest Lindgren, author of *The Art of the Film* (1948)—a straightforward study of film aesthetics by the curator of the British Film Library—spoke for many of his colleagues when he contended that movies had become the "art of our age." Although film critics wrote about a subject "patronized by a vast popular audience, inarticulate, unorganized, and unaware of its power," he believed they also had a responsibility to treat films seriously and work to convince the public of this fact.[14] Penelope Houston, a member of a younger generation of critics, seconded the notion that for too long movies had existed in an intellectual dead zone, receiving nothing but scorn from cultural critics. Writing in *Sequence,* Oxford University's undergraduate film society journal, Houston declared, "we must assume that films deserve serious criticism, only if we accept the cinema as an art form."[15]

Even though "serious" film critics would never be as widely read as their colleagues in major newspapers or popular magazines, they self-consciously had begun to distinguish themselves from the more popular—and they believed, mundane—reviewers. For example, Ernest Callenbach, an American contemporary of Penelope Houston, conducted a survey for *Hollywood Quarterly* of critics who wrote for the large daily newspapers in Chicago, Los Angeles, Washington, and New York to uncover their intellectual approach to criticism. In regard to popular movie reviews, he concluded, "such stuff creates a fraudulent and hypnotic haze of mock evaluation, and it is unfortunate that it is circulated so widely."[16]

Not one of the critics Callenbach questioned had come from the movie industry and only a couple admitted to reading books on films. All said they had some familiarity with serious film journals, though. "Most of them imagine themselves to be writing from the standpoint of the common man, but" Callenbach complained, "a discouraging proportion do not think that their work has any marked effect on their readers." He found the whole enterprise discouraging since "reviews seldom display awareness of the film as a medium," and most critics operated within "the theatrical tradition," rather than treating movies as "a peculiar genre, marked by mobility, ellipsis, and material symbolism." He declared: "The great public of this country is subjected to a barrage of cursory evaluation which tends to stifle rather than stimulate the application of imagination to motion picture fare."[17]

So, what was the job of a "serious" film critic? The editors of *Sight and Sound* put that question to ten critics, including Dilys Powell and

Catherine de la Roche, who both wrote for large daily newspapers, and Ernest Lindgren and Roger Manvell, scholars who published in film journals. Some of the more revealing responses were prompted by a question about balancing the interests of the audience with that of the critic. Both Manvell and Lindgren, the most independent members of the group, argued that remaining honest to their own taste took precedence over pleasing their audience. By contrast, critics who worked for newspapers said they wrote to entertain and inform their readers as much as to satisfy their own predilections. Powell pointed out, however, "you can't do justice to all the contributors to the week's films in a thousand words; and if you could the words would be unreadable and therefore useless to everybody." De la Roche added: "It may be technically more difficult to give analytical constructive criticism in a readable, entertaining form. But in itself the task of being as fully truthful in appraising a film as possible is, as I see it, an equal responsibility to both the film and the reader."[18]

These British critics also reflected on recent trends in French film criticism, especially the attention given to directors and the value of their input in the criticism of movies. Manvell argued that "critical evaluation is itself a creative activity. . . . Criticism is expression through words not motion pictures." He also wrote that insight provided by directors was useful. Dilys Powell dismissed the French approach, saying: "there is no reason to believe the directors would do any better than the professional critics. They would know more, but knowledge is not enough. Criticism is a writer's business and writing (though nobody recognises this nowadays) is a skilled profession, requiring for its proper practice discipline, devotion and a lifetime. To suppose that any director can write is about as sensible as to suppose that any writer can direct. Anyhow, as it is too much pompous bosh is written about the cinema."[19]

A primary source for such "bosh" was *Cahiers du Cinema,* the mouthpiece for a group of French critics who expanded the scope of film criticism by introducing new ways to understand and communicate cinematic experiences. Lo Duca, André Bazin, and, Jacques Doniol-Valcroze founded the journal in 1951 and gathered around them younger critics, including François Truffaut, Jean-Luc Goddard, Claude Charbol, Jacques Rivette, and Eric Rohmer, who would later become important filmmakers of the French New Wave (*la nouvelle vague*). The critics of the French school followed two basic principles. The first was a rejection of aesthetics based on montage—a technique made famous by Soviet directors in the 1920s and 1930s in which a director told a story by coupling scenes so that visual images conveyed literal ideas. This approach was effective as a political tool when Soviet directors contrasted scenes portraying the communist ideal with shots of the evils perpetrated under capitalist imperialism. In place of such an approach, French critics identified with a director's *mise-en-scène* or the arrangement of each individual shot as a work of art itself. The visual creation, they argued, superseded the intellectual content of a scene. As Fereydoun Hoveyda explained in *Cahiers,* "the specificity of a cinematographic work lies in the form rather than in its content, in the *mise-en-scène* and not in the scenario or dialogue."[20]

The second principle was a method of criticism made famous by François Truffaut in his 1954 article entitled "A Certain Tendency in French Cinema," in which he introduced the manifesto *la politique des auteurs* (or the author's politics or world view). Later dubbed the auteur theory by American critic Andrew Sarris, this approach grew into an argument that film "should ideally be a medium of personal artistic expression and that the best films are therefore those which most clearly bear their makers' 'signature'—the stamp of one's individual personality, controlling obsessions, and cardinal themes." When Truffaut wrote his piece, however, he intended it as a critique of post–WWII French filmmakers, whom he faulted for relying on written scenarios rather than filmic vision. Directors such as Claude Autant-Lara, Jean Delannoy, René Clement, Yves Allegret, and Marcel Pagliero had compromised their artistic integrity as filmmakers, Truffaut believed, by adapting trendy topics for the screen rather than creating an "authentic" work of cinema. The sum of such work was "an anti-bourgeois cinema made by the bourgeois for the bourgeois." He and many of his fellow *Cahiers* critics wanted cinematic authorship to depend on a director's ability to conceive, write, and direct an idea from beginning to end. These critics hoped to reveal something about life that only the visual magic of movies could illustrate. They emphasized what they believed were the essential qualities of films in order to distinguish the art of filmmaking—through the art of film criticism—from other artistic endeavors.[21]

Once this generation of French critics turned toward filmmaking, they did so, as one historian remarked, as "the first film-educated generation of film-makers in history." Most of the major figures in this movement had learned film history and filmmaking by attending exhibitions at the Cinémathèque Française. They made films as they had critiqued them, as personal expressions, thus challenging the audience to see movies in a different way. But unlike their criticism, which initially had limited exposure outside of France, their movies were international hits. At the Cannes Film Festival in 1959—the most prestigious of international festivals—Truffaut's movie *400 Blows (Les 400 Coups)* received the Director's Prize, and his contemporary Alain Resnais's film, *Hiroshima mon amour,* took the International Critics' Prize, thereby firmly establishing the Frenchmen as forces to be reckoned with. Their success as filmmakers helped legitimize a critical position—whether or not they followed it themselves—that could not be easily dismissed as naïve or foolish.[22]

Nevertheless, a stubborn paradox still pervaded auteur criticism. Members of the *Cahiers* group had developed their hyper-awareness of directorial styles in part by watching American movies of the 1930s and 1940s—westerns, gangster pictures, and comedies. It was a great coup, in other words, to find within a Hollywood production the signature of a single artist. Of all the movie industries in the world, America's had consistently been the most impersonal and collaborative. But that perspective, French critics argued, had developed out of criticism that concentrated on individual movies rather than a series of pictures by a single director. Thus, by watching dozens of films by a single director, an astute critic might discover a director's *mise-en-scène.* If this approach was mildly unorthodox, claiming that Hollywood productions were art was outright revolutionary. No known or accepted artistic standards had made it possible to accommodate mass culture in this way. The French critics were not simply blurring the line that divided the arts from the movies, they were suggesting that it had never existed, that movies made for commercial purposes—to entertain the masses— had always been art.

That concept could be vexing to those who considered movies as anything but art. Moreover, the new language used by the French critics could seem downright ridiculous to reviewers accustomed to writing for a popular audience. Yet the *Cahiers* critics had revealed something profound about the era in which they wrote. Since many in the audience had been raised as much on movies as on literature, a substantial population had begun to discuss movies in terms typically reserved for novels, plays, and poems. Many enthusiasts expressed their love for movies in language that seemed intentionally chosen to obscure the fact that they had made so much of a medium traditionally worth so little. A question thus remained: Did elevating movies to art require couching one's appreciation in linguistic and ideological codes?

Gerald Pratley, writing in *Hollywood Quarterly,* observed the somewhat disturbing implications of this trend. In his position as a movie reviewer for the Canadian Broadcasting Company, Pratley had to keep in mind the large audience he reached over the radio. He had become sensitive to language that failed to be both intelligible as well as insightful. The French Ciné Club at the University of Toronto asked him to join a discussion on Jean Cocteau's film *Orpheé.* Pratley found the movie senseless, which made him hesitant to accept the invitation. "On second thought," he explained, "it seemed a brief summary of my ideas about this type of film might help those who, like myself, wish to bring about a more rational consideration of such pictures in the appreciation of the film."[23]

Pratley watched the film a few times thinking that perhaps he had been unduly harsh. No, his initial response had been accurate: The movie had "no truth in its murky depths" and it was "not particularly well-made." Anticipating the response, Pratley added that defending his opinion typically led to an "endless argument about what is bad taste, what is sense, what is beauty, what is truth, and so on, with those persons who delight in rejecting the accepted standards of judgment in order to embrace and justify the unintelligible." What compelled him to attend the French Ciné Club was the shift then taking place in film criticism that served to rationalize poor filmmaking by exaggerating artistic merit. "The devotees of the unusual film," he argued, "elevate their absurdities out of all proportion to their value. They convince themselves that the peculiar artists are getting out of the rut and pushing the frontiers of the cinema into a glorious future." But when the public fails to respond positively to "abstractionists" such as Cocteau, snobbish cliques "like to think that in associating themselves with the abstractionists, they are elevating themselves above the mass of the people who are honest enough to reject such works as being without value and importance. To write adverse criticism results in further publicity, in which, of course, they revel."[24]

Hollywood Quarterly ran another article on Cocteau a year later that was intended as a defense of the French filmmaker but also served as another illustration of the growing estrangement between critic and audience. In "A Dialogue Between the Movie-Going Public and a Witness for Jean Cocteau," Raymond Jean (the witness) testified to all of the worst traits Pratley had identified in the new critical circles. Jean was an assistant professor of French literature in France and an associate professor of Romance languages at the University of Pennsylvania. He had published in many French journals, including *Cahiers du Cinéma*. In Jean's mind, the public was clearly at fault for its inability to understand Cocteau's significance. A clear example of the growing division between film enthusiasts and the public was evident in a passage in which the "witness" attempted to explain why the public failed to grasp the director's work. "You are trying to understand," says the witness. "Are you sure you are trying to see what is going on in front of you? What Cocteau is reproaching you for is your inattention, your lack of eagerness to look closely at what took months of meticulous work to prepare. In his films, the least image missed, he says, ruins the whole."[25]

Jean further observed that the public cared only about getting lost in "marvelous . . . supernatural fairy tales," so evident in "the sumptuous and facile productions of American westerns and musicals." Cocteau's films interested those who appreciated "quality and technique"—Cocteau had even gone "beyond the *avant-garde*." His gifts, Jean believed, were apparent to all those who *wanted* to notice them. Yet "people refuse to believe that these qualities of his can be reconciled with his avant-garde spirit, with his aesthetic originality, and with his love for the beautiful. Clown or serious artist, only you make the distinction."[26]

Of course, the point had become that once "you," the audience, made such a distinction, that decision placed you among a group of moviegoers who subscribed to an ideology particular to their tastes. To be cinematically literate meant accepting the "bosh" of critics such as Jean. To reject his rationale placed one in the odd position of being ignorant of film art—an idea that was the intellectual mangling of the notion that movies were a popular art. Thus, a certain tendency in film criticism had begun to take hold and to reflect a new sensibility among a generation of moviegoers who gradually separated themselves from those who accepted movies as art but did not make this an elitist enterprise.

The significance of French film criticism, it seems to me, was not so much its insight into movies but its ability to illustrate a shift toward the intellectualization of mass culture and democratization of criticism. Those who adopted the French approach were curious cultural rebels because they viewed movies from an elitist perspective but had reached that position by undermining an older cultural authority upheld by critics of mass culture. Auteur critics had rewritten cultural standards so that their criticism of movies—a popular art—had become an elite endeavor.[27]

André Bazin, a member of the inner circle of the *Cahiers* group, provided a thoughtful critique and defense of auteur criticism. As one of the founders of the premiere French journal of criticism, Bazin was in a good position to distinguish overblown rhetoric from serious content and significant contentions. In an April 1957 article entitled "On the *Politique des Auteurs,*" he suggested that, on balance, the French critics made contributions that were legitimate enough to prevent him from becoming a detractor rather than merely a gentle critic. The *politique des auteurs,* he contended, "has the merit of treating the cinema as an adult art, and of reacting against the impressionistic relativism which still prevails most often in film criticism." Yet it also had a tendency, Bazin wrote, to slide toward "an esthetic cult of personality" because the approach had yet to be explained in any systematic way. Bazin thus found it "unfortunate to praise wrongly a work which does not merit it [and] reject an estimable film because its maker has not up until now produced anything good." His intention for writing the critique, he concluded, was "not at all to deny the role of the *auteur,* but to restore to it the preposition without which the noun is only a lame concept. '*Auteur,*' without doubt, but *of* what?"[28]

Indeed, it often seemed that the auteurists emerged only because they had previously been obscure or derided by other critics or enemies of auteur criticism. Without any tangible basis for such praise, the evaluation of directors and films might become so arbitrary that critics themselves would slowly grow irrelevant. While aesthetic criticism had helped a number of French critics discover how they wished to make movies, it also promised to further estrange critics from the audience that watched them. In England, a group of critics hoped to turn criticism into a tool to influence the public by clarifying the role movies played in shaping social norms.

In the mid-1950s, filmmakers and critics in London had also devoted a good deal of attention to movies but rejected the auteur critics' emphasis on hyper-aestheticism. Issuing their own set of manifestoes, the British Free Cinema movement had rediscovered the importance of class relations to the health of British society and began demanding that others be "committed" (the catchword of the movement) to social change. A similar sensibility had characterized the rich British documentary film movement during the 1930s and 1940s that had merged social realism with mass media. In the early postwar era, however, British commercial films began to sink into mediocrity, resembling bad spin-offs of Hollywood productions. In the mid-1950s, critics Lindsay Anderson and Karel Reisz demanded that British movies return to depicting "the significance of the everyday" and to wield the medium of film as an instrument rather than belittle it as an amusement. Much like their French counterparts, Anderson, Reisz, and others would go on to direct the type of films they praised with their criticism.[29]

In 1956, Lindsay Anderson issued the seminal statement on commitment for *Sight and Sound.* Entitled "Stand Up! Stand Up!" Anderson's article was meant to shock complacent critics who wrote for major dallies and to challenge the French school of avant-garde criticism and its British adherents. He quickly established himself as the most resolutely "committed" of *Sight and Sound*'s contributors.[30]

John Russell Taylor, a critic for the London *Times,* wrote the letter that inspired Anderson's spirited manifesto. Taylor suggested that committed criticism, although energetic, was not "the be-all and end-all of criticism." Moreover, practicing such criticism did not "absolve critics from the necessity of reaching some aesthetic judgment for the benefit of people who just happen to love the film for its own sake."[31]

For his part, Anderson believed that because movies had become meaningless to the audience, critics needed to inject something more than aesthetics into their criticism. The wide acceptance of movies as art, he argued, "had been won at the price of diluting that original enthusiasm" for the significance of films. "To a remarkable extent, denigration of the cinema, denial of its importance and its significance, has become common among those who write about it professionally." It was fashionable, once again, for mainstream critics to dismiss movies as inconsequential since the label of "art" had become largely meaningless. And while movie critics had earned respect among other cultural critics, their opinions seemed to matter less and less to the audience. In an attempt to make movies and criticism relevant to contemporary life, Anderson called on writers to commit to a moral position. "The essence of the matter," he believed, "is in the importance we attach to our principles, and the extent to which we think they are relevant to our enjoyment of art." In other words, one had to question an artist's point of view as well as one's style, because, "in the best art, anyway, style and commitment are inseparable."[32]

Anderson pointed to Taylor and Alistair Cooke as popular but weak critics who could explain what they liked about a movie but who seemed unwilling to defend why a movie deserved to be made or seen. They represented the liberal perspective "that tolerantly estimates every work on its merits." But it was also a position that Anderson believed undercut serious critics by leading the readers to regard criticism as frivolous. "Scorn of 'highbrow nonsense about art and culture' is only round the corner from here, and so is the pursuit of 'fun.' It is the 'dull' talent that the critic really disapproves of: he wants to be entertained." Sounding a bit like a latter-day Oliver Cromwell, Anderson demanded that standards be observed to prevent "fundamental issues" from being "baulked." Where was the line between objectivity and personal convictions or aesthetic and moral judgment? Anderson asked. Why should critics who were clearly influential in society reject their power to affect their surroundings? In other words: "Why, should anyone be content to be a *mere* critic?"[33]

Anderson also found fault with French critics writing in *Cahiers du Cinema* and a younger generation of British critics writing in *Oxford Opinion* and *Film.* If one took their position to an extreme, auteur critics contended that each scene in a movie had enough material in it to determine whether or not a director was a genius. Although Anderson and his colleague Penelope Houston had initially favored aesthetic criticism while at *Sequence,* both came to bristle at favoring form over content. Yet to the auteurists, committed critics were equally fanatical in their demands for ideological films and criticism.[34]

Anderson did not doubt the sincerity of liberal critics or the intelligence of auteur critics, but he had become impatient with their passivity toward a society wracked by social problems. "The cinema is not apart from all this; nor is it something to be denigrated or patronized," he wrote. "It is a vital and significant medium, and all of us who concern ourselves with it automatically take on an equivalent responsibility." He looked for critics to take a stand on social issues rather than pretend movies and criticism had no effect on life. "There is," he declared, "no such thing as uncommitted criticism, any more than there is no such thing as insignificant art. It is merely a question of the openness with which our commitments are stated. I do not believe that we should keep quiet about them."[35]

Two years after Anderson made his stand in the pages of *Sight and Sound,* the journal published a discussion among four of Britain's most important critics—Paul Rotha, Basil Wright, Lindsay Anderson, and Penelope Houston—who discussed what they called "the critical issue." After decades of trying to gain respect, film critics had made it acceptable to take films seriously, but their victory now seemed hollow. Basil

Wright insisted that what was "vitally important about the 'thirties is . . . the total commitment . . . to critical writing and attack writing." Anderson agreed that the 1930s were "a period which is just more creative, in which there is more feeling of progress, and you therefore put yourselves in the service of that progress . . . which is not, I think, the feeling of today." What bothered Houston and Anderson about contemporary society was the lack of solidarity among young critics. Anderson lamented that "in any kind of extremist or uncompromising statements one is trying to make, one is not backed up by a lively younger generation."[36]

Indeed, film criticism had become so mundane that it had even lost the distinction of rebelliousness. "I . . . think we have reached a stage," Anderson contended, "at which the cinema has become respectable, which it was not in the 'twenties and hardly in the 'thirties, and that always somehow takes the excitement out of anything. It has created a large but essentially passive public of film appreciators." What was needed, Basil Wright claimed, was "an anarchic paper, run by a group of probably rather scruffy young men between 17 and 22 who will . . . generally stir up the whole thing." Anderson thought: "What we need is something at once more edgy and more personal. Perhaps only a new movement can provide this? But not necessarily 'anarchistic.' The criticism we desperately need should be enthusiastic, violent, and responsible, all at the same time."[37]

Jonas Mekas decided to provide such an outlet. Mekas had begun *Film Culture* in 1955 as an independent American film journal for serious writing on the movies. When an "underground" movie culture developed in New York City, Mekas responded to its rhythms by changing the emphasis of his journal to promote independent and experimental films. In a 1959 editorial he announced the establishment of the "Independent Film Award" created to honor the "New American Cinema" (NAC). This was Mekas's attempt to place domestic filmmakers alongside their international counterparts. The NAC, he declared, possessed a "spirit that is akin to that which guides the young British film makers centered around Free Cinema, a spirit which is being felt among the French newcomers . . . and a spirit which is changing the face of the young Polish cinema." He called for "breaking the frozen cinematic ground . . . through a *complete* derangement of the official cinematic senses."[38]

Yet Mekas was looking to break more than simple cinematic ground, he wanted to bulldoze older ideas of culture. He would later declare that he didn't "want any part of the Big Art game. The new cinema, like the new man, is nothing definitive, nothing final. Our art is 'confused' and all that jazz, jazz, jazz. But we refuse to continue the Big Lie of Culture. To the new artist the fate of man is more important than the fate of art, more important than the temporary confusions of art." In a rejoinder to Mekas's overblown declarations, Edouard de Laurot replied, "Paradoxically, the most salient effect of the New American Cinema's anarchic rebellion has been to reject precisely those values they needed most: experience, craft, and a sense of métier." Faced with their shortcomings, the NAC "have sought security in the enthusiastic praises of their uncritical friends."[39]

Penelope Houston had similar misgivings about auteur critics, a topic she explored in a long piece for *Sight and Sound.* In it, she made clear her profound distaste for auteur criticism because it debased the art of watching movies. Auteur critics, she argued, had not simply rejected the idea of "commitment," they had championed a position with no redeeming social value. As she saw things, "There are no good or bad subjects; affirmation is a word for boy scouts; social significance is a bore; don't expect a film to present you with sympathetic characters; don't even, if one takes it far enough, look for character; don't have any truck with anything that smacks of literature. Cinema, by this definition, means first and foremost the visual image; and the critic's response is to the excitement it can communicate." According to Houston, movies had lost their value as an art for either critics or the audience. "To the generation which has grown up during the last few years," she lamented, "art is seen as something for kicks: films which stab at the nerves and the emotions. Violence on the screen is accepted as a stimulant and anything which can be labeled as slow or sentimental is suspect. The attitude is far from being one of disillusionment or defeat: it is more simply of disinterest in art which does not work on one's own terms, and an inevitable belief that those terms are the only valid ones."[40]

The intellectual disputes over movie criticism had reached a feverish pitch, even if very few people outside a rather elite moviegoing public took notice. What made that debate important, however, was that its influence would soon be felt in mainstream movie culture. Moreover, arguments concerning the definition of film as art echoed a modernist sensibility that was slowly taking on the shades of a post-modern discourse. Postwar movie criticism illustrated just how much the presence of movies had disturbed older ideas about culture and, more importantly, traditional methods of criticism. Even though critics were beginning to talk past each other, above the public, and beyond their counterparts in other fields, they had also showed that the moving picture world was a good deal larger than previously imagined.[41]

Ernest Callenbach, the new editor of the *Hollywood Quarterly*, which had been recently—and aptly—renamed, *Film Quarterly*, attempted to assess new trends in filmmaking and criticism by proposing a new "general line" for critics. "For better or worse," he wrote, "the cinema is no longer merely a contrivance for the commercial debauching of the masses; it is now the subject of solemn aesthetic and social analysis." Callenbach pointed to John Grierson, the famous British documentarian, as the most fully developed critic because he understood both the mechanical and aesthetic aspects of motion pictures. Only those critics who considered the economic, structural, and technical aspects of movie production as well as the aesthetic and social functions of film would be useful to the effort to educate the public. "If we wish to interpret and criticize film accurately and sensibly," Callenbach argued, "we must face up squarely to the conditions of the industrial world in which they are manufactured and distributed—just as the better critics already face up to the general social context in which films appear." Callenbach's rationale hardly made peace among movie critics but his suggestions clearly influenced a generation of scholars interested in the emerging field of film studies.[42]

In an editorial entitled "Turn On! Turn On!" Callenbach offered a way across the critical impasse. "We need critics," he insisted, "for whom the cinema is like bread or wine or women: who crave it, who are passionate lovers and haters, who know that the art demands all their intelligence and all their care, and that even that will never be enough; critics who are devoted enough to know that the profound can lurk in the trivial, and vice versa . . . who are willing to immerse themselves in a film as desperately and totally as if it were their own life—and then come back and write of it for us, who may (if we are open and free) understand what the experience has been, and what it signifies."[43]

William S. Pechter, a contributor to *Film Quarterly* as well as to the *Kenyon Review*, was not "turned-on" by Callenbach's proposal. Pechter had simply grown tired of a debate that threatened to turn British periodicals into "trade journals for movie critics." Although he shared little in common with either side, Pechter seemed especially frustrated with "those intransigent rebels" whose criticism "is always made to sound like art for art's sake run amok." Generally fed up, Pechter probably spoke for many when he declared: "one thing I know we do not need is more programs and manifestos. What we do need [is] to be more intelligent; to write better, as though we thought that language might be as valid and significant a medium as the film; and to stop talking about ourselves, as though we had unique, important problems." "I am presently readying a major document on the crisis, consisting of a title and no pages," he concluded smartly. "I would like to call it, simply, 'Shut Up,' but I suppose it shall have to be retitled 'Shut Up! Shut Up!'"[44]

Pechter's response reflected a broader sensibility that viewed intellectualizing movies as nonsense. And yet, because film criticism was vogue and critics felt free to engage the medium with increasing enthusiasm, mass culture in general began to move from the shadows of the art world into the intellectual limelight—even if critics spoke about the lively arts out of the corner of their mouths. An example of the variety of approaches to this once inconsequential subject was a collection of essays edited by sociologists Bernard Rosenberg and David Manning White.

In *Mass Culture: The Popular Arts in America* (1957), Rosenberg and White provided one of the first overviews of mass cultural criticism in America. "Mass culture has reached into the Academy," they explained, "both by its pervasive influence and as a subject of serious study. Gradually, academicians and detached intellectuals are being drawn into the vortex by a suction force none can resist." Among the contributors unable to resist this attraction were heavyweight intellectuals such as Dwight Macdonald, Clement Greenberg, Leo Lowenthal, David Riesman, George Orwell, Edmund Wilson, Paul Lazarsfeld, Theodore Adorno, Irving Howe, and Ernest van den Haag. The editors also included pieces by Alexis de Tocqueville, Walt Whitman, and Jose Ortega y Gasset meant to illustrate the historical basis for serious treatment of the people's arts. The volume also provided an important forum for critics who had pioneered an intellectual fascination with mass culture, among them Gilbert Seldes, Robert Warshow, Herbert Gans, and Marshall McLuhan.[45]

Rosenberg and White qualified their position on mass culture by being critical of its effects even if respectful of its cultural weight. For Rosenberg, mass culture threatened "not merely to cretinize our taste, but to brutalize our senses while paving the way to totalitarianism. And the interlocking media all conspire to that end." White was decidedly less apocalyptic about the effects of mass culture. He conceded "there can be no defense (either on esthetic or moral grounds) for certain aspects of mass culture which are banal, dehumanizing and downright ugly, both in form and content." But White also believed that mass culture offered only a new way to dupe a majority of the masses into paying attention to basically forgettable and therefore relatively harmless things.[46] Both perspectives reflected the strange relationship intellectuals had with mass culture. If many of them found it either distasteful or distracting, then why devote time and effort to discussing it?

In a famous review of this book, art critic Harold Rosenberg offered an answer. "The common argument of the mass-culture intellectuals that they have come not to bathe in the waters but to register the degree of its pollution does not impress me," he wrote. "I believe they play in the stuff because they like it, including those who dislike what they like." Many critics, he contended, subscribed to corrupted cultural standards—they were "kitsch critics of kitsch" using "false arguments about . . . false products." Rosenberg suggested that such attention to mass culture accorded it more legitimacy and, in turn, undermined the arts that deserved serious attention. By constantly discovering the significance of mass culture, such critics had helped "to destroy the distinction between that spurious mental and aesthetic substance known as 'kitsch' and art, good or bad."[47]

Indeed, the film journals of the 1950s had illustrated the problems inherent in treating mass culture seriously. "One of the grotesqueries of present-day American life," Rosenberg believed, "is the amount of reasoning that goes into displaying the wisdom secreted in bad movies while proving that modern art is meaningless." What Rosenberg feared was not simply the elevation of movies and mass culture to higher artistic ground (a process he found irresponsible) but the gradual eclipsing of art (a prospect he found unfortunate) and the growing irrelevance of criticism (a development he found already afoot). In the coming years, such concerns would not be simply prescient but wholly realized. Differences between art and mass culture would melt away, and disappearing with them was the idea that criticism should define separate cultural spheres. Movies continued to play an important part in these developments as two critics, in particular, dueled for authority over movie criticism.[48]

Andrew Sarris, Pauline Kael, and the Duel for the Soul of Criticism

American essayist Phillip Lopate remembers that as a nineteen-year-old student his passion for films ran very strong. In 1963 he agreed to run a film society at Columbia University and needed a way to justify his selections to a crowd of cinema enthusiasts. Lopate discovered his holy grail in the work of film critic Andrew Sarris. Sarris "seemed to cherish movies because they spoke to one's half-buried desires," Lopate recalls fondly, "but then cherished most those with an 'adult' (one of Sarris's favorite words) perspective, which acknowledged the necessity for sacrifice, whether gallant or otherwise." Sarris was gallant and Lopate was smitten with him. For a slightly awkward college student with desires that tended toward the adolescent instead of the "adult," discovering a kindred spirit in Sarris allowed Lopate to embrace movies in ways that seemed both intellectually daring and systematic. That effect on moviegoers underscored Sarris's unique style of criticism and sparked his meteoric rise to fame.[1]

By his own admission, Sarris was surprised and unprepared for such a reception. In the mid-1950s, Sarris had himself been a graduate student in English at Columbia University. In 1958, however, his life, somewhat like Lopate's, was changed by the movies. Eugene Archer, a friend of Sarris's and fellow future movie critic, received a Fulbright Fellowship to study in Paris. Archer began spending an inordinate amount of time with the cinema radicals who gathered at the Cinémathèque Française and who wrote for *Cahiers du Cinema*. In letters he sent back to Sarris, Archer recounted discussions he had with this group about long-forgotten Hollywood directors. Intrigued, Sarris began reading the French film journal and was somewhat overwhelmed by the audacity of the French critics in treating Hollywood movies and directors with respect typically reserved for art and artists.[2]

Exposure to this criticism affected Sarris deeply. He writes, "a long sojourn in Paris in 1961 reassured me that film not only demanded but deserved as much faith as did any other cultural discipline." Indeed, Sarris had experienced a religious conversion of sorts, remarking that he came to accept "the sacred importance of the cinema." But his new faith had made him, happily, "not merely a cultist but a subversive cultist with a foreign ideology." The element of foreignness was vital to Sarris's attraction to the French approach and the attractiveness of his own approach among movie enthusiasts in the United States. Rather than remain on the fringes of American movie culture, however, Sarris moved into the center of debates over criticism, taking his craft from the shadows of disrespect into the spotlight of popular relevance.

Two other trends also contributed to Sarris's rapid rise. First, just as he began publishing his first pieces of criticism using the auteur theory (as it came to be known), the French New Wave had begun to break over the United States. As Sarris remembers, "by the time the 1959 Cannes Film Festival introduced *The 400 Blows,* by a twenty-nine-year-old stormy petrel, François Truffaut, the English-speaking world was primed for a surge of cinematic Francophilia." Criticism promoted by the *Cahiers* group was greatly enhanced and legitimized by its members' international success behind the camera. Sarris's reputation grew in strength because of his association with this group.

A second trend had more to do with conditions in the United States. In 1958, three years after James Agee's death, an edited volume of his movie criticism became available. This marked the first time an American film critic's work had been compiled and marketed for popular consumption. As a well-known writer for the *Nation* and *Time*—the former a leftist journal of opinion, the latter America's most popular newsweekly—he had communicated a love for the pictures and a respect for the magic of the moviegoing experience that distinguished him from his mainstream contemporaries

Yet the publication of Agee's criticism had come at the end of a decade in which film critics had earned respect as intellectuals. Besides the critics writing for serious film journals, Gilbert Seldes continued to provide astute analysis of the implications of television and motion pictures. Otis Fergunson, Manny Farber, and Parker Tyler wrote for the *New Republic* and the *Nation,* and had taken movies seriously a generation before that sensibility had become widely accepted. Such critics had, along with Agee, helped establish a tradition of criticism that Sarris and others of his generation would logically build upon.[3]

In an article for *Sight and Sound* in which he compared Agee to French critic André Bazin, film historian Richard Roud provided a glimpse into the changes movie criticism was undergoing. Roud argued that in the United States, James Agee wrote movie reviews for a population that came increasingly to respect movies as art but dismissed film theory. In France, Bazin wrote within "a milieu where art, aesthetics and form are taken far more seriously than they are in Britain and America. He wrote for an audience which was passionately interested in the cinema." Thus, Roud concluded, "the tradition in which Bazin wrote is more fruitful, more valid, and more fundamentally serious that that of Agee."[4] Andrew Sarris would help change the American perception of movies while he dueled with his most able detractor, Pauline Kael.

The two critics emerged in the late 1950s, one on the East Coast and the other on the West Coast, and would move quite a bit beyond their predecessors by popularizing the notion of movies as art. Sarris began writing for the small but influential journal *Film Culture* and soon moved on to the *Village Voice,* now New York City's largest free weekly newspaper. Based in San Francisco, Pauline Kael was Sarris's opposite in temperament, writing style, and regional sensibility, and launched the most forceful, useful, and significant attack against Sarris's auteur criticism. The debate between these two critics established the parameters of American movie criticism for at least the next two decades. Moreover, the two critics had something else going for them. As historian Ethan Mordden observes, "it was as if the logistical and cultural apparatus for the intellectual conditioning of cinema occurred just as the movies became individual enough to need it. The intelligent moviegoer didn't just talk about the latest film; he talked about the latest film's reviews."[5]

Andrew Sarris began as a contributing editor for *Film Culture* in 1955, the journal's first year of publication. He did not, however, become an activist for the New American Cinema as Jonas Mekas moved the journal toward promoting avant-garde or underground American filmmakers. Sarris had instead delved deeper into the history of Hollywood, using the auteur theory as a guide to identifying great directors. The influence of French critics who had written for *Cahiers du Cinema* was evident in Sarris's writing. By 1961, when Sarris wrote a long article on Hollywood directors for *Film Culture,* he must have also understood the misgivings that many critics had about that approach.[6]

His article entitled "The Director's Game" was on one level a contribution to the debate between British critics and the *Cahiers* group over the auteur theory, but it was also an attempt to rehabilitate the reputations of unsung directors.

As Hollywood prepared to release its summer schedule, Sarris asked if it was "possible to predict with any degree of accuracy, which of these projects will ultimately materialize as the worthiest artistically." It was possible, he contended, "if one stipulates that the director is king and that the past offers any guide to the future." By such logic, Sarris dismissed all but seven pictures, leaving those directed by men he considered significant. The group consisted of Howard Hawks, Stanley Kubrick, Robert Wise, Vincent Minnelli, Joseph C. Mankiewicz, Anthony Mann, and Carol Reed.[7]

Like his French counterparts, Sarris had grown tired of reading staid praise for movies with "solid, liberal" aspirations. Critics at large daily newspapers had rarely embraced movies with any passion, or taken a chance on a director who could enchant an audience even if his movie failed to "say" anything. Sarris explained: "Those of us in America who have embraced 'Cahiers' rules, with limited reservations, have done so partly because the deepest meanings of the film medium have become completely disassociated from the traditionally balanced criticism of causes and effects, partly because 'Cahiers' reinforced our suspicions of propaganda posing as art, and ideologies posing as ideas, and partly because we approved of critics who lived, breathed and devoured cinema not as shame-stricken fugitives from reality but as devotees of an art which no longer required the defensive analogies of the older more fashionable cultural disciplines."[8]

Also like the French critics, Sarris had become a devotee of older Hollywood films and had taken to watching them dozens of times. His criticism reflected an encyclopedic knowledge of movies. Before the mid-1950s, the world had yet to meet that kind of film buff. However, with the opening of the Museum of Modern Art's Film Library, the rise of art-house theaters, and the discovery of older films by television producers, it had become possible to see a movie multiple times and intensely study it.

Sarris also believed he had something profound to share with the moviegoing public. In the past, serious American movie critics had discussed movies as sociological subjects, fascinated by what they revealed about popular tastes. Movie aesthetics rarely received extended and serious consideration. Reviewers in large daily newspapers and weekly magazines had done little better. "The absence of critical theory in America beyond a vague distrust of Hollywood and an exotic attachment to the lower," Sarris contended, "perpetuates an atomistic chaos, film by film, caprice by caprice. Each work is either a happy or unhappy accident, and that is the end of it." He hoped to advance a new understanding of movies by incorporating both historical references and theoretical explanations into reasons why a movie seemed good or bad, and why certain directors seemed especially proficient. He wanted to include discussions about the creation of scenes and the positioning of cameras, as well as what a movie seemed to mean through its plot twists and characters.[9]

Although this approach sounded reasonable, in practice it could also deteriorate into a parody of itself. One can find such failings within an example Sarris provided. He took Nicholas Ray's movie *Party Girl* as "the acid test of *La Politique des Auteurs.*" Sarris argued that Ray was more than merely a director of "B" pictures; he was an artist whose work—all of it—deserved respect. Auteur critics found in many of Ray's pictures a moral tension between his characters. Of course, one might imagine that without such tension most movie plots would seem a bit thin. Nonetheless, Sarris pronounced Ray a genius for his ability to take a forgettable picture and turn it into something a person would choose to watch multiple times. In one particularly excited paragraph, Sarris effectively exposed the failings, excesses, and misguided passions of his theory:

> On its own terms, *Party Girl* is a garish blend of the Hollywood musical and the gangster melodrama. Cyd Charisse's flashing sequins and Corey Allen's checkered suits are swept together into a memorable riot of color, and Ray's flair for cinematic movement lingers in the mind long after the trivial plot details and the atrocious acting have been forgotten. Far from being a collection of "x" [the reader is never told what "x" signifies] images, *Party Girl* is a flow of "x^3" movements, and nothing is more vitally cubistic or visually dynamic than Cyd Charisse going into her dance. It is possible to dismiss the film as the limited triumph of form over content, but in Ray's wild exaggerations of décor and

action, there arises an anarchic spirit which infects the entertainment and preserves the interior continuity of the director's work. One may choose to confront or to ignore the disturbing implications of *Party Girl*, but the choice involves more than one film and one director. It involves the entire cinema, past, present, and future.

That last line absolutely distinguishes Sarris from his American predecessors and contemporaries. His enthusiasm for movies was not only unmatched, it was contagious. He had created the impression that what he offered wasn't so much criticism but revealed truth. Sarris concluded that most "American producers, audiences, and critics" had failed to see what he did in Ray's work because "what is interesting in American cinema has to be concealed" from such groups. Even though Sarris failed to suggest who did the concealing or why anybody would choose to do so, he had presented movies and his criticism as another world. He had illustrated the malleable bounds of criticism. Using the proper tools, one could see through the apparent poverty of a movie like *Party Girl* to the profound dynamics at its core. Since other critics and, for certain, the movie industry itself, rejected such enthusiasm, Sarris's approach was even somewhat rebellious.[10]

Sarris continued his polemic in subsequent issues of *Film Culture,* the most famous being his "Notes on the Auteur Theory in 1962." He broke the article into two parts: the first section justified the theory; the second section explained the theory. To those enthusiasts put off by traditional American disdain for abstract movie criticism, Sarris's work must have seemed positively groundbreaking. Here was a way, at last, to defend movies as art and film critics as specialists. Even so, Sarris also admitted that "without the necessary research and analysis, the *auteur* theory can degenerate into the kind of snobbish racket that is associated with the merchandising of paintings." Although ranking directors, or any artists, might seem arbitrary and pointless, Sarris insisted: "because it has not been established that the cinema is an art at all, it requires cultural audacity to establish a pantheon for film directors. Without such audacity, I see little point in being a film critic." Thus Sarris advocated criticism based on the audacity to make claims as much as on the validity of those claims.[11]

Sarris also believed that in order to correct past wrongs, such as snubbed directors whom he considered worthy of extensive review and

praise, he needed the authority of a film theory to bolster his propositions. After all, he intended to elevate Hollywood directors rather than
foreign filmmakers—the latter had traditionally received more attention
from American critics. Here again, Sarris believed he was breaking new
critical ground by employing the "*auteur* theory primarily as a critical
device for recording the history of the American cinema, the only cinema in the world worth exploring in depth beneath the frosting of a few
great directors at the top."[12]

Not surprisingly, Sarris seemed to hold rather low opinions of his
fellow critics. He reasoned that because the United States lacked repu-
table film theorists, his contemporaries would be hard pressed to object
to his theory. To do so, he argued, would be "to assume we have anyone
of Bazin's sensibility and dedication to provide an alternative, and we
simply don't." Sarris argued that most American critics had perpetuated
rather than sought to overcome the philistinism that had prevented Hollywood movies from achieving a status comparable to European films.
His theory, therefore, could help Hollywood overcome its inferiority complex.[13]

Sarris described auteurism as three concentric circles, each pertain-
ing to a level in the "pantheon" of directors. The outermost circle addressed technical competence. If a director had "no technical competence,
no elementary flair for the cinema, he is automatically cast out from the
pantheon of directors." The second circle related to a director's ability to
"exhibit certain recurring characteristics of style, which serve as his signature." The innermost circle, although the most important, was also the
most vague, having to do with "interior meaning" or "the tension between a director's personality and his material." If in his career (all the
directors considered by auteurists were men) a director's work shot
through each of these circles, he would gain admittance to the highest
level of the hierarchy of auteurs. "How do you tell the genuine director
from the quasi-chimpanzee?" Sarris asked. "After a given number of films,
a pattern is established. Only after thousands of films have been revalu-
ated will any personal pantheon have a reasonable objective validity." In
short, "Sometimes, a great deal of corn must be husked to yield a few
kernels of internal meaning."[14]

Referring to that last line, Pauline Kael replied, "Perhaps a little more
corn should be husked; perhaps, for example, we can husk away the word
'internal' (is 'internal meaning' any different from 'meaning')." Kael's critique of Sarris's theory ran fourteen pages long in the spring 1963 issue

of *Film Quarterly*. By most historical accounts, Kael eviscerated Sarris's argument. While it might not have been difficult to poke holes in Sarris's theory, Kael also used her critique as a broadside against the rising tide of quasi-theoretical film criticism.[15]

Kael quickly dispatched Sarris's logic. She was unimpressed with the men Sarris had included in his directorial pantheon, wondering what had qualified Raoul Walsh, for example. "Would Sarris not notice the repetition in the Walsh films without the *auteur* theory?" Kael asked. "Or shall we take a more cynical view that without some commitment to Walsh as an *auteur*, he probably wouldn't be spending his time looking at these movies." Indeed, Kael took offense at Sarris's justification of theory. "The greatness of critics like Bazin in France and Agee in America," she snapped, "may have something to do with their using their full range of intelligence and intuition, rather than relying on formulas."[16]

Kael believed Sarris had done more than simply insult other critics; he had harmed American film criticism in general. Sarris had aided those critics in England and the United States who perpetuated theories ripped out of their original context. "The *auteur* theory, which probably helped to liberate the energies of the French critics," said Kael, "plays a very different role in England and with the *Film Culture* and New York *Film Bulletin* auteur critics in the United States—an anti-intellectual, anti-art role." It was one thing to use one's critical expertise to convince a skeptical nation that movies were more important than mere amusements. It was something quite different, Kael explained, to employ theoretical tools to help legitimize a sensibility held among cliques of film enthusiasts. "It is not merely that the *auteur* theory distorts experience," she argued, "but that it is an aesthetics which is fundamentally anti-art." How was one to guess what art was and was not based on a logic that seemed hidden to all other critics? "Interior meaning," she added, "seems to be what those in the know know. It's a mystique—and a mistake. The *auteur* critics never tell us by what divining codes they have discovered the élan of a Minnelli or a Nicholas Ray or a Leo MacCarey. They're not critics; they're dopesters. There must be another circle that Sarris forgot to get to—the one where the secrets are kept."[17]

Kael and Sarris did, however, share common ground when it came to love and respect for movies. This might explain the ferocity with which Kael took apart Sarris's theory. She found the auteur theory detrimental to the success won over cultural conservatives and art snobs who had shunned movies for generations. Thus she could understand French critics championing film noir, since traditionally only movies with clear liberal themes had won any respect in French intellectual circles. But aestheticism could be taken too far. Kael believed that "it is good for us to be reminded that our mass culture is not altogether poisonous in its effect on other countries." Auteur critics, though, had turned bad movies into great achievements through a strange devotion to particular directors. "It must be black comedy for directors to read this new criticism," she wrote, "and discover that films in which they felt trapped and disgusted are now said to be their masterpieces. It's an aesthetics for 1984: failure is success."[18]

Kael also contended that auteur criticism reflected many of the worst characteristics of film buffs. By subscribing to a great-man approach to filmmaking, auteur critics had not only raised "trash" (one of Kael's favorite descriptive terms) to the level of art, but they did so with a strange male chauvinism. By championing directors at the expense of producers, screenwriters, and, perhaps most importantly, actors, the auteur critics had shunned many women who exercised considerable influence over the movies. Actresses such as Lillian and Dorothy Gish, Mary Pickford, Bette Davis, and others had pictures written for them. Screenwriter Anita Loos was a top Hollywood scenarist in the early days of the studios, Natalie Kalmas helped develop Technicolor, and Dorothy Arzner was a director. The auteur theory also illogically overlooked the immense power of the great studio chiefs such as David O. Selnick, Irving Thalberg, and Louis B. Mayer. Even worse to Kael, auteur critics failed to recognize her favorite members of the movie community: screenwriters of the 1930s and 1940s. Auteur critics simply romanticized figures they wanted to emulate (not unlike a generation of male New Left activists who paid homage to Lenin, Malcolm X, Che Guevera, Ho Chi-minh, and Mao Tse-tung).[19]

The early 1960s, moreover, had witnessed the further erosion of traditional artistic standards in the widespread attempt by artists and critics to redefine art. Movies had a role in this by representing the high art of mass culture. The line between high art and popular art had blurred over the century and seemed in danger of disappearing completely if the process continued in the direction that auteur critics seemed to want to take it. Kael found the situation disheartening because, without standards, the musings of auteur critics could be accepted on face value, removing the leverage needed to expose them as frauds. Auteurists, "like the pop artists, the New York Realists with their comic strips and

Campbell's soup can paintings, are saying, 'See what America is, this junk is the fact of our lives. Art and avant-gardism are phony; what isn't any good, is good. Only squares believe in art. The artifacts of industrial civilization are the supreme truth, the supreme joke.'" She lamented a period "when men who consider themselves creative scoff at art and tradition." Of course, the usefulness of this new sensibility lay in its ambiguity. One could apply it at will to almost any work of art, although it was useless for expressing oneself in clear, effective terms. Kael warned that other critical approaches "will be wiped off the cinema landscape if they can't meet the blasts of anti-art with some fire of their own." She proposed to fire back.[20]

Andrew Sarris evidently felt the heat, saying later, "I was somewhat taken aback by her apparent conviction that she had done me a favor by blasting me in print. She insisted that I should be grateful for her having shown me the error of my ways." Kael explained that when she wrote the piece she "thought of it as good intellectual fun—you know a debate. I had Chick Callenbach [editor of *Film Quarterly*] send a copy to Sarris so that he could write a reply. I was very surprised to discover how hurt he was by it." Callenbach found the whole incident remarkable because "neither Pauline nor Andy had a theoretical bone in their bodies." To Callenbach, Kael was "just felt deeply offended by [Sarris's] attempt at system-making, and its threat to the immediacy of reaction which she saw as the basis of film love."[21]

Instead of a direct rebuttal, Sarris drafted two new pieces on the auteur theory. The first was an elaborate exposition on Hollywood directors entitled "The American Cinema," taking up sixty-eight pages in an issue of *Film Culture* that appeared the same month as Kael's critique. Wanting to "resurrect" directors from the past, Sarris felt "the excavations and revaluations must continue until the last worthy director has been rescued from undeserved anonymity." It was archeology masquerading as criticism.[22]

His second piece, entitled "The Auteur Theory and the Perils of Pauline," was a weak rejoinder to Kael's argument, mostly because Sarris never directly identified Kael's "perils." Rather, he cobbled together past articles suggesting that his work spoke for itself. He did chastise *Film Quarterly*, though, for lumping all auteur critics into one group as if they followed "the same 'line' and share the same aesthetic theory." He argued that even though the "auteur theory is the most efficient method of classifying the cinema, [it] was never intended as an occult ritual."[23]

Sarris played an intriguing intellectual game. He argued that his theory ranked directors as other critics ranked authors, but he also claimed that auteurs differed from authors because the former were cinematic and the latter literal. How, one might have asked, could he have it both ways? Sarris contended that determining the "authorship" of a movie was not analogous to literature. "Research and analysis are indispensable for sound *auteur* criticism," he explained, "[so] after a given number of films, a pattern is established, and we can speak of [directors] as we speak of artists and authors in other media." Sarris thus would "smash" the tradition of criticizing movies as literary exercises and introduce a criticism of cinematic form. He explained that his theory would help moviegoers notice a director's style—predicated on bunches of ideas spread over a series of movies—which was cinematic rather than literal. It was attractive, furthermore, because it seemed a critic could make the rules and dismiss the contradictions. It was, in short, not so much a theory as an approach to watching and cataloguing movies that allowed the viewer to adopt the cultural authority of the critic by using the correct terms and codes.[24]

Although the question of who authored films was not a new issue, Sarris had done something profound by couching this old debate in new cinematic terms.[25] He acknowledged that stories rarely originated with directors, but because the director's job was to translate a work of words into a series of pictures, critics need not analyze the content of films, only the "styles" of the directors. Auteurs were directors, therefore, who took a script, no matter how detailed, and gave it a personal twist. For many American film critics, auteur criticism smacked of aestheticism— how could one separate form from content? Sarris believed, and rightly so, that critics had rarely discussed films in purely aesthetic terms. But to him, form had to be held in higher regard than content, if only to distinguish cinematic from literary analysis.

The number of responses generated by the Sarris-Kael debate testified to the increasing sense of urgency that surrounded movie criticism.[26] Two writers in particular contributed substantively to the discussion. The first was Marion Magid, a literary critic who attempted to make sense of popular fascination with Sarris's approach. The second was Dwight Macdonald, long one of America's most able cultural critics as well as a regular film critic for the popular middlebrow magazine *Esquire,* who attempted to account for the damage Sarris had wrought.

Magid began her review by recounting a discussion among a panel of movie critics at the New York Public Library in 1963. The critics plodded along, addressing American movie criticism until Dwight Macdonald stood up and made a thunderous statement about Andrew Sarris: "A Messiah he may be, but a film critic, never!" Macdonald then denounced Sarris "as a 'Greenwich Village Tsarris' issuing cinematic 'ukases' rather than reasonable critical estimates." Magid remembered that the audience erupted, one faction in cheers and applause, another faction in boos and hisses, while "the uninitiated remained silent in presumable bewilderment." She explained, "this battle, known as the Auteur Controversy, has rent film criticism into opposing camps." It had "pitted East Coast against West, brought about agonizing reappraisals on the editorial pages of existing film magazines, and infiltrated critical discourse about the movies with a host of new words, attitudes, and mannerisms as alluring to their users as they are infuriating, when not incomprehensible, to most people on the outside."[27]

But why had a theory originally developed by a group of French critics suddenly turned into a transnational phenomenon? Magid believed it had something to do with the mystical quality of the theory's foundation—"*mise-en-scène,*" or the "movieness" of movies. The auteur theory apparently gave its practitioners an air of authority without requiring them to undertake the type of critical analysis that burdened critics of other arts. One could be highbrow about a lowbrow medium without really explaining why. One need only compose a list of directors and justify one's entries with auteurist language in order to enjoy the support of like-minded critics. Championing directors alone did not generate instant critical acceptance or denunciation, however. Magid pointed out that in the Auteur Controversy, the most intense battles stemmed from the selection of directors rather than the reasons for choosing them. For example, "the position of any film journal *vis-à-vis* the Auteur Controversy can be gauged almost automatically by its editorial line on [Alfred] Hitchcock; a review of a new Hitchcock film is almost invariably made the occasion for a larger ideological statement. Generally speaking, blanket endorsement up to and including *The Birds* is the sign of total Auteur orientation; severe reservations about *The Birds* coupled with amused toleration for *Psycho* signifies a fundamentally anti-formalist orientation"[28]

To Dwight Macdonald's certain delight, his review of Hitchcock's *The Birds* did not endear him to auteur critics. After panning the movie in the first part of his October 1963 *Esquire* review, Macdonald turned to what he called "Advanced Bird-Watching." He identified two members of the auteur group—Sarris and Peter Bogdanovich—who had "issued ex cathedra panegyrics [on Hitchcock] that almost reconcile one to [the stodgy *New York Times* critic] Bosley Crowther." Both Sarris and Bogdanovich had praised Hitchcock's latest effort as yet another masterpiece. Macdonald, unimpressed, explained, "It's not that one disagrees with such judgments, it's that there is no basis for discussion since they use methods of thought and rules of evidence not common in the outside world." Again, critics who rejected the auteur approach rarely did so based on its conclusions, but on the explanation one gave for those conclusions. Macdonald would concede that all critics were entitled to hold any opinions they wanted, but he did not believe that "one man's opinion is as good as the next one's. Before the ultimate is reached, a critic goes through a process of defining, describing, reasoning, and persuading which is drawn from his own special experience and knowledge and which may or may not persuade his readers that his judgment is more accurate . . . than other judgments, according to *their* experience and knowledge."[29]

Macdonald had approached movies as a critic of broader American culture, not simply as a film critic. He was one of the famed "New York Intellectuals"—a group of contentious people who began on the political Far Left during the depression and became in the postwar era severe critics of mass culture.[30] Macdonald made his initial exploration of mass culture for *Partisan Review,* the unofficial organ of the New York Intellectuals begun under editors William Phillips and Philip Rahv. Even though many members of this group had professed an allegiance to the "common man," most did not accept "his" culture because it seemed to drain attention away from finer arts. Historian Paul Gorman argues that throughout the 1950s Macdonald had become less concerned with social change than with "preserving artistic achievements" he believed were threatened by the creeping ooze of mass culture and "kitsch." Macdonald's most forceful statement about the demise of traditional artistic standards came in 1960 with the publication of a long article in *Partisan Review* entitled "Masscult and Midcult."[31]

Macdonald identified two troubling features of contemporary American culture: the pervasive acceptance of mass culture or "Masscult," and a corrupted version of high culture he termed "Midcult." Prior to the explosion of mass mediums, it was inconceivable that a majority of Americans could share an experience almost simultaneously. However, with the appearance of radio, movies, and television, a new era had dawned in which artists produced for mass taste rather than for a higher artistic calling. The commercialization of art had changed not simply the standards for judging it but the process of creation as well. For example, "before a proper Hollywood film can be made," Macdonald contended, "the work of art has to be defeated." He considered Masscult "not just unsuccessful art. It is non-art. It is even anti-art." The popularity of Hollywood films made this situation even more dangerous because mass culture operated under the guise of democracy. "Masscult is very, very democratic," Macdonald admitted, "it refuses to discriminate against or between anything or anybody. All is grist for the mill and all comes out finely ground indeed." In short, Macdonald found Sarris's adulation of low-quality Hollywood pictures to be not just silly, but dangerous.[32]

In defending auteur criticism, Sarris had used language normally associated with criticism of high art. This approach smacked of a Midcult sensibility. Macdonald explained that "Midcult has it both ways: it pretends to respect the standards of High Culture while in fact it waters them down and vulgarizes them. It presents itself as part of High Culture." Sarris had used the auteur theory to elevate and legitimize the treatment of movies most critics, even those sympathetic to treating films with respect, had found entirely forgettable. Sarris had championed his criticism as unorthodox, even avant-garde, when in fact its real distinction was to blur the difference between the avant-garde and the mainstream.[33]

Macdonald's mass culture critique represented one side in a struggle to define art and the vocabulary used to describe art. Critics had begun to divide once again over artistic taste. As modernists had rejected the genteel tradition by embracing the avant-garde, cultural rebels of the 1960s looked to break with austere modernists by embracing movies as their art. They did so, however, by rejecting methods of determining taste, rather than by embracing new standards. The auteur theory frustrated Macdonald because he could not argue with its adherents—they spoke in a different language or simply refused to agree on the terms of debate. They seemed unmoved by challenges posed so forcefully by Pauline Kael, or humorously by Marion Magid, or indignantly by Macdonald. These challenges seemed beside the point to a generation of film critics who had discovered a way to gain respect for movies and themselves. It was ironic, nonetheless, that just as film criticism had achieved legitimacy, film critics became mired in an epistemological quagmire. Pauline Kael was particularly sensitive to that development.

Kael wrote as a "cold-water critic"; she was skeptical of almost anything another person accepted too easily. She earned her reputation for being extraordinarily tough to please and a writer with uncommon rhetorical skills. She also made enemies; the woman's magazine *McCall's* fired Kael after a few months as its movie reviewer for blasting *The Sound of Music* (1965) as a "sugarcoated lie that people seem to want to eat." If Julie Andrews failed to win Kael over, Andrew Sarris did not stand a chance.[34]

The differences between Kael and Sarris ran deeper than their critical approaches, though. Kael was born and raised in and around San Francisco. Sarris came from New York City. Kael attended the University of California's Berkeley campus and began her career as a movie critic on KPFA, San Francisco's public radio station. In the late 1950s, she wrote for *Film Quarterly* as well as for *Sight and Sound*. Sarris began his career writing for the leftwing *Village Voice* and the avant-garde *Film Culture*. He undoubtedly attended screenings of the latest independent and experimental pictures at Amos Vogel's Cinema 16 and at least sympathized with the militants of New York's cinematic underground. Kael ran her own movie house, the Cinema Guild and Studio (at the time perhaps the only two-screen art house in the nation), and compiled program notes for her patrons. In other words, Sarris had to respond to the strong impulses of New York's movie community, whereas Kael developed in an atmosphere devoid of similar influences.[35]

Yet both shared one vital characteristic: They related to the audience as few critics had before or since. They did, however, differ remarkably in how they brought the audience to the movies. Kael could express her love for movies without the type of challenges Sarris faced from other critics and filmmakers. Her arguments rose and fell on the effectiveness of her prose and the enthusiasm of her reviews. Sarris also loved films, but he did so in an environment hostile not merely to Hollywood but to the idea of art as well. Perhaps Sarris believed it necessary to cloak his fascination with Hollywood in a foreign theory—French no less—to help him overcome forces unsympathetic to his position.

Sarris's writing reflected an undercurrent of the early 1960s that sought to carry the last vestiges of traditional criticism out to sea. Kael, on the other hand, represented a second undercurrent whose headwaters lay with the modernists. Her criticism struck against cultural conservatives who dismissed movies as mere amusements and film critics as inconsequential hacks, but she also sought to uphold the core of critical traditions if only to build her own legacy on its foundation. Even though

New York's modernists may have influenced Sarris, his criticism was independent of older critical rules. And while Kael may have been independent of trends taking shape in New York, Paris, and London, she depended on modernist traditions to support her authority as a critic. Sarris commented, revealingly, that "what I do journalistically . . . is say, 'Well, this is how I see it, and you may see it differently, and I have to give it to you so that you can calibrate and relate it to your own experience." Rather than meet popular taste head-on, Sarris ceded cultural authority to the audience, preferring to relate to them through a shared enthusiasm for movies as art. Kael, on the other hand, maintained her position between the movies and the audience, issuing declarations about what was good and what was not.

Phillip Lopate regards Pauline Kael's "body of criticism as foremost an achievement in American letters . . . alongside Edmund Wilson and H.L. Mencken."[36] Indeed, Kael operated as more than merely a movie reviewer; she distinguished herself as a cultural critic who possessed the authority to shape cultural standards. She also blasted those who took themselves and mass culture too seriously. Much like Gilbert Seldes, Kael expected a great deal from movies, but her expectations never ran to the ideological or theoretical. Sitting before a movie in a darkened theater, one might feel that experience exists in a cultural vacuum. Kael was at her best when she opened a door to the outside world, allowing a complex culture to surround movies and inform criticism of them.

In 1956, Kael contributed an essay entitled "Movies, the Desperate Art" to a collection on modern writing edited by the editors of *Partisan Review*. In it she established a trademark of her criticism, blasting away at both sides of an issue. She dismissed the bland liberalism of Hollywood's "idea" pictures of the 1950s, targeting Stanley Kramer's movies as sophisticated but intellectually hollow. Kael imagined that the audience for such fare "are educated beyond the fat production values of routine pictures [but] still want the fat of visible artistic efforts . . . the fat of 'important ideas' and paraphrasable content." She found that such efforts only corrupted the capacity of movies to provide good entertainment or make provocative comments. Avant-garde films could be just as bad, however. "The poisonous atmosphere of Hollywood premieres is distilled to pure pretension at avant-garde premiers," she contended. "Object to the Hollywood film and you're an intellectual snob, object to the avant-garde films and you're a Philistine." Sometimes, Kael believed, you had to be both.[37]

Kael refused to suffer esoteric film critics gladly as well. In her review of Siegfried Kracauer's book *The Nature of Film: The Redemption of Physical Reality* (1960), Kael had fun with Kracauer's muddled attempt at profundity. "Siegfried Kracauer is the sort of man who can't say 'It's a lovely day,'" Kael submitted, "without first establishing that it *is* day, that the term 'day' is meaningless without the dialectical concept of 'night,' that both these terms have no meaning unless there is a world in which day and night alternate, and so forth. By the time he has established an epistemological system to support his right to observe that it's a lovely day, our day has been spoiled." Unimpressed by the authorial verbiage, Kael also chided Paul Rotha and the Museum of Modern Art's Richard Griffith, two authorities on film history, for contributing blurbs to the dust jacket of Kracauer's book as if they had actually read it, understood it, and liked it. She found their support indicative, however, of a trend in criticism to buy the fallacy that movies had an "essence" unique among all other arts. This assumption allowed theorists to launch bizarre (and reductive) statements about the "true" nature of movies and, conversely, to condemn certain films as somehow being "false."[38]

In December 1964, Kael capped her rise from relative obscurity on the West Coast with a long essay for the popular, widely read monthly *Atlantic.* By that time she had also won a Guggenheim Fellowship that she used to work on *I Lost It at the Movies,* her first edited volume of film criticism, which featured the article "Are the Movies Going to Pieces." That piece not only gave Kael her widest exposure yet, but also helped situate her intellectually between Macdonald's mass culture critique—perhaps the last statement of the modern era—and Susan Sontag's "One Culture and the New Sensibility"—perhaps the first statement of the postmodern era.

Kael began her article by revisiting a recent episode with a group of friends. On television was an old monster movie, the sight of which provoked a good deal of chatter about the relative merits of different horror movies, monsters, and atrocities. During the conversation, a young man who taught in the English department of a nearby university remarked that the greatest horror movie he had ever seen was *The Beast with Five Fingers*—a wholly forgettable picture. Bewildered, Kael pressed the young man for an explanation. "Because it's completely irrational," he said. "It doesn't make any sense, and that's the true terror." Kael found his reply indicative of a wider trend among the younger generation of moviegoers who had outgrown the need for logic in movies. "Perhaps now," she mused, "'stories' have become too sane, too explicable, too common-place for the large audiences who want sensation and regard the explana-tory connections as mere filler. It may be that audiences don't have much more than a television span of attention left." Indeed, had Theodore Dreiser's worst fears come to pass—had America produced a generation that blindly accepted a "dumb downed" art?[39]

Kael believed something had changed in audience tastes between the mid-1950s, when demands for smart pictures seemed to improve mainstream production, and the early 1960s, when obscure, incoherent films became cause for celebration among a talented, artistic, and pre-sumably intelligent part of the population. "I am interested in the change from the period when the meaning of art and form in art was in making complex experience simple and lucid," she explained, "to the current ac-ceptance of art as technique, the technique which . . . makes a simple, though psychologically confused, story look complex, and modern be-cause inexplicable." Kael had criticized art-house audiences for mistak-ing "lack of clarity as complexity; clumsiness and confusion as style," and basing preferences on standards that bore little relation to thought-ful consideration.[40]

Kael was particularly critical of the New American Cinema because it had turned film criticism into autobiography, making every person's opinion equal to the next. Mekas, of course, had propounded this line loudly in *Film Culture.* His ravings would have been contained, Kael be-lieved, if critics such as Susan Sontag had not given them intellectual respectability. Kael pointed to Sontag's review of Jack Smith's *Flaming Creatures* (winner of the 1963 *Film Culture* Independent Film Award) as an apt example of "a sensibility based on indiscriminateness, without ideas, beyond negation." Kael thought that by "treating indiscriminate-ness as a value, Miss Sontag had become a real swinger. Of course we can reply that if anything goes, nothing happens, nothing works."[41]

Kael's stance evidently dated her in the eyes of the younger genera-tion. One young disciple of the "New Sensibility" told Kael that she be-longed to the "Agee-alcoholic generation" that was unable to comprehend what the LSD/pot generation found so easy: to accept everything. Of course, Kael figured, "if we mention that we *enjoy* dramatic and narra-tive elements in movies, we are almost certain to be subjected to the con-temptuous remark, 'Why does cinema have to *mean* something? Do you expect a work by Bach to *mean* something?'" Fair enough, but if one did not ask anything of art or the artist what would happen? Would art cease to exist? Kael suggested that we would be undermining art by "rejecting critical standards . . . accepting everyone who says he is an artist as an artist and conferring on all his 'noncommercial' production the status of art." Kael concluded: "Miss Sontag is on to something, and if she stays on and rides it like Slim Pickens [from *Dr. Strangelove*] it's the end of criticism."[42]

Reflecting on the debate between himself and Pauline Kael, Andrew Sarris contended that while his work placed him within the cultural vanguard alongside Susan Sontag, Kael had distinguished herself by seeming "to articulate the fears of the cultural establishment over the surge of an undiscriminating barbarism" By lumping Kael in with yet another part of the older generation, Sarris meant to emphasize her complicity with those who "did not want to see the cinema, particularly the American cinema, elevated to the level of one of the fine arts or humanities. In this respect *I Lost It at the Movies* functioned as an unending diatribe against film scholars and film scholarship." Sarris was right: Kael did fear a time when movies stopped being "the only art which everyone felt free to enjoy and have opinions about," because if "they become cinema, which people fear to criticize just as they fear to say what they think about a new piece of music or a new poem or painting . . . they will become another object of academic study and 'appreciation,' and will soon be an object of excitement only to practitioners of the 'art.'"[43]

Susan Sontag had burst on the intellectual scene with her effort to democratize criticism of the arts. In two seminal essays published in the mid-1960s, Sontag sought to overcome what she perceived as a tradition of literary oppression. In "Against Interpretation," Sontag argued that Western culture's obsession with interpreting works of art—particularly literary works—had forced critics to search for meanings. Interpretation had drained criticism of its spontaneity; Sontag proposed ways of getting it back. She argued that critics should focus on "sensory experience" rather than textual interpretation to illustrate how a work of art is "*what it is, even that it is what it is,* rather than to show what it means." Because film critics worked with a visual medium, she said their criticism should stress the way the movie felt or looked rather than be "arrogant" and try to explain what it meant.[44]

In "One Culture and the New Sensibility," Sontag declared, "The purpose of art is always, ultimately, to give pleasure." She contended that if "the new sensibility demands less 'content' in art, and is more open to the pleasures of 'form' and style, it is also less snobbish, less moralistic—in that it does not demand that pleasure in art necessarily be associated with edification." In a postliterary (some might say postliterate) culture "the model arts" had become "music, films, dance, architecture, painting, sculpture," because they had "much less content, and a much cooler mode of moral judgment." She concluded that such changes did not mean "the demise of art, but a transformation of the function of art," from its "magical-religious operation" and commentary on "secular reality," to "an instrument for modifying consciousness and organizing new modes of sensibility." Thus, Jack Smith's *Flaming Creatures* was "strictly a treat for the senses. In this is the very opposite of a 'literary' film. Smith's crude technique serves, beautifully, the sensibility embodied in *Flaming Creatures*—a sensibility which disclaims ideas, which situates itself beyond negation."[45]

Sontag had responded to an older brand of cultural authority that she believed unfairly stifled appreciation of popular arts. The New Sensibility she and others propounded would redefine art outside the traditions of American criticism in order to open the nation's culture to its livelier aspects. However, by dismissing the notion that cultural authority existed at all, Sontag had joined Sarris in undercutting the reason critics had to take part in society. Without discriminating tastes, American culture would become—as Macdonald suggested and Kael feared—awash in Masscult with Midcult standards. The element of persuasion had been removed from criticism in favor of a more pluralistic approach to the arts. Interpretation could then become personal, and the personal would then become political and ideological. Historian David Steigerwald argues that "United States culture in the sixties did not mark the conquest over 'tradition' but, instead, it constituted the realm where the shift from modern to postmodern society was clearest." Indeed, critics lost to the artist the only thing that mattered: some authority over the audience.[46]

Even so, Sontag and others remained relevant, and in fact became vital, to the debate over movies. Why? The reason lies within the unique role movies played during the 1960s. It was a period marked by the redefinition of art and criticism—before it was widely accepted that "art" no longer existed, before critical judgment became elitist. It was an ambiguous but exciting and even heroic era. The debate over movies as art seemed to strike a chord within a society redefining the meaning and means of authority. Even the title of Sontag's book of essays, *Against In-*

terpretation, signaled a direct assault on tradition. When asked what art was, Andy Warhol reportedly replied: "Art? I don't believe I've met the man." By the early 1960s it was clear that few critics or artists were brave enough or naïve enough to claim that they knew what constituted art and what did not.[47]

The debate between Sarris and Kael had exposed some of the fault lines of this new era. Both critics understood that movies served as a bridge between the worlds of high and low culture. Both also furthered the notion that movie criticism was a legitimate intellectual pursuit. They differed, however, over how to define the critic's job within the new era. On one hand, Pauline Kael had established her criticism as an important link between the audience and the movie screen—exercising her authority over both the product and the audience. She interpreted the movies for the audience and reflected on audience reaction for those who produced films. Sarris, on the other hand, had helped democratize criticism by advocating a redefinition of critical and artistic authority. In Sarris's moving picture world, everyone had the potential to be a critic and all moviemakers were artists. He did not believe, of course, that all the inhabitants of this world were equally proficient at either critiquing movies or making them. His vision rested on an assumption that was quite revolutionary: that critics and artists did not necessarily look a certain way. Thus, a young Phillip Lopate could speak with as much authority about movies as learned *New York Times* critic Bosley Crowther. Similarly, a Hollywood director such as Howard Hawks could garner just as much serious consideration as any other director. Vital to Sarris's approach was the use of a new vocabulary that had the power to reveal art where it had never been thought to exist before.

Yet this redefinition of art and criticism could seem somewhat mystical—based, as it was, more on one's emotion than on a rationale that functioned beyond oneself. An example of this can be found in an exchange between Andrew Sarris and a couple of his readers in an English version of *Cahiers du Cinema* that he edited. After reading that people had trouble understanding the auteur theory, Sarris wrote that he "would be the first to admit that much of *Cahiers* has always been elliptical, elusive, esoteric and even downright obscure. In a way that's what I've always liked about the magazine. It opens more doors than it closes, and it is often most stimulating when it is most outrageous."[48]

That elusiveness was a large part of the appeal Sarris's criticism had for many people. Moreover, at the same moment that Sarris offered his new brand of criticism, a new generation of movies appeared that deserved it; elusive criticism would be used to understand obscure films. And although that convergence frustrated many older critics, it ushered in a heroic era of moviegoing for a younger generation.

8

The First New York
Film Festival and the
Heroic Age of Moviegoing

In February 1962, Jonas Mekas, the fiery editor of *Film Culture* and dean of New York City's experimental filmmakers, observed in his *Village Voice* column a significant confluence in the moving picture world. Opening within a week and no more than a block away from each other were *La Notte* and *Last Year in Marienbad*. The first was from Michelangelo Antonioni, an Italian director who had won international fame the previous year for *L'Avventura*. The second film was from Alain Resnais, a French director who, with his 1960 picture *Hiroshima mon amour*, had become even more of a darling than Antonioni among critics, art-house fans, and judges at international film festivals. Dwight Macdonald, in a telling bit of criticism, gave *L'Avventura* the highest praise of the day when he declared it "the best picture I've seen since *Hiroshima Mon Amour*." With *La Notte* and *Marienbad* opening at the same time and in the same area, Mekas believed (with some trepidation since audiences for the cinematic underground had dwindled because of foreign competition) that many New Yorkers would regard this as "the richest block in town, a gold mine, for months to come. And it will be difficult to decide which of the two films is greater."[1]

In the early 1960s, new movies from European directors such as Antonioni, Resnais, Luchino Visconti, Federico Fellini, François Truffaut, Jean-Luc Goddard, Ingmar Bergman, Tony Richardson, and (soon) Roman Polanski had become the currency of a growing, thriving movie culture. When a new film from one of these directors appeared, moviegoers—mostly young and self-consciously hip—rushed to theaters to collect and share experiences. The quicker one saw the latest art-house sensation the sooner one could begin to trade reflections and interpretations about it. That feeling of expectation, desire, and fulfillment made this age one of "heroic" moviegoing. One referred to "films" rather than movies. The cinema was not mass culture, it was art, and heroic moviegoers had risen above the faceless viewers who had allowed themselves to be duped again and again by slick Hollywood productions.

American essayist Phillip Lopate remembers: "when the first ads appeared announcing the premiere of *La Notte*, I had worked myself into such a fit of anticipation that my unconscious mind jumped the gun: I began dreaming, for several nights in a row, preview versions of *La Notte*."[2] For Lopate (a Columbia University undergraduate at the time) as well as other enthusiasts of his generation, movies not only affected one's consciousness but entered a person's subconscious as well. Essential to the new American movie milieu was the fact that many foreign films were made by recognized auteurs that accommodated multiple interpretations. In other words, as *Saturday Review* movie critic Hollis Alpert noted, the fact that such films were "so deeply obscure" insured that they would be "so widely discussed."[3] But what was happening to moviegoing? Was it evolving into an activity made over by intellectuals and the young cultural chic?

During the early 1960s, critics seemed to thank the movie gods for a deluge of films that challenged them to write treatises on life and art rather than mere movie reviews. Dwight Macdonald thought fans of Antonioni's *L'Avventura* resembled "devotees of Joyce and Eliot.... They have discovered a movie that is unlike any other they have seen, one that comments on modern life in the intimate, subjective terms that hitherto have been found in books." Macdonald was so impressed by the differences between these latest European pictures and Hollywood's typical output that he composed a "position paper" on Antonioni. He argued that people flocked to the Italian director's films for the same reason they used to read James Joyce: audiences wanted to struggle with difficult art. "The odd thing," Macdonald explained, "is that some of us enjoy doing some work, perhaps because we are used to books and music and paintings that require some effort from the consumer." Jonas Mekas compared Antonioni to Leo Tolstoy because the filmmaker forced his audience to stand with him between life and death. Entertainment, it seemed, was no longer the point; a filmmaker now had to speak directly to the human soul.[4]

For many moviegoers, a movie with elusive intelligence was particularly appealing. One was intrigued by the mysterious (or absent) plots and therefore not bothered by the lack of a director's or screenwriter's intentions. Critics who wrote for such an audience were therefore quite free to read a great deal into these movies. Stanley Kauffmann, a movie critic for the *New Republic,* became philosophical about films of this type. Of *La Notte* he wrote: "The film exists in an ambience that is post-Hitler, post-Stalin, post-Bomb, in a society caught between the far-reaching but iron-lined avenues of Marxism, and, on the other hand, a creeping corpulence fed extensively by military preparations to deter Marxism." After comparing Antonioni to William Butler Yeats, Jackson Pollock, Bertold Brecht, Samuel Beckett, and (again) James Joyce, Kauffmann explained that Antonioni had freed movies from their narrative structure, allowing the audience to reach disparate conclusions about the significance of scenes and characters—something not possible with Hollywood movies. Such films, Kauffmann concluded, had hastened a revolution in movies akin to what abstract expressionists and absurdists had done in other mediums.[5]

On the other hand, *Marienbad* was almost poetic in its allusions and illusions. For Kauffmann, the film "tried to isolate and reproduce the emotions of its situations, drawing (as all our minds do constantly) in the past and present into combinations that may never have happened and may never happen that influence us nonetheless. The film is an attempt to make visible the intangible—the lightning play of mind and memory and impulse." Again, Kauffmann compared Resnais to his counterparts in literature, painting, and the theater, adding that as "Archibald MacLeish's familiar line tells us that a poem should not mean but be; a film, Resnais obviously thinks, should not mean, but see."[6]

Pauline Kael, a critic who wrote during the heroic age of moviegoing but was not quite of it, found *Marienbad* a "mess." She noted that Resnais and screenwriter Alain Robbe-Gillet had publicly disagreed over the meaning of their film. But "who cares," cried Kael, "enthusiasts for the film start arguing about whether something really happened last year at Marienbad, and this becomes rather more important than what happens on the screen in front of them—which isn't much." She found it artistically and intellectually irresponsible to appeal to the "whatever you think is right" approach. Artists had some obligation, she believed, "to bring their vision to you." Instead, these movies "are important not because they are great movies (they are not) but because of the way people are responding to them." Nevertheless, they had captured the audience's attention. "They are telling people what they want to hear," Kael noted, "which . . . means they are obscuring problems in a way that people like to see them obscured."[7]

Hollis Alpert held a similar opinion, observing that "some of the most fervent critical huzzahs, and some of the most worshipful audience appreciation, are now reserved for films so tantalizingly elusive in their meanings, so deeply obscure, that six people can discuss a particular movie and not seem to be talking about the same movie at all." As a result, almost any work of art could be considered culturally significant as long as at least a few people agreed it was. For Alpert, the fact that "movies too are being made that cannot be easily understood and are being welcomed accordingly . . . is an admission of sorts that cinema has gained entry into the conclave of the serious arts." He recorded a series of esoteric pronouncements from the pages of mainstream publications such as *Time*, the *New York Times*, and the *New York Herald Tribune* that had praised European films in a vocabulary typically found in film journals.[8]

Indeed, many people had come to accept movies as perhaps the most vital art of the day. If this was the case, however, what had happened to the idea of art? Clearly the terms in which one spoke about movies had changed. Was that because the way one considered or defined art had changed as well?

In the 1960s, movie culture was imbedded in an art world that was also undergoing significant shifts. Art historian Arthur Danto has argued that by 1962 modern art no longer existed. Although it was still possible to create "modern" art, artists had moved beyond or perhaps simply discarded the assumptions that had guided modern artists since the early twentieth century. What distinguished the period that followed the modernist epoch was "the dawning sense that absence of direction was the defining trait." It was, he has suggested, "a period of tremendous experimental productiveness in the visual arts with no single narrative direction or the basis of which others could be excluded." Artists and critics had no easy time declaring what was part of the modern canon— or even revolutionary—and what was merely commercial or inconsequential. That ambiguity allowed the definition of art to drift beyond the bounds of criticism and *a priori* constraint.[9]

For Andy Warhol and other culture benders, such ambiguity was positively liberating and lucrative. They had created Pop Art, something art critic Harold Rosenberg reacted against not because he thought so little of it but because he was forced to listen to others praise it incessantly. Art itself, he believed, had become subservient to the image of the artist. Whatever a self-proclaimed artist did immediately became art, Rosenberg contended. "The vision of transcending the arts in a festival of forms and sensations rests upon one crucial question, 'What makes one an artist?'" That issue, he suggested, "is never raised in the post-art world, where it is assumed that the artist is a primal force, a kind of first cause—and that he therefore exists by self-declaration." As the artists broke free from their creations—effectively undermining the ability of critics to contest a work's meaning—artists were able to assume almost any role they wished, including that of commercial hucksters. Rosenberg concluded that the "de-definition of art necessarily results in the dissolution of the figure of the artist. . . . In the end everyone becomes an artist."[10]

Unlike other movements in art, Pop Art affected the audience as much as the artists. Hilton Kramer, a more conservative contemporary of Rosenberg's, claimed that the public for art had become immeasurably broader because of Pop. "Pop Art actually addressed itself to the largest possible audience," he believed, relieving it of "all the legendary difficulties that modernist art had always been said to interpose between the public and its ability to accept new artistic vocabularies." To be "with it," all the public needed to know was where and what *it* was. There was no longer any obligation to understand what *it* meant. In regard to the most famous of Pop Artists, Kramer argued that Andy Warhol "was under no obligation to spell out the 'significance' of his subject; he had only to identify it. Significance, such as it was, inhered in the mere act of transferring the subject from 'life'—which is to say, the media—to 'art,' and any suspicion of the didactic was, in any case, incompatible with the strategy of kidding the products."[11]

Pop artists, it seems to me, had built on a trend clearly started by movie critics who took objects traditionally treated as one type of culture and, by placing them in a new cultural and epistemological environment had given movies new meaning. Around this time, linguist Umberto Eco reasoned that by changing the descriptive context, "a new cloud of meaning thickens around the object." While society redefined what an object meant, the ambiguity around it increased, leading to a reconsideration of the object itself and, Eco believed, to a discovery of "certain properties which it already had but which, through the mechanics of transposition, show themselves more clearly, and have become more important, more obsessive." The gradual inclusion of movies among the arts, then, became part of the changing definition of art, but it was the language as much as the form or content that created a new definition of both. It was still unclear, however, whether developments in the worlds of film and criticism had revealed something significant about either art or the movies.

At the same time the language of cultural criticism changed, the public's relationship with high culture was also evolving. An institution that did much to relocate the place of the fine arts in American society was New York City's Lincoln Center for the Performing Arts. On September 23, 1962, Leonard Bernstein, a self-consciously popular conductor, led the New York Philharmonic in its inaugural appearance of the season. That event belied the temper of the era: At last America's oldest symphony orchestra, which was founded in 1878 by conductor Leopold Damrosch and had merged with the Philharmonic Society of New York in 1928, had become part of a civic institution that intended to popularize, rather than "sacralize" the fine arts. The Lincoln Center's new president, Pulitzer Prize–winning composer William Schuman, sought to make the arts both financially secure and culturally vibrant—rescuing them from the margins of society by returning them to the people. Containing three halls to house the New York Philharmonic, the Metropolitan Opera, and the Vivian Beaumont Theater, the Lincoln Center worked to bridge the divide between the arts and the masses.[12]

Schuman assumed his presidency on January 1, 1962, at the age of fifty-two. He had previously been the president of the Juilliard School of Music, which had also become a constituent of Lincoln Center. As part of the country's cultural elite, Schuman was among those with the cultural capital to popularize elite cultural institutions. Acknowledging that historically a tension had existed between the masses and the arts, he suggested that while the creation of art was a process normally devoid of commercial concerns, appreciation of art did not necessarily exist apart from the cultural marketplace. In fact, by the mid–twentieth century it had become vital for the arts to have both public and private support. Mass entertainments had stolen part of the audience for the fine arts, making it necessary for institutions such as the Lincoln Center, and earlier the Museum of Modern Art (MoMA), to attract patrons. Thus, much like the MoMA, the Lincoln Center hoped to enliven the fine arts by "democratizing" appreciation of them. "The arts in our society," Schuman explained, "enrich life, not because of the limitations imposed by criteria for mass acceptability, but rather by the opportunities offered by mass exposure and education. A society which . . . has the potential to insure accessibility to all of the riches of art, and, at the same time, guarantee artistic freedom, is a dynamic society."[13]

If during the twentieth century a majority of the American people had grown distant from the nation's artists, institutions like the Lincoln Center intended to reunite them. Mass culture had drawn people away from fine art, but the techniques of mass culture could be appropriated to get part of that audience back. By doing so, however, the new cultural elite had to consider what the public expected from art. Schuman argued that one could not consider the arts as merely another form of entertainment. "There must be courage to face even predictable failure if there is conviction of artistic worth," he said. "There are precious few artists, managers or laymen who are willing to meet this dilemma or who can afford to." Schuman wanted people to understand that appreciating the arts meant accepting both the bad and the good, the difficult and the enjoyable. That proposition would, however, force institutions to search for ways to make the difficult seem enjoyable and the bad to appear good.[14]

August Heckscher, Pres. John F. Kennedy's special adviser on the arts, spoke directly to the type of venture the Lincoln Center had undertaken. Heckscher had been a strong advocate for public support of the arts since his work in the Eisenhower administration, and by 1962 had become director of the Twentieth Century Fund. In a special issue of the *New York Times Magazine* promoting the Lincoln Center, Heckscher argued that the Center had an opportunity to solve a modern American dilemma: democratizing appreciation of the arts without necessarily undermining their quality. "The inevitable question arises," he observed, "whether excellence can be transmitted to a vast population without debasing it. From that sobering question critics of modern culture have gone on to indict nearly everything that is being done, or could be done, to develop the arts in a highly industrialized society." He sensed it was futile to act as if mass mediums and mass culture had not affected and could not help the arts. "The chance exists," he believed, "that we may come out into a period of creativity and enjoyment such as no other nation has quite known—not a period characterized by the imitative and traditional qualities of folk art nor by the withdrawn beauties of an aristocratic patronage, but by the liveliness, the sense of innovation, variety and vigor which goes with democracy at its best."[15]

Unwittingly, Heckscher had made a quintessential argument for accepting Midcult. Indeed, the Lincoln Center would be the realization of Dwight Macdonald's bane: a cultural institution that hoped going to the symphony or opera would become an experience comparable to seeing a movie. Even if one failed to understand the arts or even appreciate the skill required to produce them, one could still *enjoy* the arts. In the end, democratizing appreciation of the arts also meant democratizing taste and expectations. However, rather than expect patrons to understand why something was art, the Lincoln Center had bought into the assumption that no one really knew what art was any longer.[16]

In a speech before the Academy of Political and Social Sciences, Heckscher spoke about art and entertainment as if there was little difference between the two. "We are rapidly discarding the idea that works of art are created for the private enjoyment of the wealthy individual," he observed. "We see them instead as the expression of common values, made for a public purpose and at home in the open area." The custodians of culture who wielded critical authority fifty years earlier would have found such a sentiment downright vulgar. But in the new world of Pop Art and the Lincoln Center, art was not so easily defined, mass culture not so easily dismissed, and cultural authority not so easily accepted.

It thus was not surprising that the Lincoln Center intended to promote movies as art. On March 28, 1962, Eugene Archer, the second-string movie critic for the *New York Times* behind Bosley Crowther, reported William Schuman's announcement that films would become part of the Lincoln Center's repertoire. Schuman claimed it was "a cultural necessity" to exhibit films at the Center in order to "advance the popular acceptance of the motion picture as a significant form of twentieth century art." According to Archer, film director Elia Kazan would lead an advisory board created to investigate the best way to integrate movies into the Center's mission. When asked the types of films he considered suitable for exhibition, Schuman responded with an ambiguity befitting the notion of movies as art. He thought retrospectives of "old classics from America and abroad" would suffice, as well as "foreign films of artistic merit that, for commercial reasons, have not been acquired for American distribution." He also emphasized "that the Center would concentrate on films that are artistic but not abstract, avant-garde or 'arty.'" He cited one of Hollywood's latest releases, *The Hustler,* as an example of the kind of "popular art" the center would include.[17]

Many among New York City's movie community welcomed such news, including established figures of the city's cinematic elite. Symon

Gould, director of the Cinema Arts Guild (established in 1925), encouraged Schuman to bring the best films of the day to the Lincoln Center. To help that along, Gould suggested that Schuman consider Amos Vogel, founder of the city's largest film society, Cinema 16. Gould thought "some basis of co-operation between your Center and its cinematic plans should be created with that of Cinema 16 which numbers several thousand members in its roster and which has demonstrated . . . an amazing perspicacity in film-selection which in my view has contributed materially to the success of the number of film-art theatres through its pioneering in this area. Such a liaison I submit would materially solve the question of financial support for your project." For his part, Vogel was willing to discuss the matter with Schuman, but the Lincoln Center's president postponed their meeting until he and his staff had crafted their own vision of a film program.[18]

Schuman and Richard Leach, the Center's executive director for programming, had already begun to consult various New York film authorities. Schuman corresponded with Robert Gessner, a professor of communication arts at New York University, about establishing a film society for the Center. Schuman also entertained a joint venture with Time-Life to sponsor a year-round film series. Yet the person who clearly had the greatest influence during these early days was MoMA's Richard Griffith. Neither Schuman nor Leach had any expertise in films. Griffith, on the other hand, was a film scholar and curator of the museum's Film Library. After working with Griffith for a few months, Schuman told John D. Rockefeller III, chairman of the Lincoln Center's board of directors, that he intended to develop a film festival in collaboration with MoMA—a project that would display classics from the museum's vaults as well as more recent cinematic sensations.[19]

Schuman originally proposed making motion pictures a constituent of the Center, but he encountered stiff opposition from the board of directors. "It had been my feeling, strong feeling," Schuman later explained, "that Lincoln Center could have been erected a hundred years ago, with all the constituents in place, and the only new constituent that could be added was film, because film was a twentieth century art form that hadn't existed before." When he made his pitch for films, however, "it was received very coldly" by the board. He remembered "various persons saying that film was not a lively art, and I countered with the fact that it was livelier than lots of things that went on" at the Lincoln Center. Amos Vogel recalled Schuman telling him that the board thought "film was for the boobs." Someone remarked that if the Center included films, "we might as well have baseball." Eventually, Schuman explained, "my view prevailed, and they wanted to know how I wanted to do it."[20]

Schuman, like MoMA's first director Alfred Barr, ran up against traditional cultural authority. Yet unlike Barr's experience thirty years earlier, Schuman could justify including films at the Center by appealing to institutions such as MoMA that had done much to establish the notion of movies as art. Moreover, Richard Griffith suggested that Schuman contact James S.C. Quinn, the director of the British Film Institute, to get advice from the people who ran London's annual film festival. On a trip to England in the summer of 1962, Schuman met with Quinn and the program director of the London Film Festival, Richard Roud. Smartly, Schuman had sought connections with institutions that would help not only the practical but also the artistic nature of the Lincoln Center's film festival.[21]

At the same time that the Lincoln Center reached out to Europe, Richard Leach had begun courting Hollywood. Ralph Hetzel Jr., executive vice president of the Motion Picture Association of America, entered negotiations over the industry's participation in a film festival. Although Hollywood's power over the motion picture world had been the standard against which all previous international film festivals had rebelled, Leach hoped to secure the support of the Motion Picture Association of America in order to score a Hollywood movie for, at least, opening night. Through his discussions with Hetzel, Leach concluded that the Lincoln Center could count on a film festival that would include American movies in addition to the usual international fare.[22]

If Leach had insured that the Center's festival would have an American angle, Schuman's visit to London made it international. Schuman met with Richard Roud, Quinn's chief assistant, to discuss the feasibility of a formal partnership between the London Film Festival and the Lincoln Center. Schuman later wrote to Quinn: "It is natural for us to turn to you for some guidance in formulating plans for our own first film festival. . . . It is my thought that we might be able to avail ourselves of some of the work accomplished by your staff in the selection of films and in the handling of the myriad of details concerned in their presentation." While not wanting to duplicate the London Film Festival, Schuman believed that the Lincoln Center would benefit "artistically" from collaborating with the BFI. Quinn gave his tacit agreement to the proposal, believing, as Schuman had suggested, that it would also be worthwhile to exchange representatives to continue negotiations. At this point, both Schuman and Leach clearly hoped for a collaborative effort and thus came to find Quinn's right-hand man Roud important to a proposed film festival.[23]

In November 1962, a few weeks after the London Film Festival, Quinn traveled to New York to meet with Lincoln Center executives—primarily Leach—and hammer out a structure for the collaborative film festival. The Lincoln Center would use its twenty-three-hundred-seat Philharmonic Hall to show a two-week international festival of films that had already been selected by Roud for the London Film Festival. Leach explained, "their selections would be subject to our approval, and, conceivably, to that of an advisory committee, predominantly 'industry,' to be appointed by us." The schedule of films would change daily, so that people would see fourteen different programs. Since the Philharmonic Hall was nearly four times larger than the one used by the BFI, Leach proposed to "content ourselves with one, or at the outside two, daily showings." He hoped to find a "really exceptional new film—ideally, an American film—to open the first joint festival." Leach estimated the festival would gross around $100,800 over its twenty-eight shows, out of which the BFI would get a percentage for consulting and Roud would receive an honorarium. Leach and Quinn also agreed to employ "a specialist in the cinematic field who would serve as liaison between us and London and supervise the artistic, technical, and financial details of the New York Film Festival."[24]

By the late winter of 1963, a number of key players were in place. Schuman and Leach had received official approval from Sylvester Gates, chairman of BFI's board of directors, to cosponsor with the Lincoln Center and MoMA the first New York Film Festival. This group had also settled on a ten-day period from September 10–19, at the end of the Center's summer schedule but before the beginning of the New York Philharmonic's fall season. The Center's board of directors had also approved the hiring of Amos Vogel on a part-time basis from March 12 to August 1, then full-time through the festival.[25]

As founder of the eclectic film society Cinema 16, Vogel had introduced a generation of New Yorkers to a generation of independent and experimental filmmakers. Among those whose work was first shown in the United States by Cinema 16 were Stan Brakhage, Kenneth Anger, Robert Bresson, John Cassavetes, Tony Richardson, and François Truffaut. Founded in 1947, Cinema 16 had amassed thousands of members and made Vogel, as he has said, a "known quantity" in New York. By the spring of 1963, though, Cinema 16 was in financial trouble. Archer Winsten, movie critic for the *New York Post*, expressed dismay that Cinema 16 was reportedly $20,000 in debt and would close by April 1 if something were not done to save it. "Cinema 16," Winsten explained, "is a forerunner, an artistic plow, a device for getting pictures from all over the world shown in New York, pictures that could not make their own way by reason of predicted box-office strength." Vogel had a "cinematic critical intelligence so all-encompassing in taste, so devoted to the proposition that controversy is the breath of life, so keen and tireless in seeking quality work from all over the world that the sum-total of the product shown is incomparable."[26]

The trouble was that Cinema 16 had had a devoted group of patrons who purchased subscriptions to yearlong programs. That approach had worked while the number of art-house theaters remained small, but by the late 1950s and early 1960s, box-office returns for commercially marketed art-house pictures sent Cinema 16 toward financial ruin. Cinema 16 had done much to cultivate moviegoers and filmmakers for alternative cinema, but it could not compete against the quasi-commercial, quasi-alternative movies.[27]

By the spring of 1963, therefore, Vogel was open to offers of employment. He had already contacted Schuman more than a year earlier but had received no response save a brief note in May 1962. With the arrival of Richard Roud and the solidification of the arrangements with the BFI, the Lincoln Center needed a point man to handle things in New York. A few years earlier Roud had made a visit to Cinema 16 to look at American experimental films. He and Vogel had spent a pleasant afternoon and evening establishing a good personal relationship. Vogel explained that they were both, after all, "sort of like film nuts." Richard Griffith also undoubtedly knew Vogel and his work at Cinema 16, and Symon Gould had strongly recommended that Schuman consider joining forces with New York's largest film society. That last fact was probably not lost on Schuman and Leach, who knew that the Festival needed to generate a large popular turnout to win over the Center's board of directors. Years later, Roud claimed it was in fact at his request that Vogel was offered the position of director of the 1963 New York Film Festival.[28]

While Vogel managed the administrative details in New York, Roud was busy selecting films for two festivals. Roud was born in Boston, educated at the University of Wisconsin, and a Fulbright scholar who had studied in France. He recalled that Schuman was understandably relieved that the film festival's program director had American roots as well as European credentials. But the Lincoln Center was also getting a genuine cinephile. Roud had moved to London to teach English, remaining there to become a regular contributor to *Sight and Sound* and *Films and Filming*—both highly regarded British film journals. His astute criticism and reputation as a film historian had helped him become, by 1959, director of the National Film Theatre and a year later the program director for the London Film Festival. In this capacity he had also frequented European film festivals, especially the big three—Cannes, Venice, and Berlin. He was, like Vogel, a known quantity, except that his province was Europe rather than New York.[29]

By the time the Lincoln Center hired Vogel, six short months remained before the festival's opening night, and Roud and Vogel had yet to meet in the same city. Roud was off with Quinn visiting European film festivals and collecting titles to send to Vogel. Vogel was busy coordinating the advertising, cultivating a relationship with Hollywood and film distributors, and fretting over possible problems with customs and the New York State censorship board. Besides pleading with Roud to make his decisions quickly, Vogel also reminded him of "the importance of American films for the festival; especially as regards opening night." Moreover, Vogel stressed that the longer Roud took to send films to New York, the less time Vogel would have to arrange agreements with custom agents and censors.[30]

Amazingly, William Schuman, with the help of August Heckscher, had secured a pledge of no censorship. Louis M. Pesce, director of the Division of Motion Pictures in the New York State Department of Education, had decided that "in the light of the charitable and educational nature of Lincoln Center . . . the Division of Motion Pictures has no jurisdiction over films that may be shown as part of the Film Festival." This was a coup, because New York censors had been notorious for their prudish approach to movies. Foreign films with nudity had oftentimes suffered a censor's cut. However, as part of a civic works project as well as a nonprofit institution with the backing of New York governor Nelson Rockefeller and New York City mayor Robert Wagner, the Lincoln Center was not a small, independent theater. Schuman called this agreement a "milestone in the recognition of the film as an art form. . . . American audiences, like their counterparts abroad, will now be able to experience works of cinematic arts as their creator intended."[31]

On April 30, 1963, Schuman officially introduced the New York

Film Festival at a press luncheon. He explained that the Festival would be a cultural rather than a commercial exhibition of major international achievements in motion pictures. It would run in conjunction with a program of older films shown at MoMA and would work in close cooperation with the London Film Festival. Schuman also noted that he wanted American films in the festival program in addition to the best from European festivals. The combination of Hollywood films and European prize-winning pictures immediately distinguished the New York Film Festival from others in the world. Although the United States had film festivals in San Francisco and Boston, neither had the support of the American movie industry or the kind of financial backing that the Lincoln Center enjoyed. To many people, the New York Film Festival would be the first American film festival.[32]

Critics noted with relish Schuman's ability to skirt New York censors. As Jim Greene of the *Brooklyn Tablet* joked, the "180,000,000 downtrodden censor-weary beatniks [will] benefit from the r-e-a-l-l-y adult foreign productions, not just those with BB [Brigitte Bardot] and Gina [Lollabrigida]. We can hardly wait for American moral standards to soar." Many reports also acknowledged approvingly that the Lincoln Center intended to focus on films rather than the stars, parties, and awards for which Cannes and Venice were famous.[33]

Archer Winsten found the festival important because of the size, wealth, and influence the Lincoln Center could bring to bear on the treatment of films as art. Yet he was even more impressed by the absence of censorship. "It is possible," he mused, "that some 20-odd films will contain one view of the human body which is commonplace to the world but rare, prohibited and therefore pornographic here. If so, there is an explosive potential here that might sell out the 2300 seats of Philharmonic Hall in a single rush." He also reasoned that with prices set reasonably between $1.50 and $3.50, young film enthusiasts would have no excuse for failing to support the festival. However, Winsten worried that with Roud selecting films, American movies might get overlooked. As Schuman had remarked during the luncheon, Roud had been responsible for bringing films of international fame to London's Film Festival, although none of them had been American.[34]

A month later, Schuman and Leach finalized Hollywood's involvement by forming a sponsoring committee on which sat many of the industry's biggest names, including John Ford, Samuel Goldwyn, Elia Kazan, Arthur Mayer, Otto Preminger, David O. Selznick, Jack Warner, and Darryl Zanuck. The Lincoln Center had offered the chairmanship of the committee to MPAA president Eric Johnston, but he turned it down. Instead, presidential adviser August Heckscher agreed to become chairman. The Lincoln Center had spun a web of connections within a group that wielded considerable power and influence. The festival had the support of Hollywood, the MPAA, and the Independent Film Importers and Distributors of America; New York's avant-garde film community, the London Film Festival, MoMA's Film Library; the president of the United States, the governor of New York, and the mayor of the city. Eric Johnston provided an appropriate blessing: "such a festival, under the auspices of the Center, provides new dimension to the significance of the motion picture in the realm of culture and of art, as well as its worldwide recognition as an entertainment medium."[35] The New York Film Festival had pulled together an extraordinary amalgam of institutions to honor movies. Considering that only forty years earlier the U.S. Supreme Court had declared that motion pictures were no more than commodities, the festival illustrated how far movies had come.

By July 1, the Center had announced the selection of two Italian films for the program: Ermanno Olni's *I Fidanzati* and, to be shown at MoMA, Luchino Visconti's 1947 classic, *La Terra Trema*. Vogel reminded Roud, who was still in England, that "it will be necessary for us to look for a few bigger-name films. Always bear in mind that the film milieu .. . is on a lower level here; and so, both from a publicity and audience viewpoint, we will have to have some better known guideposts to lean on." Vogel wanted this first program to be popular so that "we can then go on to greater heights." He was also sensitive to the possibility that MoMA could overshadow the Lincoln Center's program because the museum was to show film classics.[36]

Two weeks later, the Lincoln Center announced four additional titles: *Knife in the Water* by the young Polish phenomenon Roman Polanski, Chris Marker's *Le Joli Mai*, Takis Kanelopoulos's *The Sky,* and Brazilian director Glauber Rocha's *Barravento*. In keeping with the theme of a festival of festivals, each selection had been accompanied by an announcement of the awards won by the director and the picture. However, Symon Poe of Twentieth Century Fox informed Vogel that his choice for opening night, Visconti's *The Leopard*, winner of the 1963 Palm d'Or at Cannes, would not be available. Poe offered *The Condemned of Altoona* in its place, but Vogel rejected it. Instead, Vogel and Roud decided to open with Luis Buñuel's *The Exterminating Angel*.[37]

Throughout the summer of 1963, publicity about the Festival had remained somewhat thin. The Lincoln Center had asked all New York film critics to hold off on publishing reviews of pictures scheduled for the festival. It was clear from exchanges between Vogel and Robert Hale, the Center's public relations director, that the Center believed critics could significantly affect ticket sales. Thus, Vogel and Hale made a list of the critics they thought the Festival should court. Among those mentioned were Vincent Canby and Abe Weiler of the *New York Times;* Archer Winsten, Bob Salmaggi, and Judith Crist of the *New York Herald Tribune;* Brendan Gill of the *New Yorker;* Dwight Macdonald of *Esquire;* Hollis Alpert of *Saturday Review;* and Andrew Sarris of the *Village Voice.* Although Hollywood barely acknowledged movie criticism, it was clear to a man such as Amos Vogel that critics could determine popular response to nonmainstream movies.[38]

A couple of weeks before the festival opened, Richard Roud publicized and defended the Festival in a *New York Herald Tribune* column that was usually the province of Judith Crist (who would later claim that New York needed a film festival like it needed more traffic). Roud aptly summed up what the film festival represented in American culture. He argued, interestingly, not so much why movies belonged in the Lincoln Center but how illogical it was to keep them out. In other words, because art had lost so much of its traditional meaning, it had become unnecessary to defend movies in terms of artistic standards. After all, Roud observed, "the borderline between art and non-art has become so blurred most people have stopped looking for it." The rise of television had also helped make films seem more artistic. "Ever since television has really taken over in the country," Roud explained, "movies are becoming more and more a 'minority' art—just as the theater became a 'minority' art when movies took over some fifty years ago." Thus, not only had television become a medium against which to contrast movies, it also had pushed movie studios to improve on the product they made for theaters.[39]

What truly made the New York Film Festival unique, Roud suggested, was that it elevated all movies to the level of art. He explained that for years "there have been some who would recognize that the experimental film, the avant-garde film had a right to the name of art. But anything that came out of a large studio, or that was, God save us— *popular,* forfeited for those very reasons any claim to art." To Roud, such an attitude ran "fundamentally counter to any real appreciation of the film." As a visual medium, movies had directly challenged the way society judged its art. Roud claimed that while subject matter, dialogue, and script were "obviously important . . . they are not crucial." At least they were no longer crucial in an age when meaning and art no longer needed to connect.

In other words, movies could be considered art simply by being visually arresting, rather than intellectually substantive. While that might seem sensible, such an idea also made it possible to consider French New Wave directors as the successors to Joyce and Tolstoy. One need not be a cultural conservative to believe that more than different artistic mediums separated Alain Resnais and Leo Tolstoy. Nonetheless, Roud declared that with the New York Film Festival, movies were "respectable at last." Indeed they were, but did one accept that proposition because movies had achieved respectability or because the meaning of art had been redefined so severely that Hollywood pictures could be considered art?[40]

Fittingly, Larry Rivers, part of the New York School of Pop Art, painted a billboard announcing the New York Film Festival. The piece stood on Broadway and West Sixty-fifth Street in front of the half-finished Lincoln Center complex. Here was yet another example of art imitating popular culture. A collector named Joseph A. Hirshhorn had already purchased Rivers's piece for the relatively substantial sum of $14,000. Critic John Canaday observed that "the deftness of Mr. Rivers's arrangements of apparently scrambled letters will be lost on most people . . . but this deftness and sportiveness should delight the kind of person who is a potential customer for a film festival."[41] Indeed, the New York art public welcomed the idea that billboards were a place to display art and had come to expect the inclusion of movies in cultural institutions that also housed symphony orchestras and opera companies.

On August 25, the first advertisement for the New York Film Festival appeared in newspapers. Tickets went on sale the next day, and, as Vogel predicted, the festival appealed to the crowd that had patronized his film society and had become the chief audience of New York's arthouse cinemas. Leach reported that three times as many people had bought tickets holding a *Village Voice* ad as those carrying the one placed in the *New York Times*. Nevertheless, the audience for the first show was an interesting mix.[42]

On September 9, 1963, the first New York Film Festival opened to a sold-out house. John Gruen of the *New York Times* described a scene of Lincoln Center patrons and film stars in black-tie and gowns mingling with "intent-looking young men and women of a decided beatnik persuasion." One young man even showed up in shorts. Amos Vogel recalled that the audience "was predominantly very young and bohemian, but some of it also was much more middle class and staid. It was very varied." Stanley Kauffmann thought those attending had "generated the keenest sense of interest that I have felt (outside of music and ballet audiences) since the proletarian plays of the thirties, the feeling that they were there because nothing could have kept them away." Wilfrid Sheed reported for *Commonweal* that "there seemed to be a feeling that the art of cinema was at the crossroads; Mr. August Heckscher, the royal messenger, read a Presidential blessing on the first evening and the air was heavy with self-conscious portent from there on in."[43]

Opening the festival was Luis Buñuel's *The Exterminating Angel,* a film about a group of rich people dressed very much like the crowd that sat in the Philharmonic Hall who are trapped within a richly ornate living room. Wilfried Sheed believed that Buñuel intended his film as an allegory on the suffocating power of the Catholic Church, but he also imagined that as the "characters putrefy, in mysterious captivity, you are likely to become restless yourself. You won't be able to leave the Lincoln Center after it's all over, that's what the film symbolizes." And that, in fact, was what happened. The hall was so crowded following the movie that people had trouble exiting. According to Vogel, he and Roud had selected Buñuel's film because of its obvious reflection on the expected audience—though not exactly the one that appeared—that first night. Yet they had not planned on the joke going quite that far. After assessing the scene, Hollis Alpert was unsure whom the joke was on, the audience or the organizers. Alpert remarked that while the atmosphere that night was "remarkably unstuffy," a friend of his also asked, "For God's sake, what did it mean?"[44]

As Alpert had smartly noted in 1962, such films needed to be a bit obscure in order to play like art. The audience, after all, wanted to work at interpretation even if there really was no right or wrong way of interpreting the film. Perhaps more importantly, though, was the large, excited, and varied crowd that had attended a film festival. Certainly such a popular outpouring marked the acceptance of movies by nation's economic elite as well as the culturally rebellious. *New York Times* critic Bosley Crowther gushed that the tremendous public response "was nothing short of a full-blown cultural phenomenon." He had written before opening night that "the enterprise calls for celebration ... because the idea behind it is progressive, mature and artistically sound." In an editorial, the *Times* declared, "The Lincoln Center–Museum of Modern Art showings dignify movies in this country; tell the world that we too are interested in cultural efforts. Hopefully, our own serious filmmakers will be encouraged and recognized."[45]

One of those independent filmmakers had made the only disreputable scene of the entire festival. Adolfus Mekas, Jonas Mekas's brother, stood up before the screening of his film *66 Hallelujah Hills* and, after being handed his notes by a young woman in a bikini (recalling images of Cannes or Venice), gave a mock acceptance speech that mimicked winners at the Academy Awards. He thanked Thomas A. Edison, Sergei Eisenstein, and D.W. Griffith, among others, for helping his career. Although the Center's executives failed to find humor in this prank, Mekas did draw some attention to the fact that the New York Film Festival was not without its own contradictory elements of commercialism and pretension.[46]

Yet the 1963 Festival had clearly scored with audiences. Eugene Archer reported that the Lincoln Center had taken in more than $90,000, selling out more than 85 percent of its twenty-one programs. Perhaps the most significant indication of the Lincoln Center's accomplishment, though, was to make the cover of *Time* magazine. Appearing on the last day of the festival, *Time* declared that cinema was an international art. "By its taste and high excitement, by the quality of most of its films and the intelligence of its sellout crowds," *Time* concluded, the festival "may well mark for Americans a redefinition of what movies are and who it is that sees them." *Time* maintained that since the rise of television, "the movies have suddenly and powerfully emerged as a new and brilliant international art, indeed as perhaps the central and characteristic art of the age." *Time* even quoted François Truffaut urging young people to "be free, free of prejudice, free of old culture of technique, free of everything, to be madly ambitious and madly sincere!" The younger generation of movie buffs (*Time* estimated that 80 percent were under thirty years old) "believes that an educated man must be cinemate as well as literate. And it is a mass audience; financially, the new cinema is a going concern." Echoes of ideas advanced decades earlier by pioneering film critics Vachel Lindsay and Iris Barry could be heard in *Time*'s declaration that film "is the whole of art in one art, and it demands the whole of man in every man.... The art of the future has become the art of the present."[47]

Other critics, though, seemed underwhelmed by the festival and expressed a qualified skepticism. To Stanley Kauffmann, the reception of many of these movies had illustrated what he termed the "anti-Hanslick syndrome." Hanslick was a nineteenth-century Viennese music critic who had the misfortune to overlook some of the era's major figures. "The twentieth century," Kauffmann contended, "keenly aware of these conservative errors, is trying to atone for them by embracing every crankishness as creative, every incompetence as liberation from tradition." Judith Crist found most of the festival pretentious: "Night after night one could conclude only that this was a chapter meeting of Cinema 16; the 'in' boys were in their glory, the little jokes were bringing forth the snickers; the inertia of technique, the vacuum of soul, the limited mentality were the order of the day." Although most critics admitted to liking at least one or two films, Ronald Steel's assessment of the Festival in the weekly *Christian Century* was indicative of much of the criticism. Steel liked Polanski's *Knife in the Water* and Joseph Losey's *The Servant* (both were also crowd favorites and were released commercially based on that reaction), but he found *The Terrace* a "runner-up for general boredom." That film, he noted, was nothing more than "Leopoldo Torre-Nilsson's latest exercise in cinematic incompetence," and was made worse by "a little speech of breathtaking pretentiousness from the director himself."[48]

Among the younger generation, however, the festival seemed to represent an experience that was greater than the movies themselves. Traveling down from Morningside Heights, undergraduate Phillip Lopate had ventured to the Lincoln Center as a sort of pilgrimage. Lopate explained that "to be young and in love with films in the early 1960s was to participate in what felt like an international youth movement. We in New York were following and, in a sense, mimicking the café arguments in Paris, London and Rome, where the cinema had moved, for a brief historical moment, to the center of intellectual discourse, in the twilight of existentialism and before the onslaught of structuralism."[49] Lopate's sentiment had grown out of "a whole apparatus [that] had sprung up to support [a] moviemaking renaissance: the art-house circuit, new movie journals, museum and university studies, and, like a final official seal of legitimacy, the establishment of the New York Film Festival." It was an era "of high hopes, with the conviction that we were entering a fat time for movies." Some wondered if American culture had not grown a bit flabby from its diet of mass culture.[50]

A cycle of sorts was completed on the night of September 13, 1963, when an audience sat in the Philharmonic Hall watching *All the Way Home,* the sole American feature in the New York Film Festival. The movie was based on James Agee's novel *A Death in the Family* and began with a little boy named Rufus taking a walk with his father to see a picture show. In Agee's depiction of early-twentieth-century America, a person went to the movies to escape the realities of the outside world; nothing intruded on the pure comedy of Charlie Chaplin or the heroics of William S. Hart's cowboys. By 1963, though, Rufus had made it to the other side of the screen. He had entered the moving picture, and the world that sat before him barely resembled the one he and his father had inhabited only fifty years earlier. It was not just that the people in the audience had become predominantly middle class and educated, but that they sat in a hall built for orchestras and attended a festival sponsored by the cultural elite, supported by Hollywood, blessed by the nation's president, and intellectualized by critics.

The moving picture world had changed not so much because the pictures themselves were different, but because the world—and the words—around them had evolved. It seemed that a kind of cultural inversion had taken place. In an earlier era, movies had been seen as a threat to the health of both the nation's youth and its established culture. By the early 1960s, it seemed that the youth and the culture had come to threaten the health of moviegoing by substituting an older passion for movies with an almost religious devotion to "the Cinema." That development characterized a generation of moviegoers reared in an intellectual environment that was disconnected from older notions of art and movies. It would be both a wildly inventive and pretentious group. It would be known as the "film generation."

9

The Film Generation Goes to School

In his article entitled "The Film Generation," Stanley Kauffmann attempted to assess the phenomenon of a "generation that has matured in a culture in which the film has been accepted with serious relevance, however that seriousness is defined." He argued that as young people broke free from traditional cultural authority, they encountered a world that afforded them opportunities not previously available. Phillip Lopate has suggested that his generation "had no real perspective, which is why we called on movies to be our language and our knowledge, our hope, our romance, our imagination and our life." But, as Kauffmann observed, that sensibility possessed a dangerous "ambivalence toward tradition . . . a hunger for art as assurance of origins together with a preference for art forms that are relatively free of the past."[1]

The first New York Film Festival marked a turning point in the history of movies much as Andy Warhol's arrival in 1962 came to represent the end of modern art. A cultural inversion had taken place. Only fifty years earlier, movies had been considered mere amusements; by 1963 they were art. At the beginning of the twentieth century, cultural critics had regarded art as a barometer of social health, but by 1962 one was hard-pressed to define what art was. As the art world slowly descended into a period of ambiguity, marked by trends that seemed literally outside of the "pale of history," movies assumed a position at the heart of American culture.[2]

During the 1960s, critics and audiences came increasingly to view movies with a single vision. As an older view of Hollywood faded into the haze of the New Sensibility, new groups of American producers and, more importantly, directors emerged with the determination to meld

Hollywood's substantial financial resources with the intention of remaking a commodity into an art. While it was no longer odd to imagine that art could be popular, it was still ironic to consider that art could be something created by an industry. Movie directors had become artists and movies were no different from the latest production of a Verdi opera or a Beethoven symphony—all three could be seen at the Lincoln Center, after all.

While the perception of movies underwent profound changes between 1909 and 1963, the effects that development had on the mainstream movie culture came later. When *Time* ran a cover featuring movies as *the* international art, it marked a point after which it was increasingly common for major newsweeklies, journals of opinion, and popular periodicals to treat movies and their filmmakers as cultural treasures. It was a development that canonized directors not merely among auteur critics but throughout the vast movie audience. It conferred legitimacy on filmmakers who are accepted as contemporary geniuses. It was the combination of cultural and financial forces of this era that shaped the reputations of directors such as Stanley Kubrick, Arthur Penn, Robert Altman, Mike Nichols, Francis Ford Coppola, Martin Scorcese, and Woody Allen. Although prior to 1963 moviegoers had referred to a picture by its star, its director or even its producer, after 1963 audiences saw films as the creation of single artistic soul and spoke about many movies as cultural events. Consider the sensations sparked by Kubrick's *Dr. Strangelove,* Penn's *Bonnie and Clyde,* Altman's *M*A*S*H,* Nichols's *The Graduate,* Coppola's two-part epic *The Godfather,* Scorcese's *Taxi Driver,* and Woody Allen's *Annie Hall.* Such works and their creators began replacing older heroes in literature, poetry, and drama in the minds of both film aficionados and the younger generation as a whole.

In December 1963, *Life* ran one of its large pictorial essays on the state of movies, entitled "Everybody Wants to Say It in Films." Readers learned that movies had "found a mind, and this once bland entertainment medium, the citadel of the sure-shot, is moving to explore the nature of man and his ideas." Rather than looking to write the great American novel or the protest manifesto, "people everywhere who have something to say want to say it with movies." Yet the reason for this had as much to do with changes among those who sat in front of the screen as with those who produced what was on it. At newsstands, magazines devoted to movie stars and gossip shared space with journals of a more serious bent, such as *Film Quarterly* and *Sight and Sound.* What this conjunction illustrated, *Life* explained, was that a new generation of movie-goers liked "intellectual, sophisticated, and aggressive films, and when they find one they talk their heads off about it, thereby propelling them before large audiences."[3]

Likewise, film festivals attracted a wider variety of moviegoers and continued to promote the perception that movies were an art vital enough to view and discuss at length. Amos Vogel, director of the New York Film Festival, believed that the success of the Lincoln Center's endeavors reflected and contributed to "a new cultural phenomenon: the belated official acceptance of film as serious, though not necessarily solemn, art." *Saturday Review* movie critic Hollis Alpert thought there was a *"lingua franca* at festivals, a trading of ideas," that encouraged a constant reassessing of what movies mean to society as both an art and as entertainment. At the 1963 New York Film Festival, *Life* reported that even an impromptu panel of film critics (not even directors) drew a standing-room-only crowd.[4]

Movies served as the perfect vehicle to shuttle between the worlds of art and media—and the perfect medium to combine the two. Film (rather than the more folksy word, movies) was considered by the younger generation to be *the* art of its era. Anthony Schillaci, a colleague of media guru Marshall McLuhan's at Fordham University in New York City, argued that the older generation and the nation's leaders in education, the arts, and politics had to understand that "seen through young eyes, film is destroying conventions almost as quickly as they can be formulated. Their hunger is for mind-expanding experiences and simultaneity, and their art is film." Another observer, this time from the self-proclaimed "hip" under-thirty generation, explained that movies had helped shift American culture from a literate world to a "filmic" one. He attributed that shift to an expression of a "new sensibility, one which is defined in part by its very lack of guilt about not being well-read and, on the other hand, by its overtly positive enthusiasm about film." *Time* magazine believed a result of the cultural shift toward a filmic society was that film-makers had replaced novelists as the nation's artistic stars. "Film has all but replaced the novel as the chief topic of cultural talk on the campus and at many cocktail parties," the magazine contended.[5]

A sign of the changing times for movies was an event held at the 1964 New York Film Festival devoted not to movies, filmmakers, critics, and audiences, but to film scholars. The American Council on Education in cooperation with the Motion Picture Association of America and the Lincoln Center ran a conference in October entitled, "The Study of Motion Pictures as a Contemporary Art in College and Universities." David C. Stewart, director of education programs for the National Council on the Arts as well as a consultant to the American Council on Education, was made the director of that project. Three assumptions guided the commission's work: first, that "motion pictures are a major, contemporary artistic expression;" second, "their cultural value lies far beyond pure entertainment;" and third, "higher education ... should contribute to the development of a more informed and discerning film audience." While such an explanation might have seemed self-evident to the community that had taken movies seriously since the medium's inception, recognition of movies as art by the education community represented another landmark on the trajectory of movies into art.[6]

Not a group to test mainstream tolerance, the education community found it imperative to offer film as an academic subject. After all, educators of the 1960s were dealing with the Film Generation. Stewart observed: "In light of the amount of informal but serious attention given to the art of motion pictures during the last decade, a time when the talents of European film directors were being enthusiastically applauded in this country, it seems curious that film study has not developed more rapidly." Indeed, movies had assumed a role in American culture unprecedented for a medium primarily thought of as entertainment. Stewart recognized the peculiar mixture of responses movies received, at once derided and elevated by intellectuals the world over. He also understood that film studies were going to develop with or without the formal sponsorship of educational institutions. Thus, he wanted his project to help organize and influence the 846 courses—a staggering figure when compared to statistics of only a decade earlier—already being taught in academic year 1963–64.[7]

Not all educators, however, were as enthusiastic about teaching "the movies." Robert Steele, a professor of film at Boston University since 1958 and the president of the Society for Cinematologists, attended the conference at the Lincoln Center as both an educator and a filmmaker. He hesitated to endorse the approach Stewart took because he believed the project was being driven by a fad—enthusiasm rather than thought. "Film studies should be kept as a privilege and for the privileged few who are ready," he argued. "The function of a good teacher is to discourage film as a course of study for the non-avid. There are film societies and cinemas galore for the non-serious film student." Incorporating film studies into a formal university curriculum would, he believed, ultimately compromise the integrity of educating serious students as well as dumb-down the notion of art itself.[8]

Steele made his opinions known in print shortly after this initial conference. A far more substantial and effective attack came from Pauline Kael. In October 1965, Stewart assembled another conference on film studies, this time held at Dartmouth College in New Hampshire, to discuss the data amassed during the previous year. From the conference's proceedings, Stewart hoped to compile a source book for teachers across the United States who would teach courses on some aspect of film. The conference was a chance for scholars to explain their prototypical course offerings. It was also a chance to criticize the idea of film studies.

Kael's talk, entitled "It's Only a Movie," was one of the three given that questioned the sensibility of formal film studies. While neither a scholar nor even a film scholar, Kael's criticisms still appeared as the most relevant because she dealt directly with the paradox of movies as a mass art. Kael had established a style in which she observed the audiences as much as the movies they watched. For critics concerned solely with whether a film met the criteria of art, Kael's criticism had become frustratingly glib. In her view, movies were special not because a professor told us so, but because movies connected with "us"—the audiences sitting together in darkened theaters. To Kael, the educators gathered at Dartmouth were simply in the dark.

After listening to professors discussing the study of film, Kael replied: "It goes against everything I feel about the movies, and against the grain of just about everything I believe about how we learn the arts." Discussing how to teach appreciation of movies, she believed, was akin to enforcing the rules one followed in a china store on a children's playground. Kael reveled in the fact that movies were not what educated people expected art to look like. After all, movies had gained acceptance into cultivated circles by being the right kind of antiart at the right time. Even so, Kael admonished her audience, "It's only a movie. Nobody says you have to like a movie (not, that is, until you get to the art-house age) and, as it isn't an occasion, there's no aftermath for you to fear." She believed that the whole exercise of treating movies as art was, at base, anti-intellectual. "I think," she contended, "that teenagers and college-age people may be caught up in movies because movies are a medium in which it's possible to respond in such an infinity of ways to an infinity of material without forming precise or definite attitudes, or making conscious judgments, or referring to values of any kind beyond 'cinema,' as if the medium were an end in itself." Kael warned that by trying to jump on the bandwagon of interest in movies, educators would be doing a disservice to themselves and the idea of moviegoing simply because they failed to grasp why movies were significant to young people.[9]

Students had, as Stewart and many other educators could attest, demanded that film societies and film courses be offered on college campuses. That development, according to Kael, was not unexpected. However, by legitimizing students' interest in movies through formal academic courses, the educational establishment had forgotten to ask why a movie was worthy of such treatment and had instead accepted the significance of movies as if they were a "fact of nature." Kael feared that a result of the Dartmouth conference and the policies it would endorse would be an unnecessary inflation of the importance of films, filmmakers, critics, and, ultimately, cultural trends connected with the youth.[10]

Kael ended her talk with a list of suggestions she hoped would deflate the self-importance of the gathering. She believed that making cinema respectful would be anathema to the essence of moviegoing. "Respectful is what the movies are not, and that's what we love about them." She suggested that the reason movies seemed to be more "alive" or livelier than other scholarly fields was precisely because they had eluded scholarly investigation. Nevertheless, if academic treatment was unavoidable, Kael wanted educators to show students a wide spectrum of cinema, from the grossest examples of commercial movies to the esoteric, experimental exercises of the quickly diminishing avant-garde. She cautioned against inflating mundane movies to the level of classics simply to justify a course on movies to a school's bureaucracy. The comment that echoed longest after she made it (and, I think, is still pertinent today) was the simple admonition: "If you think movies can't be killed by education, you underestimate the power of education." Kael probably had the image of an erstwhile professor lecturing a group of earnest sophomores about the artistic integrity of Alfred Hitchcock films. Yet her lament also related to scores of journals, conferences, and manifestos that began to emerge in the late 1960s and that helped turn moviegoing— what used to be an enjoyable and even inspiring experience—into an exercise of linguistic gymnastics and academic posturing. When discourse on a mass medium exists deliberately miles above the heads of the masses, such an approach comes perilously close to violating the spirit of the medium.

Kael's critique was the only one to warrant a counterattack. In *Film Heritage,* the editor of the journal, F. Anthony Macklin, shot back in a piece entitled "The Perils of Pauline's Criticism" that Kael was an anti-intellectual because it suited her role as an outsider to the academic world. Maurice Rapf, a screenwriter, director, and an attendee at the Dartmouth conference, responded that education "can't kill the movies for this generation because it's their medium and they love it." Much like Stewart's defense that the younger generation will obsess about film whether educated to or not, Rapf also argued that since the children of media had a passion for movies, the adults had better listen and respond to their wants.[11]

There was, of course, ample evidence that Kael played both sides of the debate over movies as art when it served her needs, and she had few suggestions about how to return movies to their rightful place in society—if there ever was one. It was a fact that film societies could be found thriving across the country and that students had demanded and received permission to begin formal training in all aspects of film. Why should students think otherwise when the era of the New Sensibility made it acceptable to embrace developments in media as earlier generations had embraced trends in painting? At least during the 1960s, the masters of movies, such as Jean-Luc Goddard, were recognized by their contemporaries—Goddard pulled in $1,500 an engagement while on a tour of eighteen American colleges.[12] Was not the United States simply catching up to its cousins across the Atlantic Ocean? Did not the rise of film studies reflect a long overdue concession that the movies, one of the truly original contributions Americans had made to the arts, were something of which to be proud?

In fact, many movie enthusiasts believed the time had come for the country to capitalize on its rich (both artistically and financially) cinematic tradition. In the summer 1961 issue of *Film Quarterly,* Colin Young, at the time the Los Angeles editor of that journal, made a pitch for the establishment of an American film institute. He believed that the United States lacked the benefits of centralized coordination that England had with the British Film Institute and in France with the Cinémathèque Française. There was no single organization in the United States with the power and reach to distribute and exhibit films on a nationwide basis. Without such an institution, film societies operated precariously, aspiring filmmakers had little more than a prayer of getting films distributed, and the size of audiences with a proclivity for movies outside the mainstream would remain relatively small. Young's idea was a successor to the Cinema Art Guild and National Board of Review of the 1920s, the Museum of Modern Art's Film Library of the 1930s and 1940s, Amos Vogel's Cinema 16 of the 1950s, and the film festivals of the 1960s. A natural next step of a nation that seemed increasingly enthralled with the dimensions of movies was to promote that interest through a federally supported institution.[13]

In November 1965, the federal government allocated $3 million for a national program for the arts. Seven projects would be fed by the money, including a grant of $500,000 for the establishment of an American Film Institute (AFI). Beginning in 1966, the institute took shape under the guidance of the Nation Council on the Arts. Its primary responsibilities were to aid film educators in colleges and universities, help young filmmakers finance projects, and assist archival activities of existing institutions. Pushing the starting budget to $5.2 million for the first three years of operation, the AFI quickly matched the financial reserves of its European counterparts. However, the institute's governing board possessed a striking difference: Hollywood was well represented. George Stevens Jr., the thirty-five-year-old son of Hollywood director George Stevens, was named president of the AFI and director of a twenty-two member board of trustees which had, as Hollis Alpert noted, a decidedly "Establishment coloration." That fact was not surprising since the MPAA had contributed $1.3 million, and private sources, mostly from Hollywood, had given another $1.3 million to help supplement the $2.6 million provided by the National Council on the Arts.[14]

The AFI's relationship with Hollywood was scrutinized, as was the decision not to include any prominent members of the American cinematic underground. Instead, the board of trustees was made up of educators, critics, and filmmakers such as Arthur Knight, Andrew Sarris, and a young Francis Ford Coppola. Although it failed to represent the cinematic vanguard, the AFI did hope to advance a more serious appreciation of movies. Both Bosley Crowther of the *New York Times* and Hollis Alpert of *Saturday Review* praised the AFI's worthy intentions. Crowther exclaimed that the ultimate service of the institute would be "to promote the *medium* of motion pictures and bring the public into fuller awareness of the great range and possibilities of the device of cinema. The still widely entertained image of 'movies' as something with stars that you see in theaters has to be erased," he declared, "and a new image of a means of stimulation as varied as literature and as highly respected as classic painting must be put in its place." Alpert argued that Hollywood's presence would be overridden if "what is being acknowledged is that the commercial spirit has for too long dominated the American film and that a counterforce has been long overdue."[15]

By the mid-1960s, treating movies as a lesser art or merely as an amusement had vanished for good. Both Hollywood and the federal government—two institutions that had earlier dismissed suggestions that movies were anything but an industry—had at last provided formal recognition of the new perception. The AFI did not, however, match its European counterparts in influence or effectiveness. Hollywood failed to assume the type of relationship with the AFI that film centers in European nations had with their government-subsidized film industry. Making it in Hollywood was still a long shot for the vast majority of young filmmakers. Yet the growing importance of movies in American culture ensured that the generation of filmmakers working on their craft in the late 1960s would attract more attention than ever before. Years later, this generation would be known as the "film school generation."

Film schools, those institutions that taught the production of movies rather than simply the study of the finished product, had been around since 1932 when the University of Southern California (USC) founded its film program. By the mid-1960s, film schools could be found across the United States, but three in particular dominated the scene: USC, the University of California at Los Angeles (UCLA), and New York University (NYU). The two California universities had close ties to Hollywood and had prepared many students for jobs in the industry. NYU, while located in the city where the money to finance movies originated, produced students whose chances of entering the mainstream movie business were relatively slim, but who nonetheless belonged to one of the largest film programs in the country.

Throughout the 1960s, film school students could submit their work to the annual national Student Film Festival sponsored by the National Student Association, the MPAA, and, by 1964, the Lincoln Center. In 1967, the Student Film Festival attracted an impressive audience of eleven thousand people to two venues—one at USC and the other at NYU—for the screening of student work. One observer remarked, "not only that a lot of very bright people think that film is capable of more, more, more, and that they are willing to fail big in their eagerness to succeed, but also that there is an audience." Without knowing how prescient he was, another critic thought that four student filmmakers—Martin Scorcese, John

Milius, George Lucas, and Francis Ford Coppola—stood out from the rest. In 1965, as a young NYU student, Scorcese won the student competition with a film entitled *It's Not Just You, Murray,* about life on Manhattan's lower east side. In 1968, Milius of USC won the animation category with his *Marcello, I'm So Bored,* and across town at UCLA a young and very serious George Lucas captured the drama prize with a strange, esoteric science-fiction thriller entitled *THX 1138 4EB.* That last film would be made into a feature length movie a few years later under the guidance of the greatest graduate of the film school generation, Francis Ford Coppola. Many critics suggested that if American movies were going to change, the audience for them had to evolve into a group that demanded something different from Hollywood. With that change underway, it seemed the industry would be compelled to search for new talent. A resource for new ideas about filmmaking was germinating in the nation's film schools.[16]

Movie culture as a whole had changed. It seemed that both the movies and their audiences had matured intellectually, allowing for a great variety of subjects and deeper exploration of themes. In 1967, the mainstream movie industry learned the full effects of the long movement that had made movies not only serious business but serious art. That year, moviegoers mostly under the age of thirty-five swarmed to see *Bonnie and Clyde* and *The Graduate.* Both movies gave new spins to older genres by incorporating the styles that had made European films so popular. *Bonnie and Clyde* premiered on August 4, 1967, at the Montreal Film Festival. It was an unusual picture because it turned bad guys into heroes and made violence seem humorous. *The Graduate,* released three months later, launched the career of its young leading man, Dustin Hoffman, by portraying him as a successful failure—he succeeded by subverting his parents' expectations.

In the previous decade, European films had captured an increasing percentage of the American market by providing what Hollywood would not and could not: quirky, unformulaic movies that had measures of nudity, profanity, and obscurity. By the time Michelangelo Antonioni's film *Blow-Up* appeared in 1967, with the first shot of full, frontal nudity allowed in mainstream American theaters, the European film invasion had reached its apex and would shortly fizzle out. When *Bonnie and Clyde* and *The Graduate* opened in late 1967, both movies connected with an audience—relatively vocal about its preferences—that was ready to receive them.

No European film came close to making the kind of money that either *The Graduate* or *Bonnie and Clyde* did at the box office. The combined effects of financial and critical success enabled Hollywood's version of the offbeat film to thrive and reproduce. The American movie industry adapted to the audience's new sensibility and adopted European techniques to create what was called at the time the "New Hollywood." As historian Robert Ray suggests, the New Hollywood "perfectly represented its audience's ambivalent relationship to the period's developments ... [it was] superficially radical, internally conservative." Industry executives acted as sensible businessmen when they green-lighted projects oriented toward a youth culture that other industries—such as the fashion, cosmetic, and advertising—had already begun to tap. But in doing so, Hollywood gave a chance to a new generation of filmmakers who otherwise would have been closed out of the industry. British director John Boorman recalls: "there was a complete loss of nerve by the American studios at that point. They were so confused and so uncertain as to what to do, they were quite willing to cede power to the directors." And why not? In contemporary movie culture, the director was thought to be the single greatest force in the production of movies.[17]

The film school generation was young, literate in the cinema if not in any of the other arts, and enamored with the masters of European cinema. Peter Biskind writes that New Hollywood directors had an unusual mixture of nerve and verve: they were "unembarassed—in many cases rightly so—to assume the mantle of artist, nor did they shrink from developing personal styles that distinguished their work from other directors." Somewhat ironically, "at its most ambitious, the New Hollywood was a movement intended to cut film free of its evil twin, commerce, enabling it to fly high through the thin air of art."[18]

Yet without the "Hollywood" part of that equation, these filmmakers would most likely have been underemployed and not all that "new." It was, of course, the twin benefits of merging commerce and art that drove so much of the cultural explosion of the 1960s. That merger made artists such as Andy Warhol into millionaires, radicals such as Abbie Hoffman into celebrities, and movie directors such as Stanley Kubrick and soon Francis Ford Coppola into artistic heroes, all within their own time. The perception that movies had become not simply big business but big art had an effect on those who dwelt between the industry and the audience: film critics.

Although *The Graduate* topped all movies in box office returns for

1967, it was *Bonnie and Clyde* that reflected the most dramatic shift in the perception of what movies meant to audiences. When the movie opened in Montreal, Bosley Crowther, the venerable *New York Times* movie reviewer, hated it. He could not understand why the crowds who viewed it with him seemed to love it. "Just to show how delirious these festival audiences can be," he wrote, *Bonnie and Clyde* was "wildly received with gales of laughter and given a terminal burst of applause." The critic had misread a trend that overtook movie culture by 1967. Audiences at film festivals were, in the past, clearly different from the mainstream crowds who watched movies elsewhere. Not any longer. Crowther dismissed the film for its excessive violence and for the glorification of two notoriously vile criminals. Letters poured into the *New York Times* chiding the reviewer for being narrow-minded and literal to a fault. The letters, moreover, reflected a generation responding to the war in Vietnam as well as the growing power of youth culture. One person suggested that Bonnie and Clyde "did all of the normal American things . . . and the violence which was their stock in trade is also an integral part of the American scene (as can be evidenced in our own times, from Detroit to Danang)." Another took a direct shot at Crowther: "*Bonnie and Clyde* was wonderful," he wrote. "The audience in the theater went crazy. Now I realize why Mr. Crowther feels so defensive. Soon everyone will know that his reviews can't be trusted." Perhaps the most apt response to Crowther came in an ad for *Bonnie and Clyde,* for it spoke over the critic's objections directly to the audience: "They're young . . . they're in love . . . and they kill people."[19]

Contributing to the sense of a culture in flux, two of the nation's largest weekly magazines, *Newsweek* and *Time,* devoted cover stories to the perceived rebellion in American society. In November 1967, *Newsweek* ran a cover with a naked Jane Fonda (from her movie *Barbarella*) with the caption: "Anything Goes: The Permissive Society." Inside, readers were treated to pictures and commentary on new attitudes toward sex. The permissive society's outlines were etched, the article contended, "in the increasing nudity and frankness of today's films, in the blunt, often obscene language seemingly endemic in American novels, in the candid lyrics of pop songs and the undress of the avant-garde ballet, in erotic art and television talk shows, in freer fashions and franker advertising." To explain why the United States seemed to be in the grip of a moral crisis, journalist Max Lerner was quoted as arguing that the nation was in "a late senate period. The emphasis in our society today is on the senses and the release of the sensual. All the old codes have been broken down." The public had shattered old taboos about expression, which filtered quickly into the commercial and art worlds, which in turn further fed the public's appetite and increased its tolerance for sex.[20]

Following quickly behind was *Time* magazine's cover story, introduced with a silk screen of *Bonnie and Clyde* from Pop artist Robert Rauschenberg under the caption: "The New Cinema: Violence . . . Sex . . . Art . . .". To the article's author, Stefan Kanfer, representatives of the New Cinema were "not what U.S. movies used to be like. They enjoy a heady new freedom from formula, convention and censorship. And they are all from Hollywood." To explain the rise of the New Cinema, Kanfer pointed to the convergence of movie culture and the youth culture. "The growing mass audience has been prepared for change and experiment both by life and art," he argued. "It has seen—and accepted—the questioning of moral traditions, the demythologizing of ideals, the pulverizing of esthetic principles in abstract painting, atonal music and the experimental novel." A picture like *Bonnie and Clyde* occupied a cultural space made over by the receding of older cultural pretensions. In such an environment, critics were free to explore the ambiguous distinctions between art and entertainment.[21]

Perhaps the critic best suited to discuss the intriguing convergence of art and commerce that made *Bonnie and Clyde* a significant cultural moment was Pauline Kael. Her infamous nine-thousand-word essay published by the *New Yorker* helped establish her as that journal's new movie critic. She had always been someone who intuitively understood both sides of the motion picture screen. She was a moviegoer that other critics had faulted for paying too much attention to the audience watching the movie rather than what that audience was "seeing." Yet to understand why *Bonnie and Clyde* had hit with such force, a critic had to engage more than simply the movie. After all, this picture was no better than many other gangster movies. Simply looking at the screen would not explain the excitement it generated.

Kael was not interested, as was Crowther, in critiquing the movie's immorality because she did not expect movies to raise the morals of moviegoers. Kael was not interested, as were auteur critics, in dissecting the style of director Arthur Penn because she did not treat movies as a fine art. The reason the audience was "alive" to *Bonnie and Clyde,* she suggested, had to do with the type of visceral experience it produced. The movie had "some connection with the way we reacted to movies in childhood," she believed, "with how we came to love them and to feel they were ours—not an art that we learned over the years to appreciate but simply and immediately ours."[22]

For Kael, the movie connected with American audiences because it played upon the period's unique movie culture psyche—the popularity of the gangster genre, the recent trend of antihero worship in such movies as *The Manchurian Candidate* and *Dr. Strangelove,* and the similarities to styles used by foreign filmmakers. But the cultural significance of *Bonnie and Clyde* and Kael's review of it lay in the dynamics unique to mass art. The movie evoked emotional responses that were spontaneous and immediate, vital but not enduring. Kael praised the movie for its ability to be the best type of mass art; the kind at which a critic can hear bursts of laughter, audible gasps, and brief claps of hands; the kind of art that the best movies had always been and the kind she hoped more of them would be. It was not a subject for theoretical treatment or scholarly discourse. Both the movie and its most ardent critic revealed the possibilities of transient significance. Neither would set the world ablaze with profound insight, but neither would be dismissed as inconsequential expressions of the time—the immediate, vibrant present.

Kael's review hit with a force not normally seen in American culture. Her prose and hard-fought perspective won her admirers in the world of film criticism. One of her friends, Joseph Morgenstern, reviewer for the influential political weekly *Newsweek,* issued an unprecedented retraction on a critique in which he blasted *Bonnie and Clyde.* He began the second review stating, "Last week this magazine said that *Bonnie and Clyde* . . . turns into a 'squalid shoot-em-up for the moron trade' because it does not know what to make of its own violence. I am sorry to say I consider that review grossly unfair and regrettably inaccurate. I am sorrier to say I wrote it." Kael's excitement convinced Warner Brothers (after constant prodding from the movie's lead actor Warren Beatty) to release *Bonnie and Clyde* a second time. In the fall of 1967 the movie brought in a modest $2.5 million, the following spring it took in another $14 million. Pauline Kael and the New Hollywood had illustrated the power of mass art.[23]

Following the success of both *The Graduate* and *Bonnie and Clyde,* a string of New Hollywood movies became commercial and critical hits. In July 1969, *Easy Rider,* a movie that cost $501,000 to produce and grossed an astonishing $19.1 million, sent shock waves through the industry as executives searched for their own answer to a low budget, youth and drug culture cash cow. The movie's slightly crazy director, Dennis Hop-

per, recalled: "We made all our money back the first week. In one theater." Other examples quickly followed that played upon either the black
humor, or youth culture, or sex, drugs, and rock 'n' roll themes of the late
1960s. Robert Altman's *M*A*S*H* took in $36.7 million and a documen-
tary about the Woodstock music festival (edited by Martin Scorcese)
brought $16.4 million, while other movies such as Bob Rafelson's *Five
Easy Pieces,* John Schlesinger's *Midnight Cowboy,* Peter Bogdanovich's *The
Last Picture Show,* and William Friedkin's *The French Connection,* won
critical acclaim and Academy Awards.

The film that signaled the next great step was *The Godfather.* In
1968, Paramount had optioned a draft of the novel by New York writer
Mario Puzo, but had let the novel sit dormant until it became a bestseller.
By 1970, Paramount executives were seeking a director to make a movie
based on Puzo's book. After a number of filmmakers rejected the project,
the studio turned to Francis Ford Coppola, a man with experience in the
industry but no hit to his name. The studio figured that as an Italian-
American, Coppola would have an innate feel for the movie's subject
and thus lend authenticity to the plot and production. Coppola, although
reluctant to accept the assignment, had recently failed to finance his own
studio, named Zoetrope, and needed money to repay his Hollywood lend-
ers. He accepted the job while on a cruise across the Atlantic and set to
work by literally breaking the book down into sections and taping them
to the windows of one of the ship's rooms.[24]

Throughout the production of the film, Coppola reportedly believed he had failed at every aspect of his job. He had won small victories
along the way, though—among them persuading Paramount to cast Al
Pacino and Marlon Brando, and getting the studio to finance location
shoots in New York City and Sicily. When production wrapped in September 1971, Coppola again sailed for Europe expecting to leave his
troubles behind.

The Godfather opened in Manhattan on March 15, 1972, and people
stood six abreast in block-long lines. The movie was an unmitigated commercial and critical success. By mid-April it was bringing in $1 million a
day. After its first run it had taken in $86.2 million, making it the highest
grossing movie in history. By the end of its second run, *The Godfather*
had earned over $150 million—establishing Coppola as Hollywood's most
lucrative and powerful director. Peter Biskind writes that the movie "hit
a cultural nerve. It was all things to all people, which is perhaps, as mar-
keters would soon realize, a sine qua non for blockbusters."

Indeed, the distribution pattern for Coppola's movie broke new ground. It opened in 316 theaters, adding fifty more by the second week, and it played in five first-run theaters in New York City alone. Never before had a movie enjoyed such broad and aggressive distribution. That approach ensured that if the movie were a hit with audiences, its success with critics would have little effect on its overall popularity. In the future, movies such as *Jaws* and *Star Wars* would gross the unheard-of sums of hundreds of millions of dollars by flooding the market with products that had mass appeal. Satisfying critics became a secondary concern. Ironically, *The Godfather*, made by a veteran of the film school generation and a leader of the New Hollywood, ushered in the era of the blockbuster.[25]

Pauline Kael began her review of Coppola's movie by declaring: "if ever there was a great example of how the best popular movies come out of a merger of commerce and art, *The Godfather* is it." The theme of art that entertains ran through a number of reviews, including Vincent Canby's in the *New York Times:* "Francis Ford Coppola," he exclaimed, "has made one of the most brutal and moving chronicles of American life ever designed within the limits of popular entertainment." William Pechter wrote that the movie possessed "that special excitement and authority available to a film which is both a work of artistic seriousness and one of truly popular appeal, a mass entertainment made without pandering or condescension." Similar to *Bonnie and Clyde*, Coppola's films existed for the moment and while it did it was truly and abundantly significant.[26]

And yet, since these were the days of Andy Warhol's factory mass-producing priceless works of art, contradictions inherent in the merging of mass culture and art persisted. Peter Biskind recounts in his book *Easy Riders, Raging Bulls* a scene that followed a party at agent Freddie Fields's house outside Hollywood. Hot directors Coppola, Friedkin, and Bogdanovich happened to pull up alongside each other at a stoplight. The first two were in Coppola's Mercedes 600 stretch limousine, a gift from Paramount because *The Godfather* had grossed over $50 million. Bogdanovich was in his Volvo station wagon with his wife Polly (whom he would soon give up for Cybill Shepherd). Well-lubricated from the party, Friedkin poked his head though the limo's sunroof in order to quote the rave reviews he had received for directing the Oscar-winning movie *The French Connection*. "Not to be outdone," Biskind writes, "Bogdanovich poked his head out the window of the Volvo, recited a line from one of his reviews which he had apparently committed to memory.

Francis, large and bearded, thrust himself through the sunroof and bellowed, "*The Godfather,* a hundred and fifty million dollars!" One and all, struggling artists in action.

Even though this example illustrates the vulgarity of Hollywood, it also highlights the paradox of taking movies seriously. At long last, movies had earned respect that consistently eluded them for most of the century. Moreover, the first generation of filmmakers and filmgoers to mature under the new movie culture had performed brilliantly, producing some of the greatest movies of all time and recognizing those achievements. Yet the underside of this renaissance revealed a growing detachment from reality.

Stephen Farber reflected on the financial success of *Midnight Cowboy* and *Easy Rider,* arguing, "I really don't think this audience is any more enlightened than mass audiences of the past, though it does seem to be slightly more tolerant of movies it doesn't fully understand." Farber believed that the movie industry and the audience's relationship with it had not changed all that much over the years—no matter what the 1960s generation thought of the over-thirty population. "There is really no point in idealizing the young audience," he contended. "If a movie happens to feed their fantasies, they will embrace it." Much of the perceived radicalism found in movies such as *Easy Rider, Alice's Restaurant,* and *Medium Cool* had been around in the American past for a long time. More recent movies simply played on contemporary fantasies, just as popular movies of the past had constructed myths on the foundations of the American West, heterosexual romance, and moral heroes. The most important difference was preference for antiheroes over heroes and antimyths over myths.[27]

Theater critic Robert Brustein had taken note of that change in attitude in a long, quite prescient essay published in *Film Quarterly* in 1959. Brustein observed a fading of more traditional Hollywood screen fantasy and a rise of cinematic realism in pictures such as *On the Waterfront, Baby Doll,* and *The Long Hot Summer.* To account for that trend, Brustein believed that television had stolen an increasingly larger percentage of the movie audience and foreign films had begun to make money by updating older Hollywood genres with scenes from the youth culture. In response to shifts in demographics and taste, Hollywood began raiding the reservoir of "realist" talent on the New York stage, sets changed to locations, stars became method actors, and the magic of moviegoing took people to the streets of their time rather than to Oz. In an attempt to put this in perspective, Brustein argued that new movie realism was no less fantastic than the fantasies of earlier movies. "Now the anti-hero is the central character in the anti-myth in which the 'real' is juxtaposed with the 'illusion,' the tawdry with the grand." *Bonnie and Clyde* might be different from gangster pictures of the past, but it was no more profound. No one could deny, however, that the movie meant something important to American society—it was, after all, the movie that broke the spell of Bosley Crowther, making traditional movie criticism obsolete.[28]

Ironically, the future held a similar fate for the critics who replaced him. Trends that had made fleeting heroes of the film school generation would ultimately undermine the conditions that made its era heroic. The success of Coppola's *The Godfather* had introduced a new type of blockbuster, and even though the director had little to do with marketing his picture, the hope that art and entertainment could merge in an amicable union was simply not possible. It had taken thirty years to overcome the traditions on which Crowther's generation of critics based their authority, and an acceleration of cultural change would bite the succeeding generation of critics. That last group had benefited from the redefinition of art in the 1960s because it had given cultural authority to movie critics, allowing them to champion masterpieces on the screen. But questioning cultural authority did not cease once the film generation began writing. Instead, the rationale for criticism itself underwent significant changes, making it increasingly difficult for critics to speak to large audiences— either because moviegoers could care less what a reviewer said about a "big" movie or because critics had become increasingly irrelevant as the power to judge cultural worth grew more ambiguous. For the moving picture world, the question was no longer whether movies were art, but whither criticism?

10

Whither Criticism?

Penelope Gilliatt, a critic who split reviewing duties at the *New Yorker* with Pauline Kael, recognized that by the late 1960s and early 1970s being "filmic is always groovy." But, she asked, "Does anyone else have fatal visions of carefully educated people getting more and more groovy and less and less intelligent?"[1]

Gilliatt also clearly shared Kael's misgivings over the attitude of the film generation. As pithy as Gilliatt's observation might seem, she hinted at a paradox of that era. Although movies had accumulated cultural capital, that development had happened at the expense of more traditional notions of art and criticism. During the 1960s and early 1970s, an older generation of authorities—in fields as varied as culture, religion, education, and foreign affairs—came under fire and slowly gave up ground to groups more interested in the ability to question such authority than to create a new set of national assumptions. It was becoming increasingly apparent that in order for society and culture to "loosen up," criticism would no longer depend on a notion of cultural authority common to past generations. Being filmic would indeed prove quite timely because it was mildly rebellious, but the vogue for movies made many critics wonder what had been lost in the effort to be so groovy.

An example of the strange atmosphere that had begun to surround the world of criticism was the attention given mass media at Expo '67, the same venue at which *Bonnie and Clyde* premiered. In Montreal, the world of the arts conceded the mantle of significance (or, at least, relevance) to the world of media. Reporting for *Life* magazine, Frank Kappler observed that the sixties generation responded "to the shock effect of total-immersion, multiple-screen, multi-track movies with the same personal involvement that their grandfathers felt in reading *The Adventures of Tom Sawyer*." The exhibitions he saw fit the new catch phrase "mixed-media," or the layering of images and sounds in nonlinear formats.

Marshall McLuhan, author of seminal tracts on media such as *The Medium Is the Message, The Gutenberg Galaxy,* and *Understanding Media,* became an instant intellectual celebrity for rationalizing this postliterate world. For at least one critic of McLuhan, though, his message was mere massage: it contained little more than intuitive responses to trends that became important because they were new. Much the way universities were responding to the youth culture, McLuhan and others thought they had found something profound in the fact that a generation of Americans had been raised with televisions in their homes and movies in their lives. The perception emerged that the electronic generation was significant because it was different, with little consideration given to why that difference was significant.[2]

To cultural historian John Cawelti, those critics who explored mass culture and media had contributed to the democratization of criticism by "breaking down the walls of snobbery, elitism and status that have been implicit in our habitual cultural categories of highbrow, middlebrow and lowbrow." In a very influential review essay published in the summer of 1968, he discussed a new generation of observers such as McLuhan, Susan Sontag, and even novelist Tom Wolfe, who had illustrated the complexity and richness of cultural forms typically dismissed by intellectuals as worthless or, even worse, harmful to the rest of society. "The traditional attacks on homogenization, standardization and falsity do not mean much to [the new generation], because their own responses are both vital and complex. This does not mean that they confuse pop culture with great art. They find in it another range of experience." Indeed, if one could respond to a cultural form seriously, then the cultural form itself must be serious. Such logic, however, sounded like immature posturing to critics who had participated in the last great cultural rebellion.[3]

A famous essay written by Irving Howe, one of the deans of the New York Intellectuals, served as an autopsy for the ideas and criticism embodied by modernism. Modernist thought had been prominent for the first half of the twentieth century then suffered a kind of extinction in the second half. Howe believed that because "modernism had become successful ... it was no longer a literature of opposition, and thereby had begun that metamorphosis signifying its ultimate death." Modernist art and ideas had once been disreputable and even revolutionary, but by the 1950s modernism had earned a place in the academy and, perhaps worse, in the market. The New Sensibility replaced it—"new" because it offered a way to understand trends in such fields as movies and television that the New York Intellectuals had dismissed as trivial. Howe reviled champions of the New Sensibility not because he disliked the art or culture they praised, but because he (like Dwight Macdonald) rejected their criticism. He considered this group a bunch of nihilists who eschewed the past in favor of an intellectually weightless present. He believed the younger generation of critics went so far as to defend its criticism "through a refusal of both coherence and definition."[4] The rules for debating culture had simply vanished—and with them the reason to engage either those who disagreed with the new critics or the people who watched the stuff the new critics were elevating.

Along the fault line of sixties culture, older authorities—such as the New York Intellectuals—had collapsed. The cultural transformation of movies into art was a result of that seismic shift in culture. The obstacles that had stood in the way of movies earning respect had fallen. As fewer significant differences separated mass culture, popular culture, and art from each other, so too did the distinctiveness of critics melt away. The democratization of criticism seemed to produce a looking-glass effect: the bottom was on top and the top had fallen to the bottom. That fact prompted modernists such as Howe to attack the emergence of a new sensibility in criticism, but it also prompted two essays published no more than a month apart in early 1969 on the new culture of moving pictures.

The first was by Richard Schickel, at that point the author of *The Disney Version* and movie critic for *Life*. Schickel accepted that "film is The Thing," but was troubled by a dilemma unique to audiences in the 1960s: "Movies aren't movies anymore. They are the play-things of the New Class, those who are custodians (or, perhaps, prisoners) of the technostructure. This is, I think, no small point, for it means there has been a fundamental reordering of film's place and function in our society." In short, movies had ceased to be the "art of the masses, truly central to the lives of many people."[5]

But if movies had stopped being themselves, then what had they become? Movies had evolved into a new kind of high art for the new society that had emerged during the 1960s. Schickel believed that movies had made a natural evolution from mass amusement to high art that other cultural forms had traveled. He also noted that film had become the preferred art of "half-baked intellectuals and, the population and educational explosions being what they are, we are very shortly going to have more of them than any class of people."

This new class was quite unlike the traditional cultural elite. Demographically large, economically influential, but not necessarily intellectually rigorous, the film generation rejected the elitism of previous cultural authorities by turning one of the most nonelite aspects of American life into a symbol of cultural rebellion. When Hollywood supplanted the hero with the antihero and revised older genres to take advantage of new affinities for sex and violence, the new rebels claimed (with an aura of cultural pretension) that they had changed the moving picture world if not American society. Schickel wondered whether such arrogance had only alienated a majority of the audience for movies. Had taking movies seriously reached a point of diminishing returns? By accepting film as the latest and most vital art, had the new generation stolen the magic that made them important to the masses in the first place?[6]

The critic who consistently engaged those last two questions was Pauline Kael. In a long essay published a month after Schickel's, Kael discussed why she, an intelligent person, loved movies so much without feeling the need to rationalize that love by appealing to the gods of art. With "Trash, Art, and the Movies," Kael established herself firmly within the tradition of critics who could write intelligently about a mass art without sliding into solemn declarations of their love for it. Throughout most of her essay, Kael mused that what people like about movies has almost nothing to do with art. "There is so much talk now about the art of the film that we may be in danger of forgetting that most of the movies we enjoy are not works of art."

Was there an inherent hypocrisy in taking movies so seriously? People liked movies, Kael suggested, because there were no expectations placed on the audience to catch what had become meaningful or significant to a minority of film buffs. To drag movies into classrooms, journals, and theoretical discussions was not only to undermine the fun of moviegoing, but also to pose as an intellectual without any of the obligations or work that traditionally went along with that distinction. "If it was priggish for an older generation of reviewers to be ashamed of what they enjoyed and to feel they had to be contemptuous of popular entertainment, it's even more priggish," Kael believed, "for a new movie generation to be so proud of what they enjoy that they use their education to try to place trash within the acceptable academic tradition." An example of this strange academic hybrid was a line in museum publication declaring that Josef von Sternberg's *Shanghai Express* (1932) "was completely misunderstood as a mindless adventure" when in fact, Kael suggested, "it was completely *understood* as a mindless adventure. And enjoyed as a mindless adventure."[7]

Kael was hard on the Film Generation because she was extraordinarily sensitive to the relationship between both sides of the motion picture screen. She had used the universal "we" when writing film reviews, assuming that she could speak to moviegoers as part of a common culture in which she wrote. Kael believed that the perceptions of those who sat in theaters had the ability to influence the atmosphere in which movies were made. If that relationship lost its sense of balance and perspective, the worst of all additives could creep in: pretentiousness. "One doesn't expect an *educated* generation to be so soft on itself," she sneered, "much softer than the factory workers of the past who didn't go back over and over to the same movies, mooning away in fixation on themselves and thinking this fixation meant movies had suddenly become an art, and *their* art."[8]

Like Schickel, Kael feared that movies would lose their allure if the cinephilia ascribed to by Sontag and others seeped into and thereby corrupted the relationship between movies and moviegoers. Movies existed between the realms of official culture and pop culture. Movie critics thrived because they were engaged in an act that was mildly rebellious without threatening traditional cultural authority. While poking fun at reviewers such as Bosley Crowther, Kael and other critics remained respectful of commentators who considered movies as important but fleeting experiences. "What draws us to movies in the first place," Kael believed, "is the opening into other, forbidden or surprising, kinds of experience and the vitality and corruption and irreverence of that experience are so direct and immediate and have so little connection with what we have been taught is art." Mass art should not be found in the same places as high art, Kael reasoned, and by straining to find it there only confounded the relationship between the audience and the screen. "But it isn't easy to come to terms with what one enjoys in films," she concluded, "and if an older generation was persuaded to *dismiss* trash, now a younger generation, with the press and the schools in hot pursuit, has begun to talk about trash as if it were really very serious art."[9] With that observation, Kael watched one cast of cultural assumptions fade out, unsure of what would take its place.

Some time in the mid-1980s, during a meeting of the New York Society of Film Critics, Pauline Kael turned to Richard Schickel and sighed: "It isn't fun anymore." "Why do you say that?" Schickel replied. "Remember how it was in the 60s an 70s," Kael asked, "when movies were hot, when *we* were hot? Movies seemed to matter." Kael was right; for a relatively brief moment, movies did matter to a population that read movie critics and believed discussing movies was significant. And yet, just when movies and the critics seemed to hit an intellectual peak, those same critics had begun questioning the new role movies played in American culture. I think one, final example from this era illustrates why that was the case.[10]

Throughout the 1960s, moviegoers were at least aware of, if not engaged with, debates among movie critics. Many people understood that Pauline Kael had profound disagreements with Andrew Sarris, and that John Simon thought very little of either of them. Simon, the erudite critic for the *New Leader* during the 1960s and 1970s, wrote a twenty-five-page introduction to his collection of criticism, *Movies into Film,* in which he concluded that both Kael and Sarris, his competition, were inadequate as film critics. Simon felt it necessary to establish why films—rather than movies—deserved serious criticism. He contended that "to call film movies is, however fondly, to derogate from it; or, more precisely, to view it as an entertainment rather than as an art. The implication is that we go to the movies purely for fun, and to hell with the highbrows, scholars, and other squares who would try to turn movies into Art, with a long-faced upper-case A, and a joyous experience into a cultural obligation." Clearly seeking to dismantle Kael's anti-intellectual approach, Simon observed that if "film were merely an amusement, if it could not and should not go beyond that, there would be little need or justification for publishing a book about it—mine or anyone else's." Simon was equally unimpressed with critics such as Sarris, who turned criticism into "pseudo-learned post-prandial chatter . . . with virtually no critical standards." While both Sarris and Kael have out-shone Simon in historical longevity and influence, all three fell victim to the same plight: irrelevance.[11]

Simon's intention, it seems to me, was to justify film criticism as a craft that was respectable because filmmaking itself was an art and moviegoers should, in an educated society, be informed critics of that art. Yet what both Sarris and Kael understood, and Simon did not, was that movie criticism was a traditional craft in constant conflict with a disreputable art. The appeal of critics like Sarris and Kael came from their enjoyment of playing with that conflict and speaking to audiences who wanted something between scholarly criticism and synoptic reviews.

Many of the best writers on movies—from Vachel Linsday and Gilbert Seldes to Iris Barry, James Agee, Kael, Kauffmann, Schickel, Sarris, and Denby—have understood that as mass art, movies exist between the worlds of entertainment and art. Once the perception of them slides farther toward the world of art—and to the margins of scholarly discourse—the pleasure of reading about movies vanishes for large audiences. People clearly were interested in the transition that movies were undergoing during the 1960s. However, once the suspense ended, movies became the province of either entertainment or art. The mystique of movies as a rebellious art—the most vital art of the day—vanished, and with it fell the power critics had to move people and use discussions of movies as a protest against the critical traditions of the past. The transition of movies into art has, ironically, meant the defeat of the forces that fought hard to get film there. Ultimately, the prestige was in the fight rather than the victory.

Critical debate depends on the past remaining alive enough for the present to recognize, digest, and refute. Without something to fight against—such as the cultural authority of critics—there remains little reason to get excited. Other fields such as history and politics continue to generate debate because each generation has a core of professionals trained to do battle with each other, even if nobody else listens. Yet in order for serious discussions about movies to take place, critics need popular recognition for legitimacy. If moviegoers cease to care about the art of moviegoing, critics cease to matter. In a recent article, *New Yorker* film critic David Denby penetrated to the core of the matter: "The trouble is that critics can no longer appeal to a commonly held set of values."[12]

Champions of a new kind of cultural pluralism have, in an attempt to broaden the debate over culture, made participating in a national discussion almost irrelevant. The New Sensibility ultimately helped redefine the meaning of culture so that it no longer could address a "commonly held set of values," but instead only describe what society has produced. Today, criticism belies the expectation that standards and judgment will stay out of the way. What movie critics of the 1960s and 1970s fought for, it seems to me, was a broadening of the debate over culture to include the mass arts—not an end to criticism.

Each one of us can claim a different reason for thinking movies are significant and for considering them to be or not to be art. The question that has always mattered is not so much if movies are art, but so what if they are? To answer that second question, however, entails accepting some notion of cultural ideals against which to judge our answers. It means that we listen to critics because we believe they have something important to tell us—we invest in them a certain amount of authority. Sometimes we even like it when they use the word "we."

Of course, champions of populist criticism have had good reasons for attacking the cultural standards of the past, since expressions such as jazz and movies had been left out of pantheon of American culture. For example, historian Paul Gorman (a student of Lawrence Levine's) has argued that because Seldes failed to consider "the role of the public in initially shaping the entertainments and the subsequent tailoring of the arts to meet popular tastes, he could not understand how these forms were both artists' interpretations and social expressions at the same time." True enough, but what is not an expression of society? In other words, by including all aspects of life in one's view of culture, it becomes very difficult to recognize why anyone should care about what is included in that view. Although it is no doubt an improvement to consider "the public in all its dimensions," it surely is not wise to leave our judgment at that. For the best critics of the past, finding a way to discriminate among all the arts—from mass to fine—required preserving distinctions important to their work as critics.[13]

At one time it seemed fruitful to welcome the decline of criticism. I think from a contemporary perspective that development has been generally disheartening, not so much because critics overlooked important movements in the arts or because they made statements that were flat out wrong, but because they represented a challenge to both the artists and the public. Critics and their work have served a function in society: to remind creators and audiences that a relationship exists between us all. Moreover, as Russell Jacoby has suggested, those who currently champion the people's culture seem to end up writing for everybody but the people and, in the process, "trample the culture they supposedly love."[14] Obviously, the work of a few scholars has not created the problems under which movie critics now suffer. These scholars have only identified (or even identify with) the state of cultural criticism. But with the vanishing of cultural authority, and with it the popular relevance of criticism, a melancholy has settled over the world of the arts.

When many of America's finest movie critics began their careers, discussions about movies were part of a much larger debate over national culture and the roles artists, critics, and the public played in creating it. Unfortunately, the late 1960s marked the beginning of the end of that discussion. By the early 1970s, debate over culture had shifted from what "we" as a people want out of life to how we as millions of people live those lives. The meaning of culture has fractured into parts that no longer need to be defined within a common culture. Movies continue to be the perfect vehicle for such national discussions. Moreover, because their influence can seem overwhelmingly diffuse, it remains important to have a venue in which critics and audiences grapple with the dynamics of this mass art. When modernism showed us that art exists in everyday life—even in movie theaters—American culture expanded. When criticism helped make sense of the intersection between art and life, our discussions grew more vital and lively. It is sad, therefore, that today movie critics appear powerless to help us discover the art of moviegoing—for we miss out on the surprises that await all of us in the dark.

Notes

Introduction

1. Sontag, "Decay of Cinema," p. 60. See also Sontag, "A Century of Cinema," pp. 23–28; Schickel, "Cinema Paradiso," p. 67; Kauffmann, "A Lost Love?" p. 28; and Denby, "Moviegoers," p. 100.

2. Schickel, "Cinema Paradiso," p. 59; Sontag, "Decay of Cinema," p. 61.

3. Denby, "Moviegoers," p. 100; Sontag, "Decay of Cinema," p. 60.

4. Andrew Sarris, "Why the Foreign Film Has Lost Its Cachet," *New York Times,* May 2, 1999, sec. 2A, p. 15.

5. Danto, *After the End of Art,* pp. 13, 34, 37.

6. Roger Ebert, "Film, the Snubbed Art," *New York Times,* Oct. 27, 1997, p 22. See also Ackerman, "Pulitzer Prizes for the Cinema," p. 15; and Hubler, "A Pulitzer for Motion Pictures," p. 7–10.

7. Caryn James, "Four Directors in Seminar on Movies," *New York Times,* June 23, 1988, sec. C, pp. 17, 21.

8. Levine, *Highbrow/Lowbrow,* p. 7.

9. Macdonald, "Masscult and Midcult," in *Against the American Grain,* passim. See also Clement Greenberg, "Avant-Garde and Kitsch," in *Mass Culture,* ed. Rosenberg and White, pp. 98–107.

10. Two recent books speak directly to the paradoxical implications of democratizing criticism and culture. See Kammen, *American Culture, American Tastes,* pp. 133–61; and Jacoby, *End of Utopia,* pp. 67–99.

Chapter 1. Amusement or Art?

1. Agee, *A Death in the Family,* p. 17.

2. Lounsbury, *Origins of American Film Criticism.* Myron Lounsbury's pioneering study on early film criticism has shown that this failure was not from a lack of trying. By producing an encyclopedic view of the first thirty years of writing on film, Lounsbury's work helps to explain the aesthetic approaches of film critics long forgotten but quite influential. The critics he included were fas-

cinated by the moving picture and found it important enough to chronicle as an industry and an art. Lounsbury argued that such writing remains significant as the cultural and intellectual origins of contemporary film criticism. However, while Lounsbury collected as much as he could find about the emergence of film aesthetics, his study reflected little more than a wide diversity of critical opinions agreeing that film was indeed art.

3. Hugo Münsterberg, *Photoplay,* p. 99.

4. H. May, *End of American Innocence,* pp. 28, 30–76; and Alexander, *Here the Country Lies,* p. 33.

5. H. May, *End of American Innocence,* p. 51.

6. Alexander, *Here the Country Lies,* p. 75.

7. Paul Gorman has suggested that Oppenheim, Frank, and Brooks subscribed to a radicalism that might best be described "as a philosophical inclination toward change rather than a specific program built around one aesthetic style" (Gorman, *Left Intellectuals and Popular Culture,* p. 55).

8. Gorman finds such sentiments exasperating. The treatment of movies illustrated "just how weak was the cultural radicals' acceptance of mass arts. Such forms were useful for enlivening the art world, but were inevitably detached from the popular milieu in which they were shaped and tested" (ibid., p. 75).

9. Bourne, "Heart of the People," p. 233.

10. Among the best works dealing with the effects of mass mediums on the American population are Gorman, *Left Intellectuals and Popular Culture,* pp. 34–52, 83–107; Koszarski, *An Evening's Entertainment,* pp. 1–62; Jowett, *Film,* pp. 23–45, 74–102; Sklar, *Movie-Made America,* pp. 3–66; L. May, *Screening Out the Past,* pp. 3–21; and Czitrom, *Media and the American Mind,* pp. 30–59.

11. Patterson, "Nickelodeons," p. 11.

12. "A Democratic Art," p. 193.

13. "Birth of a New Art," p. 8.

14. Lounsbury, *Origins of American Film Criticism,* pp. 28, 12–27. Stanley Kauffmann also included a selection of Woods's criticism in his compilation of early film reviews, *American Film Criticism,* pp. 30, 34, 37.

15. Kauffmann, *American Film Criticism,* p. 37.

16. Lounsbury, *Origins of American Film Criticism,* pp. 17–20.

17. Lounsbury, "Flashes of Lighting," pp. 777, 788–89.

18. Bush, "Film of the Future," p. 172.

19. Bush, "Do Longer Films Make Better Shows?" p. 275.

20. "Lay Press and the Picture," p. 1.

21. Dale, "Film Criticism in the Lay Press," p. 1.

22. Jackson, "Moving Picture 'World,'" p. 931.

23. Harrison, "Mr. Lowbrow," p. 21.

24. Koszarski, *An Evening's Entertainment,* p. 193.

25. Johnson, "Close-Ups," p. 119.

26. Ibid., Aug. 1915, pp. 121, 123.

27. Ibid., Mar. 1916, p. 59.

28. Ibid., May 1916, p. 66; and July 1916, p. 76.

29. Johnson, "Aren't You Tired of Trash?" pp. 27, 63; and "Close-Ups," *Photoplay Magazine,* Apr. 1917, p. 101.

30. Quirk, "Art and Democracy," p. 1.

31. Quirk, "Fifth Estate," p. 17; and idem., "Realism v. Idealism," pp. 75, 76.

32. See Wolfe, *Vachel Lindsay;* Lounsbury, *Origins of American Film Criticism,* pp. 50–58, 74–77; Lindsay, *Progress and Poetry of the Movies,* pp. 1–101; Jowett, *Film,* pp. 89–90, 98–99; and Klawans, "Mute and Glorious Miltons," pp. 82–84.

33. Lindsay, *Art of the Moving Picture,* pp. 45, 47.

34. Stanley Kauffmann, "Introduction," in Lindsay, *Art of the Moving Picture,* pp. xvi, xvii; and Czitrom, *Media and the American Mind,* pp. 58–59.

35. Myron Lounsbury, "Introduction," in Lindsay, *Progress and Poetry of the Movies,* p. 3.

36. Lindsay, *Art of the Moving Picture,* p. 281.

37. Jameson, "Endowed Photoplay," pp. 26, 77.

38. Richard Griffith, "Introduction," in Münsterberg, *Photoplay,* pp. 13–14.

39. Ibid., p. 8.

40. Münsterberg, *Photoplay,* pp. 17, 100.

41. Ibid., pp. 24, 46.

42. Ibid., p. 93.

43. Ibid., pp. 95, 97–98.

44. Ibid., pp. 97, 99–100.

45. Lindsay, "Photoplay Progress," pp. 76–77.

46. Griffith, "Introduction," pp. 9–10.

47. See Freeburg, *Art of Photoplay Making,* "Preface."

48. Ibid., pp. 20, 25.

49. Ibid., p. 204.

50. Ibid., p. 267.

51. Lounsbury, *Origins of American Film Criticism,* pp. 41–47; and Jowett, *Film,* p. 58.

52. Eaton, "Canned Drama," p. 499.

53. Eaton, "Class-Consciousness and the 'Movies,'" pp. 48–56.

54. Ibid., p. 52.

55. Eaton, "Art of the Motion Picture," p. 218.

56. Ibid.

57. Ibid.

58. Ibid.

Chapter 2. Menace or Art?

1. Jowett, *Film,* p. 110.

2. Ibid., p. 113. Film historian Garth Jowett has noted that the failure of New York's mayor to secure stiffer laws against the movies said a great deal about the position movies had attained in people's lives; "The strength of public support

for the exhibitors indicated that the mayor and the religious groups and other pressure groups behind the action had grossly underestimated the importance of the motion picture house as a recreational activity for the ordinary people of New York City."

3. *Mutual Film Corporation v Industrial Commission of Ohio,* 236, sec. 230–47 (U.S. Supreme Court).

4. Hawley, *Great War and the Search for a Modern Order,* pp. 2, 12, 50; Alexander, *Here the Country Lies,* pp. 76–102; Allen, *Only Yesterday,* pp. 188–203; Douglas, *Terrible Honesty,* pp. 3–73; Dumenil, *Modern Temper,* pp. 145–200; Fass, *The Damned and the Beautiful,* pp. 291–378; Gorman, *Left Intellectuals and Popular Culture,* pp. 53–82; Green, *New York 1913,* pp. 47–128; Jacoby, *Last Intellectuals,* pp. 27–53; Lasch, *New Radicalism in America,* pp. 104–80; Nash, *Nervous Generation,* pp. 33–125; Ware, *Greenwich Village,* pp. 3–9, 422–26; and Steel, *Walter Lippmann,* pp. 245–56.

5. "Is the Younger Generation in Peril?" pp. 9–12, 58, 61, 63, 66–67, 69–70, 72–73.

6. *Chicago Tribune,* "Girls' Claim to Fame as 'Vamps' Worries School," Mar. 1, 1919, p. 13.

7. Sheldon, "Moving Pictures, Books, and Child Crime," p. 243.

8. Fass, *The Damned and the Beautiful,* p. 25. See also Davis, *Response to Innovation,* pp. 12–27, 46–63; Behrman, "Movie Morals," pp. 100–101; and "Morals and the Movies," p. 581.

9. *Chicago Tribune,* "The Police and Social Vice," July 19, 1918, p. 6.

10. Ibid., July 18, 1918, p. 6.

11. Ibid., July 19, 1918, p. 7.

12. Chicago Motion Picture Committee (hereafter CMPC), *Report,* p. 7.

13. *Moving Picture World,* "Illinois Women's Clubs Ban Sensational Pictures," Feb. 1, 1919, p. 612.

14. CMPC, *Report,* pp. 6, 8.

15. Ibid., p. 27.

16. Ibid., p. 18, 46.

17. Bourne, "Heart of the People," p. 233; Braun, "Censoring the Censor," pp. 193–96; "Yes, There Is No Art in the Movies?" pp. 73–74.

18. On the intersection between movie power and psychology see Münsterberg, *Photoplay,* pp. 96–98.

19. CMPC, *Report,* pp. 16, 17.

20. Ibid., pp. 105–106, 109.

21. Ibid., pp. 93, 95, 100, 101.

22. Ibid., pp. 80, 82, 83.

23. Jowett, *Film,* pp. 119–22. Jowett quotes the Supreme Court's 1915 *Mutual Film Corporation v Ohio* decision: "It cannot be put out of view that the exhibition of moving pictures is a business pure and simple, originated and conducted for profit, like other spectacles, not to be regarded, nor intended to be regarded as part of the press of the country or as organs of public opinion." See also Seabury,

Public and the Motion Picture Industry, pp. 143–59; Oberholtzer, "Censor and the Movie 'Menace'," pp. 641–47; Clayton, "Cinema and Its Censor," pp. 222–28; MacMahon, "Big Shears—Or Common Sense?" pp. 662, 679; Braun, "Censoring the Censor," pp. 193–96.

24. Sklar, *Movie-Made America,* p. 131. Both were part of an organization that would soon be supplanted by the more powerful MPPDA.

25. Ibid., p. 131; Schwartz, *Genius of the System,* pp. 69–157.

26. CMPC, *Report,* pp. 159, 160, 170.

27. Ibid., p. 171

28. Ibid., p. 176. See also Sklar, *Movie-Made America,* pp. 131–32.

29. CMPC, *Report,* p. 176.

30. Sklar, *Movie-Made America,* p. 132. Sklar continues: "If this is true, it is likely that the selection of Will Hays as 'czar' of the motion picture industry in December 1921 was not a sudden response to the Arbuckle and Taylor scandals of that year, but the end result of a collaboration over several years."

31. Ibid., pp. 16–17. See also Jowett, *Film,* p. 135. In 1921, two scandals rocked Hollywood. Roscoe "Fatty" Arbuckle, a very popular comedian in the 1910s, had been suspected of murder after one of his female guests died at an all-weekend party in his hotel suite. Arbuckle was never convicted of the crime, although he stood trial for it three times. During Arbuckle's first trial, director William Desmond Taylor was found murdered in his home. Both incidents destroyed the careers of all those involved and prompted producers to run for the safety of Will Hays, the new movie czar. See Sklar, *Movie-Made America,* pp. 78–85.

32. *Moving Picture World,* May 17, 1919, p. 1023.

33. CMPC, *Report,* pp. 27, 29.

34. Ibid., p. 33.

35. Ibid., p. 25.

Chapter 3. Forging a Mainstream Movie Aesthetic

1. Feldman, *National Board of Censorship,* pp. 62–66, 216–17.

2. Barrett, "Work of the National Board of Review," pp. 175–77.

3. Jowett, *Film,* pp. 135. For a more optimistic assessment see, Feldman, *National Board of Censorship,* pp. 206–19.

4. *Films in Review* is the present-day title of the NBR's journal.

5. "Censorship and the Art of the Screen," p. 6.

6. "Editorial," *Exceptional Photoplays,* Dec. 1920, p. 1.

7. Kuttner, "Better Pictures," p. 7.

8. "Aesthetic vs. Moralistic Censorship," p. 8.

9. Kuttner, "A Question of Faith," p. 6.

10. "Is It Art?" p. 3; and "More Art," p. 3.

11. Reinhardt, "Screen Visions," p. 4.

12. Spearing, "Movies," p. 4.

13. See also Lounsbury, *Origins of American Film Criticism,* pp. 133–35, 153–54.

14. Block, "Movies versus Motion Pictures," p. 892. The phrase used in regard to independent stage productions, the Little Theatre movement, was also used for movies until critics began calling it the Little Cinema movement.

15. Spearing, "A Valuable Service," p. 1.

16. Kuttner, "Editorial Comment," p. 9.

17. Kuttner, "Motion Pictures and the Photoplay," p. 3.

18. Kuttner, "A Place for the Photoplay," p. 3; idem., "Exceptional Photoplay," p. 3; and idem., "Needed—One Free Screen on Broadway," p. 3.

19. Patterson, "Signs and Portents," p. 4.

20. Kuttner, "Foreign Invasion," pp. 1–2.

21. Kuttner, "The Little Motion Picture Theatre," p. 3.

22. Ibid.

23. Gould, "Little Theatre Movement in the Cinema," p. 4.

24. Clarke, "Special Feature for the Special Audience," pp. 7–8.

25. Kuttner, "More Anent the Little Theatre," p. 5; and Kuttner, "Proof of the Pudding," pp. 3–4.

26. Gunczy, "Bloodless Revolt," p. 3.

27. See, in particular, Bakshy, "Future of the Movies," pp. 360–64.

28. H.L. Mencken, "Appendix from Moronia," in *Authors on Film*, ed. Geduld, pp. 101–2.

29. Celia Harris, "Movies and the Elizabethan Theater," pp. 29–31. See also Myron Lounsbury's discussion of Mark Van Doren's writing in the mid-1930s, in which Van Doren employs a similar comparison to Shakespeare's plays (Lounsbury, *Origins of American Film Criticism*, pp. 405–6).

30. Harris, "Movies and the Elizabethan Theater," p. 31.

31. Dwight Macdonald, "Our Elizabethan Movies," in *On Movies*, pp. 65–66.

32. Seldes, *Seven Lively Arts*, pp. 30, 286, 288.

33. Ibid., pp. 293–94.

34. Ibid., pp. 292, 297, 298.

35. Ibid., pp. 13, 16; Kammen, *Lively Arts*, p. 215; and Lounsbury, *Origins of American Film Criticism*, p. 484.

36. Seldes, "'Art' in the Movies," p. 148; and Seldes, "A Letter to the International Film Art Guild," pp. 332–33.

37. Seldes, *Seven Lively Arts*, pp. 4–5.

38. Barry, *Let's Go to the Pictures*, p. viii.

39. Ibid., p. ix.

40. Ibid., pp. 191, 263.

41. Ibid., pp. 193–94.

Chapter 4. Dreiser versus Hollywood

1. Fine, *West of Eden*, p. 2.

2. Bauer, "Movies Tackle Literature," pp. 288, 294.

3. Fine, *West of Eden*, p. 14; and Dreiser, "Real Sins of Hollywood," p. 211.

4. Kazin, *On Native Grounds*, p. 87.

5. Swanberg, *Dreiser*, pp. 105, 186; and N. Leonard, "Theodore Dreiser and the Film," pp. 8, 9.

6. Dreiser, "Dreiser on Hollywood," pp. 16, 17.

7. Quoted in Lingeman, *Theodore Dreiser*, p. 322.

8. "Statement of Theodore Dreiser, re: An American Tragedy," June 18, 1931, Theodore Dreiser Collection, Department of Special Collections, Van Pelt-Dietrich Library Center, University of Pennsylvania (hereafter, TDC), MS collection 30, box 124, folder 7053, pp. 1–3; and Schatz, *Genius of the System*, pp. 76–78.

9. Sergei Eisenstein to Dreiser, undated, TDC, MS collection 30, box 124, folder 7052, pp. 1, 2; and Ivor Montagu to Dreiser, Aug. 10, 1931, ibid., p. 1.

10. Eisenstein to Dreiser, undated, p. 1.

11. Schatz, *Genius of the System*, pp. 77–78.

12. Dreiser to Jesse L. Lasky, Mar. 10, 1931, TDC, MS collection 30, box 124, folder 7053, exhibit 7, pp. 1, 2.

13. Lasky to Dreiser, Mar. 14, 1931, ibid., folder 7054, p. 1.

14. Swanberg, *Dreiser*, p. 369. W.A. Swanberg, Dreiser's first biographer, reflected that "although this clause gave lip service to Dreiser's demands, the ultimate authority to accept or reject his advice rested with Paramount."

15. Dreiser to Lasky, Mar. 17, 1931, TDC, MS collection 30, box 124, folder 7054, exhibit 9, p. 1; and "Editorial," *Commonweal*, Apr. 22, 1931, p. 677.

16. B.P. Schulberg to Dreiser, Apr. 1,1931, TDC, MS collection 30, box 124, folder 7054, exhibit 11.

17. Although Hays was head of the MPPDA, the organization responsible for censoring thousands of Hollywood movies including *An American Tragedy*, Dreiser apparently believed he had a decent working relationship with the "Movie Czar." See, "Theodore Dreiser, Affidavit," TDC, MS collection 30, box 124, folder 7054, p. 10; and "Statement of Theodore Dreiser," p. 7.

18. Dreiser to W.H. Hays, undated, TDC, MS collection 30, box 124, folder 7054, exhibit 12.

19. Swanberg, *Dreiser*, p. 374; and Murray, *Cinematic Imagination*, p. 121.

20. Dreiser to Harrison Smith, Apr. 25, 1931, *Letters of Theodore Dreiser*, ed. Elias, pp. 527, 529.

21. Swanberg, *Dreiser*, p. 376.

22. Barrett H. Clark to Dreiser, June 16, 1931, TDC, MS collection 30, box 124, folder 7054, exhibit 23.

23. Arthur G. Hays and Arthur C. Hume to Paramount Publix Company, June 26, 1931, TDC, MS collection 30, box 124, folder 7053.

24. Dreiser to Lasky, undated, ibid., pp. 1, 3; and "Shaw Draws Fire From Hollywood," *New York Times*, Mar. 3, 1931, p. 6.

25. Dreiser to Lasky, undated, pp.17–18.

26. See statements by Albert Lasker, Robert E. MacAlarney, G.P. Putnam, James R. Quirk, Lowell Brentano, Charles Brackett, Sheppard Butler, Corey Ford, Lewis Gensler, John Golden, and Owen Johnson, TDC, MS collection 30, box 124, folder 7053; "Testimony of B.P. Schulberg," July 18, 1931, ibid., p. 12; and Dreiser to Louise Campbell, Aug. 5, 1931, *Letters of Theodore Dreiser,* ed. Elias, p. 562.

27. Judge Graham Witschief, *Theodore Dreiser v Paramount-Publix Corporation,* Aug. 2, 1931, TDC, MS collection 30, box 124, folder 7054, pp. 1, 3.

28. Dreiser to Campbell, Aug. 5, 1931, p. 562.

29. Dreiser, "Real Sins of Hollywood," p. 206.

30. Ibid., p. 208.

31. Lingeman, *Theodore Dreiser,* p. 364.

32. Swanberg, *Dreiser,* p. 377; Lingeman, *Theodore Drieser,* p. 346; Nancy Lee, "Dreiser Goes to Battle for 'American Tragedy,'" July 12, 1931, TDC, MS collection 30, box 124, folder 7053; "Editorial," *New Republic,* Apr. 22, 1931, p. 258; and "Editorial," *Commonweal,* Apr. 22, 1931, p. 667.

33. Frank Dennis, "Theodore Dreiser Is Fighting Author's and Public's Battle," *Kansas City Star,* Aug. 2, 1931, p. 6D; and "Dreiser's Fight with Hollywood," *Chicago Tribune,* Aug. 3, 1931, p. 10.

34. John P. Fort, "Dreiser's Tilt with the Cinema; Difficult Task Given the Actors," *Chattanooga News,* Aug. 15, 1931, p. 16; as quoted in "Tragicomedy of 'An American Tragedy,'" *Literary Digest,* Sept. 5, 1931, pp. 18, 19.

35. Josephson, "Dreiser, Reluctant, in the Films," p. 22; Bakshy, "Emasculated Dreiser," p. 237; and Wilson, "Eisenstein in Hollywood," p. 321.

36. Potamkin, "Novel into Film," pp. 267–68.

37. Gorman, *Left Intellectuals and Popular Culture,* pp. 119–20; and Jacobs, ed., *Compound Cinema.* See, in particular, "The Eyes of the Movies," pp. 243–69.

38. Potamkin, "Novel into Film," p. 268.

39. "Dreiser in Court Calls Lynch Liar," *White Plains (New York) Press,* July 22, 1931.

40. Potamkin, "Novel into Film," pp. 270, 273.

41. Some historians contend that Dreiser's argument with Hollywood illustrated its ideological bias. Richard Maltby believes that censors working for the MPPDA operated under the terms of an "affirmative culture." Negotiations that went on behind closed doors between producers, writers, directors, and the MPPDA shaped a set of ground rules for material found unsuitable for Hollywood—"the purveyor of fictions for mass consumption." Thus, Dreiser's novel, with its clear social message, hardly stood a chance because "its detailed actions and its thematic concerns were inappropriate to an affirmative medium." Lea Jacobs has reached a similar conclusion, arguing that, in a sense, Dreiser targeted the wrong party in his suit. The producers and especially director von Sternberg were helpless in the face of the overbearing ideology of the censors. See Richard Maltby, "'To Prevent the Prevalent Type of Book:' Censorship and Adaptation in Hollywood, 1924–1934," in *Movie Censorship and American Cul-*

ture, ed. Couvares, pp. 100, 103, 107; and Jacobs, "*An American Tragedy,*" pp. 90, 93.

42. Strychacz, "Dreiser's Suit Against Paramount," pp. 199–200.

Chapter 5. Movies into Art

1. Levine, *Highbrow/Lowbrow,* p. 149; Harris, *Cultural Excursions,* pp. 17, 225; and Paul DiMaggio, "Cultural Entrepreneurship in Nineteenth Century Boston: The Creation of an Organizational Base for High Culture in America," in *Rethinking Popular Culture,* ed. Mukerji and Schudson, p. 376. Levine writes that "the new meaning that became attached to such words as 'art,' 'aesthetics,' and 'culture' in the second half of the nineteenth century symbolized the consciousness that conceived of the fine, the worthy, and the beautiful as existing apart from ordinary society." See also Carol Duncan, *Civilizing Rituals,* p. 9, in which she contends: "what we see and do not see in art museums—and on what terms and by whose authority we do or do not see it—is closely linked to larger questions about who constitutes the community and who defines its identity."

2. Harris, *Cultural Excursions,* pp. 65–66.

3. Russell Lynes, *Lively Audience,* pp. 316–17, 321, 352, 378; Alfred H. Barr Jr., "Notes on Departmental Expansion of the Museum," June 24, 1932, box 01-02, p. 6, Early Material, Department of Film, Museum of Modern Art, New York (hereafter cited as DOF, MoMA); and Barr, "Films and the Museum," p. 1.

4. Lynes, *Good Old Modern,* p. 108; and Barry, "Film Library and How It Grew," p. 20.

5. Montagu, "Birmingham Sparrow," p. 106; Barry, "Film Library and How It Grew," p. 21; and Lynes, *Good Old Modern,* p. 108.

6. Thornton Delehanty, "Iris Barry," box 01-16, p. 4, Early Material, DOF, MoMA.

7. Barr, "The 1929 Multidepartmental Plan for the Museum of Modern Art: Its Origins, Development, and Partial Realization," box 15A, p. 1, Special Collections, DOF, MoMA; and Barr, "Notes on Departmental Expansion," pp. 5–6.

8. Barr, "Films and the Museum," p. 3.

9. Slide, *Nitrate Won't Wait,* p. 5.

10. Ibid., 6.

11. John Abbot and Iris Barry, "An Outline of a Project for Founding the Film Library," Apr. 17, 1935, box 01-05, Early Material, DOF, MoMA, pp. 5–6; and Barry, "Film Library and How It Grew," p. 21.

12. Abbot and Barry, "An Outline of a Project," pp. 8–9.

13. Ibid., p. 3. Gilbert Seldes also sought to incorporate many types of movies into a film aesthetic. See his *An Hour with the Movies.*

14. Ibid., p. 2.

15. John Reddington, as quoted in "Sanctuary for Film Art," p. 22; Barry, "Film Library and How It Grew," p. 20.

16. Frank S. Nugent, "Celluloid Pageant," *New York Times Magazine,* July 18,

1937, sec. 10.

17. Barry, "Film Library and How It Grew," pp. 22–23.

18. Barry, "Film Library, 1935–1941," pp. 5–7.

19. John E. Abbott, "Pickford Dinner Speech," Aug. 25, 1935, box 02-D, John Abbott Speeches, Library of Congress Material, DOF, MoMA, pp. 2–5.

20. Barry, "Film Library, 1935–1941," p. 5.

21. Barry, "Founding of the Film Library," pp. 2–3.

22. Ibid., p. 5.

23. Ibid., pp. 5–6; Seldes, *Seven Lively Arts;* Seldes, *An Hour with the Movies,* passim.

24. Barry, "Museum of Modern Art Film Library," p. 16.

25. Barry's influence on the formation of the French film library, the Cinémathèque, was later recognized by its founder, Henri Langlois, when he supported awarding her the Legion d'Honneur for her part in promoting film history and preservation.

26. It was generally accepted among the staff at the Film Library that Iris Barry wrote the speeches Abbott gave throughout the first few years (Lynes, *Good Old Modern,* pp. 109, 332–33).

27. Abbott, "The Motion Picture and the Museum," 1935, box 02-D, John Abbott Speeches, Library Of Congress Material, DOF, MoMA, pp. 1, 2; Abbott, "Mr. Abbott's Talk at Mrs. Pratt's," Nov. 26, 1935, ibid., p. 1.

28. Abbott, "Motion Picture and the Museum," p. 4; Abbott, untitled speech, Feb. 7, 1936, box 02-D, John Abbott Speeches, Library of Congress Material, DOF, MoMA, p. 8.

29. Abbott, "The Film as Museum Piece," 1936, box 02-D, John Abbott Speeches, Library of Congress Material, DOF, MoMA, p. 12.

30. Many writers about Barry and the Film Library believe she had such success in acquiring films because of her unpretentious approach to her assignment and the entire motion picture world. See, Richard Griffith, "Film Collection of the Museum of Modern Art," undated, box 12–10, general files, DOF, MoMA, pp. 10–13; Alistair Cooke, "To Iris Barry (1895–1969), *New York Times,* Jan. 18, 1970, sec. 2; Montagu, "Birmingham Sparrow," p. 106; and Lynes, *Good Old Modern,* pp. 225, 332.

31. Barry, untitled speech, Apr. 1936, box 01-12, Early Material, DOF, MoMA, pp. 2, 4.

32. Ibid., p. 8.

33. Lynes, *Good Old Modern,* p. 206.

34. Macdonald, "Action on West Fifty-Third Street," pt. 1, pp. 50–51, 63.

35. Ibid., pp. 46, 61, 62.

36. Frank Nugent, "Sideshow to the Fair," *New York Times,* Apr. 23, 1939, sec. 10; and Thomas S. Pryor, "Hit Show at the Museum," *New York Times,* Aug. 13, 1939, sec. 9.

37. "The Movies March On," *The March of Time* film script 5, Dec. 1939, box 02-02, general files, DOF, MoMA, p. 15. In August 1938 the *New York Times*

reported from Hollywood that MoMA's Film Library was negotiating with producers and directors "in the effort to portray accurately and interestingly the history of motion pictures in the United States." Frank Capra reportedly was set to lead a staff of esteemed documentary filmmakers that included directors Robert Riskin, Howard Eastbrook, Frank Lloyd, and A.S. Van Dyke. Walter Wanger, with the assistance of MoMA's John Abbott, would coordinate production. The documentary never materialized.

38. Museum of Modern Art, "What's Art to Me?" transcript of program no. 6, Dec. 2, 1939, box 02-03, general files, DOF, MoMA.

39. Ibid., p. 1.

40. Ibid., pp. 2–5.

41. Ibid., p. 10.

42. Ibid., p. 18.

43. Peter Catapano recently argued that MoMA's Film Library was a groundbreaking affair because it "problematized" the distinction between mass art and high art. Thus, MoMA and Iris Barry helped elevate motion pictures to a level at which institutions such as museums could control them. There is little evidence to conclude, however, that Barry had any real (or "reel") power to change how people viewed the movies—for the masses could still either accept or reject the argument that movies were art. To suggest that simply by placing movies in a museum changed the nature of movies and the public's relationship to them oversimplifies matters. See Catapano, "Creating 'Reel' Value," pp. 30–35.

44. Card, *Seductive Cinema*, pp. 102–12.

45. Alistair Cook to Iris Barry, "Report on the Film Library," Mar. 27, 1940, box A-1/A-3, DOF, MoMA, pp. 4–5.

46. Ibid., p. 6.

47. Ibid., p. 10.

48. Iris Barry, "The New Building, Gifts, Summer Exhibitions," *Museum of Modern Art Bulletin* 4 (July 1937): p. 5. A list of films shown as part of the first public exhibition in 1939 illustrated a more balanced review. See Barry, *Art in Our Time*, pp. 345–48; and Cooke, "A Report on the Film Library," pp. 10–11, 13.

49. Cooke, "A Report on the Film Library," p. 14.

50. B.G. Braver-Mann, "A Letter to Ye Editor," *New York Times,* July 9, 1939, sec. 9; and Kirk Bond, "In Defense of Mr. Hays," *New York Times,* Dec. 24, 1939, sec. 9.

51. Barry, "Film Library, 1935–1941," p. 4.

52. William Troy, "Film Library," p. 112.

53. Barry, "Series One: Class One," Sept. 28, 1937, box 09-02, Columbia University Course, DOF, MoMA, p. 4; Barry, "Motion Pictures as a Field of Research," p. 208; and Barry, "Film Library and How It Grew," p. 26.

54. Panofsky, *Transition*, p. 121.

55. Ibid., pp. 121–22; and Barry, "Film Library and How It Grew," p. 26.

56. Edward M.M. Warburg, "Unstuffing the Self-Important," in *Remembering Iris Barry*, p. 4.

Chapter 6. A Certain Tendency in Film Criticism

1. Wilson, "Spectator," pp. 3–5.

2. For a discussion of the potential of movies to serve avant-garde ends see Taylor, *Artists in the Audience*, pp. 19–29. Taylor does a commendable job illustrating how the work of Manny Farber and Parker Tyler—two important though relatively obscure American critics—helped establish a new way of looking a movies. Both reimagined movies as a high-art phenomenon, thus lending legitimacy to movie criticism and opening the door for the popularization of camp and cult spectatorship.

3. Robert Sklar, *Movie-Made America*, p. 293; Jowett, *Film*, p. 378; and Twomey, "Some Considerations," pp. 239–47.

4. Crowther, "It's the Fans," p. 30. See also Sellin, ed., *Annals of the American Academy of Political and Social Science*, passim.

5. Jowett, *Film*, p. 475. Hollywood took a serious economic hit in 1948 when the U.S. Supreme Court decided against the "Big Five" production companies—Paramount, Warner Brothers, MGM-Loew's, RKO, and Twentieth Century Fox—in a case that effectively ended a practice known as "block-booking." Major studios controlled not merely the means of producing and distributing a movie, but also the length of time it would run. Although not every small-town theater fell under Hollywood's control, the studios did own almost all the big theaters in cities. Garth Jowett explains that the "divorcement, coming as it did during a period of economic hardship for the motion picture industry, was blamed for many of the ills besetting the movies in the early fifties." Studios faced the twin economic challenge of a rise in labor and production costs and a reduction in revenue. See *United States v Paramount Pictures* (1948) in Jowett, *Film*, p. 345.

6. Stuart, *Effects of Television*, passim; Sklar, *Movie-Made America*, p. 276; Goldwyn, "Television's Challenge to the Movies," pp. 17, 42; Mayer, "Are Movies 'Better Than Ever?'" pp. 34–35; Crichton, "View from the East," pp. 44, 83; Houseman, "Hollywood Faces the Fifties," pt. 1, pp. 53, 56; Pells, *Not Like Us*, pp. 220–24; Howard, "Hollywood and Television," pp. 359–69; Houston, "Hollywood in the Age of Television," pp. 175–79; Seldes, "Impact of Television on Motion Pictures," pp. 3–6, 20. Samuel Goldwyn, producer of the movie *The Best Years of Our Lives*, which won the Academy Award for Best Picture in 1947, began an article in the *New York Times Magazine* with a revealing anecdote. In a conversation with a banker, Goldwyn had learned about the increasing number of small loans taken out by people who wanted to purchase television sets. When asked how they intended to meet the payment deadlines each month, people usually wrote: "We will save the money by cutting down on the number of times we go to the movies each week." Goldwyn, "Television's Challenge to the Movies," p. 17.

7. Hodgins, "What's with the Movies?" p. 97.

8. Ibid., pp. 97–105.

9. Arthur Rosenheimer Jr., "A Survey of Film Periodicals," pp. 338–52; and Leonard, "Recent American Film Writing," p. 73. Harold Leonard, writing for

Sight and Sound, found important research being done at the MoMA Film Library. Among the manuscripts to treat films seriously were Iris Barry's *D.W. Griffith: Film Master* (1940), Alistair Cooke's *Douglas Fairbanks* (1940), Lewis Jacob's *The Rise of the American Film* (1939), *Film Index* (1941), an extensive bibliographical index, Siegfried Kracauer's *From Caligari to Hitler: A Psychological History of the German Film* (1947), and Jay Leyda's *Kino: A History of the Cinema in Russia from 1896 to the Present Day* (1947). Leonard concluded that research centers such as MoMA had helped make such studies possible, but that the other developments had made them popular.

10. Jacobs, *Rise of the American Film,* pp. 543–82.

11. For details on film exhibitions at the San Francisco Museum of Art see *Art in Cinema,* passim; Jacobs, *Rise of the American Film,* pp. 543–44, 563–70; Amos Vogel, "Cinema 16," pp. 420–22. See also Ansell, "Cinema for the Few," pp. 177–78; Schofield, "They Built a Cathedral," p. 129; Dobi, "Cinema 16," passim; and Schreiber, "New York—A Cinema Capital," p. 266.

12. Hine, "Cinema 16," pp. 26–27, 30.

13. Noble, "A Survey of Film Periodicals," pp. 140–41, 143.

14. Lindgren, "Art of Our Age," p. 89.

15. Houston, "Leading the Blind," pp. 42–43; Manvell, "A Forgotten Critic," pp. 76–77; C. Denis Pegge, "Another Forgotten Critic," pp. 78–80; and Barbarow, "Anesthetic Film Criticism," pp. 441, 446. Among the important books on movies that came out during this time was Roger Manvell's *Film* (1946), a work that stressed the importance of addressing social themes within a mass art. Important books on abstract or avant-garde film technique and critique also appeared. Jay Leyda, an authority on Soviet cinema, collected and published essays by Sergei Eisenstein entitled *Film Form* (1949), and French director Jean Cocteau described the aesthetic and technical processes of a film artist in his *Diary of a Film* (1950). Leo A. Handel's *Hollywood Looks at Its Audience,* Hortense Powdermaker's *Hollywood: The Dream Factory,* and Gilbert Seldes's *The Great Audience,* all published in 1950, are works that represented a wave of interest in movies from a variety of relatively new perspectives. Handel used quantitative methods—an approach becoming popular at that time—to research audience taste in order to determine which themes the public would find attractive. Powdermaker, a noted anthropologist, studied Hollywood as one would a primitive society in an attempt to understand the "culture" of the movie industry. Her conclusion did not surprise many of Tinseltown's critics: The movie capital, she argued, seemed structured to produce mediocrity but not much else. Seldes's work was the most traditional of the three. As one of America's most respected cultural critics and a popularizer of the lively arts, Seldes had nonetheless become increasingly discouraged by the development of mass media. In this book he looked at the gaps between what the public seemed to want from mass media, what it received, and what it needed. He did not commend the movie industry for its contribution to popular entertainment.

16. Callenbach, "U.S. Film Journalism," p. 351.

17. Ibid., pp. 356, 357, 362.

18. "Replies to a Questionnaire," pp. 99–100.

19. Ibid., pp. 100–2. See also the regular column in *Sight and Sound* by John Grierson, "A Review of Reviews," ibid., vol. 23 (Apr.-June 1953): p. 208, 222; vol. 23 (Oct.-Dec. 1953): pp. 207–8; ibid., vol. 24 (July-Sept. 1954): pp. 43–44; and ibid., vol. 24 (Oct.-Dec., 1954): pp. 101–3. Grierson criticized *Sight and Sound* and other film journals for waxing nostalgic for older films and older critical standards. "Look . . . for a certain snobbery about the knowledge of the old," he said. "Look therefore for the building of myths in and around the 'greats,' so that it may be the more important to reveal their secret. Look for a positive distaste of the contemporary because no academic aura yet surrounds it."

20. Hoveyda, "*Les Taches du soleil,*" p. 37; and Astruc, "What is Mise-en-Scene?, pp. 53–55.

21. Truffaut, "A Certain Tendency of the French Cinema," pp. 30, 39; Hiller, ed., *Cahiers du Cinema,* pp. 5–6; and Cook, *History of Narrative Film,* pp. 456–57.

22. Cook, *History of Narrative Film,* pp. 461–62.

23. Pratley, "Cult of the Unintelligible," p. 302.

24. Ibid., p. 303, 305.

25. Jean, "Dialogue Between the Movie-Going Public," pp. 160–61.

26. Ibid., pp. 162–65.

27. Americans Manny Farber and Parker Tyler had both explored terrain similar to that of the Frenchmen, but their influence seems to have been less pervasive than that of the French critics. For a slightly different view on this issue see, Taylor, *Artists in the Audience,* pp. 73–97.

28. Bazin, "On the *Politique Des* Auteurs," pp. 14, 18.

29. Cook, *History of Narrative Film,* pp. 487–91.

30. "Front Page," p. 59.

31. Taylor, "Letter: Critical Attitudes," in *Sight and Sound,* ed. Wilson, pp. 116–18.

32. Anderson, "Stand Up! Stand Up!" pp. 63–64.

33. Ibid., p. 66.

34. Cameron and Jarvie, "Attack on Film Criticism," pp. 12–14; Armitage, "War of the Cults," pp. 25–27; and Wilson, ed., *Sight and Sound,* p. 17.

35. Anderson, "Stand Up! Stand Up!" p. 69. See also Lejeune, "On Not Being Committed," p. 9.

36. "Critical Issue," pp. 271–75, 330.

37. Ibid., pp. 275, 330.

38. Mekas, "A Call for a New Generation," pp. 1–3; "Cinema of the New Generation," pp. 1–20; and Sklar, *Movie-Made America,* p. 306.

39. Mekas, "Notes on the New American Cinema," p. 6, 14; and de Laurot, "Future of the New American Cinema," pp. 20, 21.

40. Houston, "Critical Question," pp. 160–64. Roud wrote an article in the

same issue harshly critiquing the *Oxford Opinion* group, see "The French Line," pp. 167–72.

41. Cameron, "All Together Now!" pp. 12–15; and Cameron, Perkins, and Shivas, "Oxford Opinion," p. 64. See also Vaughan and Riley, "Letters from the Trenches," pp. 9–11; Armitage, "Free Criticism," pp. 8–10; Cameron, "What's the Use," pp. 10–11; and Jarvie, "Comeback," p. 18.

42. Callenbach, "A New 'General Line'," pp. 374, 376, 379.

43. Callenbach, "Turn On! Turn On!" pp. 5, 13.

44. Pechter, "Turn Off," p. 62.

45. Rosenberg and White, eds., *Mass Culture*, p. 3.

46. Ibid., pp. 9, 14.

47. Rosenberg, *Tradition of the New*, p. 260.

48. Ibid.

Chapter 7. Andrew Sarris, Pauline Kael, and the Duel for the Soul of Criticism

1. Lopate, *Totally, Tenderly, Tragically*, p. 252.

2. Hickenlooper, *Reel Conversations*, pp. 7, 8.

3. Macdonald, "Agee and the Movies," in *On Movies*, p. 34; and Murray, "James Agee, 'Amateur Critic'," in *Nine American Film Critics*, pp. 5–23. For commentary on the significance of Manny Farber and Parker Tyler to the rising popularity and importance of film criticism in the 1960s see, Taylor, *Artists in the Audience*, pp. 14–18, 73–97.

4. Richard Roud, "Face to Face: James Agee," p. 98; and idem., "Face to Face: André Bazin," p. 179.

5. Mordden, *Medium Cool*, p. 177.

6. Bazin, "On the *Politique des* Auteurs," pp. 8–18; Roud, "French Line," pp. 166–71.

7. Sarris, "Director's Game," pp. 68–73.

8. Ibid., p. 73.

9. Ibid., p. 78.

10. Ibid., pp. 80–81.

11. Sarris, "Notes on the Auteur Theory," pp. 529–30; and idem., "High Forties Revisited," pp. 62–70.

12. Sarris, "Notes on the Auteur Theory," p. 532.

13. Ibid., pp. 533, 535.

14. Ibid., pp. 537–40.

15. Kael, "Circles and Squares," pp. 12–26; Murray, "Andrew Sarris and Auteur Criticism," in *Nine American Film Critics*, pp. 38–66, 110–40; Alpert, "Movies and the Critics," pp. 10–12, 55–56; McBride, "Mr. Macdonald, Mr. Sarris, and Miss Kael," pp. 26–34; Schickel, "Movie Studies," pp. 24–38; and Manchel, "Film Criticism and Theory," in *Film Study*, 1:122–30.

16. Kael, "Circles and Squares," p. 307.

17. Ibid., p. 311.

18. Ibid., pp. 312, 314.

19. Ibid., pp. 318–19; Schatz, *Genius of the System*, p. 5.

20. Kael, "Circles and Squares," p. 314.

21. Lopate, *Totally, Tenderly, Tragically*, p. 235.

22. Sarris, "American Cinema," pp. 1–68.

23. Sarris, "Auteur Theory and the Perils of Pauline," pp. 27–28.

24. Ibid., p. 29.

25. Mankiewicz, "Film Author! Film Author!" pp. 23–28; "Can Screen Writers Become Film Authors?" pp. 34–38; Armitage, "Role of the Director," pp. 14–19; Arnheim, "Who Is the Author of a Film?" pp. 11–13; Vidal, "Who Makes the Movies?" pp. 35–39.

26. Arthur Knight, "Auteur Theory," p. 22; Boultenhouse, "Camera as a God," pp. 20–22; Alan Casty, "On Approaching the Film as Art," pp. 28–34; "Correspondence and Controversy," pp. 57–60; Magid, "Auteur! Auteur!" pp. 70–74; Dienstfrey, "Hitch Your Genre to a Star," pp. 35–37; Phelps, "Rosencrantz vs. Gildenstern," pp. 45–50; Anderson, "Controversial Search for Value," pp. 18–19, 34; Durgnat, "Who Really Makes the Movies?" pp. 44–45; Siska, "Movies and History," pp. 27–32; Wald, "Who is the Film Author?" pp. 11–12; Staples, "La Politique des Auteurs," pp. 303–11; and Mast, "Auteur or Storyteller?" in *Film Theory and Criticism*, pp. 563–71.

27. Magid, "Auteur! Auteur!" p. 70.

28. Ibid., pp. 71, 72.

29. Macdonald, "The Birds," in *On Movies*, pp. 178–81, 337, 338.

30. Gorman, *Left Intellectuals and Popular Culture*, pp. 138–85; and Jumonville, *Critical Crossings*, pp. 151–85.

31. Gorman, *Left Intellectuals and Popular Culture*, pp. 161–70.

32. Macdonald, "Masscult and Midcult," in *Against the American Grain*, pp. 4, 8, 12.

33. Ibid., pp. 37, 50–51. See also, Boultenhouse, "Camera as a God," p. 20. He argued as a member of New York's underground film community finding Sarris's "effort to bestow on [commercial movies] a kind of authenticity . . . absurd. There are two assertions which I think are particularly wrong: one is that commercial film is a natural kind of Pop Art, the other is that commercial film conceals a director of such creative intensity that he can be regarded as an Author (in the higher sense)."

34. "Perils of Pauline," in *Conversations with Pauline Kael*, ed. Brantley, p. 3; Lopate, "Passion of Pauline Kael," in *Totally, Tenderly, Tragically*, p. 236; and George Malko, "Pauline Kael Wants People to Go to the Movies: A Profile," in *Conversations with Pauline Kael*, ed. Brantley, pp. 21–22.

35. Lopate, "Passion of Pauline Kael," in *Totally, Tenderly, Tragically*, pp. 229–32, 251–58; Sarris, "Sarris vs. Kael," pp. 1, 30–31, 70.

36. Lopate, "Passion of Pauline Kael," in *Totally, Tenderly, Tragically*, p. 249.

37. Kael, "Movies the Desperate Art," in *Film: An Anthology*, ed. Talbot, pp. 61,

71. See also "Fantasies of an Art-House Audience," pp. 4–9, in which Kael suggests "that the educated audience often uses 'art' films in much the same self-indulgent way as the mass audience use Hollywood 'product,' finding wish-fulfillment in the form of cheap and easy congratulation on their sensibilities and their liberalism."

38. Kael, "Is There a Cure for Film Criticism?" pp. 57, 58.

39. Kael, "Are the Movies Going to Pieces," pp. 61, 62.

40. Ibid., p. 64.

41. Ibid., p. 65.

42. Ibid.

43. Sarris, "Sarris vs. Kael," p. 30; Kael, "Zeitgeist or Poltergeist; Or, Are the Movies Going to Pieces?" in *I Lost It at the Movies*, p. 23; "Perils of Pauline," in *Conversations with Pauline Kael*, ed. Brantley, p. 3; and Pearl, "A Quarter Century with Kael," p. 103.

44. Sontag, "Against Interpretation," in *Against Interpretation*, pp. 5, 7, 10, 13–14.

45. Sontag, "One Culture and the New Sensibility," in *Against Interpretaton*, pp. 296, 299, 303; and idem., "Jack Smith's *Flaming Creatures*," ibid., p. 229.

46. Steigerwald, *Sixties and the End of Modern America*, p. 155.

47. Twitchell, *Carnival Culture*, p. 19. See also O'Neil, *Coming Apart*, pp. 200–5; Rosenberg and White, eds., *Mass Culture*, pp. v, 5, 17; N. Jacobs, ed., *Culture for the Millions?* pp. ix–xxv, 1–27; L. Jacobs, ed., *Introduction to the Art of the Movies*, pp. 3–38; and Steigarwald, *Sixties and the End of Modern America*, pp. 160–61.

48. Sarris, "*Cahiers* in Context," p. 6.

Chapter 8. The First New York Film Festival and the Heroic Age of Moviegoing

1. Jonas Mekas, "Movie Journal," *Village Voice*, Feb. 15, 1962, p. 11; and Macdonald, "La Notte," in *On Movies*, p. 367.

2. Lopate, "Anticipation of *La Notte*," in *Totally, Tenderly, Tragically*, p. 22.

3. Andrew Sarris, "Why the Foreign Film Has Lost Its Cachet," *New York Times*, May 2, 1999, sec. 2A, p. 15; and Alpert, "So Deeply Obscure," p. 68.

4. Macdonald, "Antonioni: A Position Paper," in *On Movies*, pp. 57, 59; and Mekas, "Movie Journal," *Village Voice*, Sept. 15, 1962, p. 11. The more conventional Bosley Crowther wrote that even "boredom is made interesting" by Antonioni. Crowther also left open the possibility of individual enlightenment: "Whether one finds it stimulating or a redundant bore will depend, we suspect, in large measure upon the subtle attunement of one's mood" (*New York Times*, Feb. 20, 1962, p. 29).

5. Kauffmann, "*La Notte*," in *A World on Film*, pp. 303, 306–7. See also Nowell-Smith, "*La Notte*," in *Sight and Sound: A Fiftieth Anniversary Selection*, ed. Wilson, pp. 163–68.

6. Kauffmann, "*Last Year at Marienbad*," in *A World on Film*, pp. 247–50.

7. Kael, "The Come-Dressed-as-the-Sick-Soul-of Europe Parties," in *I Lost It at the Movies*, pp. 186–88, 194. Kauffmann also admitted that the "fallacy of this style is that if it is followed absolutely rigorously, it leads not to art but to madness. Art that tries to set down everything, and to set it down as it occurs, must end like a man trying to pick up too much and dropping what he has." Kauffmann, "Last Year at Marienbad," p. 250.

8. Alpert, "So Deeply Obscure," pp. 68, 71.

9. Danto, *After the End of Art*, pp. 13, 16; and O'Neil, *Coming Apart*, p. 205.

10. Works that I found helpful to understanding the influence of Pop Art include, Madoff, ed., *Pop Art*; Mashun, *Pop Art and the Critics*; *Andy Warhol*; Cooke, "Independent Group"; and Rosenberg, "On the De-Definition of Art," in *The De-Definition of Art*, pp. 12, 13.

11. Kramer, "Andy's 'Mao' and Other Entertainments," in *Age of the Avant-Garde*, pp. 540, 542.

12. Levine, *Highbrow/Lowbrow*, pp. 130–32; and Schuman, "Idea: A Creative, Dynamic Force," pp. 11, 34–35, 38. The Lincoln Center was also part of a wider trend known as urban renewal, in which cities sought to sweep away slums by undertaking large-scale, government-financed reconstruction. Built on the ruins of old apartment houses in a fourteen-acre section on the west side of Central Park, the Lincoln Center sought to advance both urban and spiritual renewal. "The physical slums of any community are all too apparent, and their evil in plain enough," Schuman contended. "But a community in which the spirit is not fed—where it does not often enough encounter the perfections of the arts—is just as certainly underprivileged" (*New York Times Magazine*, Sept. 23, 1962, p. 11).

13. William Schuman, "Have We 'Culture'? Yes—and No," in *Pop Culture in America*, ed. White, pp. 40–49; and Levine, *Highbrow/Lowbrow*, pp. 85–168.

14. Schuman, "Have We 'Culture'?" in White, ed., *Pop Culture in America*, p. 49.

15. Heckscher, "Nation's Culture," pp. 15, 30–31.

16. Ibid., pp. 30–31. See also Alexander, *Here the Country Lies*, pp. 271–76; Toffler, *Culture Consumers*, passim.

17. Eugene Archer, "Lincoln Center to Show Movies," *New York Times*, Mar. 28, 1962, p. 34.

18. Symon Gould to Schuman, Mar. 28, 1962, LCA, Box 23-3-7-3, 1963, "General,"New York Film Festival, Lincoln Center for the Performing Arts (hereafter NYFF); and Schuman to Amos Vogel, May 18, 1962, ibid. Vogel has claimed in two separate interviews that he did not contact Schuman until the fall of 1962. However, Schuman's reply to Vogel on May 18 makes note of a letter he received from Vogel dated February 23, 1962, inquiring about the Lincoln Center's plans and offering his help if needed (Sharon Zane, "Amos Vogel," *Oral History*, Nov. 17, 1993, Oral History Project, Lincoln Center for the Performing Arts, Inc. (hereafter OHP, LCPA), pp. 81, 83; and Vogel, interview with author, Feb. 16, 1999, p. 1).

19. Schuman to John D. Rockefeller III, July 3, 1962, LCA, Box 23-3-7-3, NYFF 1963, "General."

20. Zane, "William Schuman," *Oral History,* Sept. 27, 1990, OHC, LCPA, pp. 198–99; and Zane, "Amos Vogel," pp. 138–39.

21. Richard Leach to Schuman, July 3, 1962, LCA, Box 23-3-7-3, NYFF 1963, "General"; and Schuman to James S.C. Quinn, July 10, 1962, ibid.

22. Leach to Ralph Hetzel Jr., July 11, 1962, ibid.; and Leach to Schuman, July 11, 1962, ibid.

23. Schuman to Quinn, Aug. 8, 1962, ibid.; Quinn to Schuman, Aug. 22, 1962, ibid.; Schuman to Quinn, Aug. 29, 1962, ibid.; and Leach to Schuman, Aug. 13, 1962, ibid.

24. Leach to Schuman, Oct. 11, 1962, ibid.; and Leach to Schuman, Nov. 27, 1962, ibid. See also Leach to Schuman, "Summary of Projected New York Film Festival," ibid.; and Leach to Quinn, Nov. 29, 1962, ibid.

25. Quinn to Leach, Jan. 17, 1963, ibid.; Schuman to Gates, Jan. 24, 1963, ibid.; Quinn to Leach, Feb. 5, 1963, ibid.; Leach to Quinn, Mar. 6, 1963; ibid.; Leach to Schuman, Mar. 8, 1963, ibid.; and Leach to Schuman, Mar. 11, 1963, ibid.

26. Vogel interview, p. 2; Archer Winsten, *New York Post,* Mar. 11, 1963, in LCA, Box 12-3-5-3, NYFF, Press Clippings, 1962–67.

27. Ibid.

28. Corliss, "70-Millimeter Nerves," p. 38; Vogel interview, pp. 1–3; Zane, "Amos Vogel," pp. 81, 83–86. Vogel has been adamant about the disconnection between Cinema 16's failing and his becoming part of the Lincoln Center. "The sequence of events is very important," he argued, "because there had been some. . . . I have noticed a story or two that indicated I closed Cinema 16 *because* I had been approached by Lincoln Center. Absolutely untrue, there is no connection" (Zane, "Amos Vogel," p. 83).

29. Houston, "Richard Roud," pp. 103–4; Corliss, "70-Millimeter Nerves," pp. 36–54.

30. Vogel to Roud, Apr. 5, 1963, LCA, Box 23-3-7-3, NYFF 1963, "General."

31. Schuman to Louis M. Pesce, Mar. 25, 1963, LCA, Box 23-3-7-3, NYFF 1963, "General"; Eugene Archer, *New York Times,* May 28, 1963, p. 33.

32. Eugene Archer, *New York Times,* May 1, 1963, p. 35.

33. LCA, Box 12-3-5-3, NYFF, Press Clippings, 1962–67.

34. Archer Winsten, *New York Post,* May 6, 1963, p. 48.

35. Letter to Committee Members, Apr. 15, 1963, LCA, Box 23-3-7-3, NYFF 1963, "General"; John Ford to Schuman, Apr. 16, 1963, ibid.; Leach to Michael Mayer (IFIDA), Apr. 29, 1963, ibid.; and Eric Johnston to Schuman, Apr. 5, 1963, ibid.

36. Vogel to Roud, July 1,1963, ibid., pp. 1–5.

37. Symon Poe to Heckscher, July 10, 1963, ibid.; Leach to Poe, July 16, 1963, ibid.; Leach to Vogel, undated, ibid.; Joseph Sugar to Vogel, July 19, 1963, ibid.; and Zane, "Amos Vogel," p. 98.

38. Robert Hale to John McNulty, Aug. 14, 1963, LCA, Box 23-3-7-3, NYFF 1963, "General"; and McNulty to Vern Armstrong, Aug. 15, 1963, ibid.

39. Richard Roud, "Film Art's New Frame," *New York Herald Tribune*, Aug. 25, 1963, in LCA, Box 12-3-5-3, NYFF, Press Clippings, 1962–67.

40. Ibid.

41. John Canaday, "Art: Larry Rivers Juxtaposing the High and the Low," *New York Times*, August 26, 1963, p. 21.

42. Leach to Schuman, Sept. 9, 1963, ibid.; Eileen Bowser to Herb Bronstein, NYFF 1963, box 9, File NYFF Organization, General, DOF, MoMA. Roud and Vogel also expressed some frustration with the handling of advertising by the Lincoln Center staff, but this seems to have been negligible (Vogel and Roud to Leach, Aug. 27, 1963, LCA, Box 23-3-7-3, NYFF 1963, "General").

43. John Gruen, *New York Herald Tribune*, Sept. 15, 1963, Section 2, p. 1; Zane, "Amos Vogel," p. 143; Kauffmann, "After the Ball," p. 33; Sheed, "Cinema's Last Stand," p. 136.

44. Vogel interview, p. 3, 6, 8; Schuman to Johnston, May 22, 1963, LCA, Box 23-3-7-3, NYFF 1963, "General"; Alpert, "One Man's Festival," pp. 18–19, 67–68.

45. Bosley Crowther, "Our Film Festival," *New York Times*, Sept. 22, 1963, sec. 10, p. 1; idem., "We Have a Film Festival," ibid., Sept. 8, 1963, sec. 2, p. 1; "The Film as Art," ibid., Sept. 10, 1963, p. 38; Eugene Archer, ibid., Sept. 9, 1963, p. 23. See also Martin Quigley, "All for Art's Sake," undated, LCA, Box 12-3-5-3, NYFF, Press Clippings, 1962–67.

46. Archer, *New York Times*, Sept. 16, 1963, p. 43; Leach to Jonas Mekas and David Stone, Sept. 16, 1963, LCA, Box 23-3-7-3, NYFF 1963, "General"; Zane, "Amos Vogel," pp. 122–23, 155–57; Vogel interview, p. 9.

47. "Cinema as an International Art," pp. 78–82.

48. Kauffmann, "After the Ball," p. 36; Judith Crist, "A Field Day for the Buffs at Lincoln Center," *New York Herald Tribune*, Sept. 22, 1963, sec. 4, pp. 1, 4; Steel, "Film Festival at the Concert Hall," p. 51. See also Henry Hart, "NYC's 1st Film Festival," pp. 449–50, 491; Sheed, "Cinema's Last Stand," pp. 136, 138.

49. Lopate, "Anticipation of *La Notte*," in *Totally, Tenderly, Tragically*, pp. 9–10.

50. Ibid., p. 24.

Chapter 9. The Film Generation Goes to School

1. Stanley Kauffmann, "The Film Generation," in *A World on Film*, p. 415; and Lopate, "Anticipation of *La Notte*," in *Truly, Tenderly, Tragically*, p. 26.

2. Danto, *After the End of Art*, pp. 14–17.

3. "Everybody Wants to Say It in Films," pp. 39–40, 43. See also Sarris, "Farthest-Out Moviegoers," pp. 14–15.

4. Amos Vogel, "Films: Fashion for the Fashionable," *New York Times*, Sept. 5, 1965, sec. 2, p. 7; Alpert, "How Useful Are Film Festivals?" p. 56; "Everybody Wants to Say It in Films," p. 40; and Kauffmann, "Are We Doomed to Festivals?"

p. 31. Stanley Kauffmann doubted, however, that festivals held as much significance as many accorded them primarily because the number of great films made each year rarely seemed plentiful enough to fill festivals, particularly New York's. Moreover, movies at festivals suffered "very badly by bearing the implied weight of being major artistic events." Yet what he objected to—the quality of the films—ultimately had little to do with the growing perception that movies were significant.

5. Schillaci, "Film as Environment," p. 8; Cohen, "New Audience," p. 8; and "Cinema: The Film Maker as Ascendant Star," p. 46.

6. Stewart, ed., *Film Study in Higher Education*, pp. 2–3. See also Stewart, "Movies on the Campus," pp. 82–83.

7. Ibid., pp. 3–4.

8. Steele, "Film Scholars at the New York Film Festival," pp. 41, 43.

9. Kael, "It's Only a Movie," p. 12. For an attack in the same spirit, see Russell Baker, "Observer: They've Snatched Bogart," *New York Times*, Apr. 1, 1965, Op-Ed sec.

10. Kael, "It's Only a Movie," p. 12.

11. Macklin, "Perils of Pauline's Criticism," p. 1; "Pauline Kael: Abuser or Abused?" pp. 43–44; and Rapf, "Can Education Kill the Movies?" p. 11.

12. Lynes, "Flicks for the Fastidious," p. 27.

13. Young, "An American Film Institute," pp. 37–50; and idem., "A Special Report," pp. 5, 15-16.

14. Vincent Canby, *New York Times*, Mar. 28, 1967, p. 51.

15. Vincent Canby, *New York Times*, June 6, 1967, p. 54; Bosley Crowther, "A Hope for New Images," ibid., June 25, 1967, p. 14; and Alpert, "Onward and Upward," p. 50.

16. Stefan Kafner, "The Student Movie-Makers," in *Film 68/69*, ed. Alpert and Sarris, pp. 247–52; Madsen, "Fission/Fusion/Fission," pp. 124–26; and Pye and Miles, *Movie Brats*, p. 47. For a more pessimistic look at the chances of film school graduates see Monaco, "You're Only as Young," pp. 15–17; and Steiner, "Europe and America," pp. 18–20.

17. Ray, *A Certain Tendency*, p. 260; and Biskind, *Easy Riders, Raging Bulls*, p. 22. See also Frank, *Conquest of Cool*, pp. 104–31.

18. Biskind, *Easy Riders, Raging Bulls*, pp. 15, 17.

19. Bosley Crowther, "Shoot-em Up Film Opens Fete," *New York Times*, Aug. 7, 1967, p. 32; "Screen: Bonnie and Clyde Arrive," ibid., Aug. 14, 1967, p. 36; "Run, Bonnie and Clyde," ibid., Sept. 3, 1967, sec. 2, p. 1; "Bonnie and Clyde—Facts? Meaning? Art?" ibid., Sept. 10, 1967, p. 7, 9; and ibid., Aug. 13, 1967, p. D11.

20. "Anything Goes," pp. 74, 75, 76.

21. Kanfer, "New Cinema," p. 67.

22. Kael, "Bonnie and Clyde," in *For Keeps*, pp. 141–42.

23. Joseph Morgenstern, "Ugly" and "The Thin Red Line," in Schickel and Simon, *Film 67/68*, pp. 25–29; and Biskind, *Easy Riders, Raging Bulls*, p. 40, 45.

24. Biskind, *Easy Riders, Raging Bulls*, pp. 91, 152.

25. Ibid., p. 163.

26. Kael, "*The Godfather:* Alchemy," in *For Keeps*, pp. 434, 438; Vincent Canby, "*The Godfather*," in *Film, 72/73*, ed. Denby, p. 3; and William S. Pechter, "Keeping Up with the Corleones," in ibid., p. 5.

27. Farber, "End of the Road?," pp. 4–5.

28. Brustein, "New Hollywood," pp. 23–28.

Chapter 10. Wither Criticism?

1. Gilliatt, "Only Films Are Truly Deep-Down Groovy," pp. 117–18.

2. Kappler, "Mixed Media," p. 28; McLuhan, *Medium is the Massage*; and Schlesinger, "Plugged-In Generation," pp. 1–2.

3. Cawelti, "Reviews," pp. 256, 259.

4. Howe, "New York Intellectuals," pp. 34, 45.

5. Shickel, "Movies Are Now High Art," pp. 32, 34.

6. Ibid., pp. 38, 44.

7. Kael, "Trash, Art, and the Movies," in *For Keeps*, pp. 201–3, 216–17.

8. Ibid., p. 226.

9. Ibid., pp. 209, 211, 215.

10. Biskind, *Easy Riders, Raging Bulls*, p. 409; Callenbach, "Looking Backward," pp. 1–10; Callenbach, "Recent Film Writing," pp. 11–32; Resnik, "A Seismic Moment," pp. 25–28, 38; Sheed, "Good Word," pp. 2, 42; and Schickel, "Movie Studies," pp. 24–38.

11. Simon, *Movies into Film*, pp. 2–4.

12. Denby, "Moviegoers," p. 98.

13. Gorman, *Left Intellectuals and Popular Culture*, p. 81.

14. Jacoby, *End of Utopia*, p. 89.

Bibliography

Archival Resources

Department of Film, Museum of Modern Art, New York.
Billy Rose Theater and Dance Collection, New York Public Library, New York.
New York Film Festival, Lincoln Center for the Performing Arts, New York.
Oral History Project, Lincoln Center for the Performing Arts, Inc., New York.
Theodore Dreiser Collection, Department of Special Collections, Van Pelt-
Dietrich Library Center, Univ. of Pennsylvania, Philadelphia.

Government Documents

Chicago Motion Picture Commission Hearings, *Report,* 1920, Chicago Histori-
cal Society, Chicago.
Mutual Film Corporation v Industrial Commission of Ohio, 236, sec. 230–47 (U.S.
Supreme Court).

Unpublished Material

Dobi, Stephen J. "Cinema 16: America's Largest Film Society." Ph.D. diss., New
York Univ., 1984.

Interviews

Vogel, Amos. Interview by author, Feb. 15, 1999.

Books

Adams, K. Gary. *William Schuman: A Bio-Bibliography.* Westport, Conn.: Green-
wood Press, 1997.
Agee, James. *A Death in the Family.* New York: Avon Books, 1959.

————. *Agee on Film.* 2nd ed. New York: Beacon Press, 1966.

Alexander, Charles C. *Here the Country Lies: Nationalism and the Arts in Twentieth Century America.* Bloomington: Indiana Univ. Press, 1980.

Allen, Frederick Lewis. *Only Yesterday: An Informal History of the 1920s.* New York: Harper and Row, 1931.

Alpert, Hollis, and Andrew Sarris, eds. *Film 68/69.* New York: Simon and Schuster, 1969.

Amberg, George, ed. *Experimental Cinema, 1930–1934.* New York: Arno Press, 1969.

Andy Warhol. Greenwich: New York Graphic Society, 1970.

Art in the Cinema. San Francisco: San Francisco Museum of Art, 1947.

Balio, Tino, ed. *The American Film Industry.* Madison: Univ. of Wisconsin Press, 1985.

Barry, Iris. *Let's Go to the Pictures.* London: Chatto and Windus, 1926.

————. *Art in Our Time.* New York: Museum of Modern Art, 1939.

————. *D.W. Griffith: Film Master.* New York: Museum of Modern Art, 1940.

Biskind, Peter. *Easy Riders, Raging Bulls: How the Sex-Drugs-and Rock 'n' Roll Generation Saved Hollywood.* New York: Simon and Schuster, 1998.

Blake, Casey Nelson. *Beloved Community: The Cultural Criticism of Randolph Bourne, Van Wyck Brooks, Waldo Frank, and Lewis Mumford.* Chapel Hill: Univ. of North Carolina Press, 1990.

Bluestone, George. *Novels into Film.* Berkeley: Univ. of California Press, 1961.

Boorstin, Daniel. *The Image: A Guide to Pseudo-Events in America.* New York: Harper and Row, 1964.

Brantley, Will. *Conversations with Pauline Kael.* Jackson: Univ. of Mississippi Press, 1996.

Card, James. *Seductive Cinema: The Art of the Silent Film.* New York: Alfred A. Knopf, 1994.

Carroll, Noël. *A Philosophy of Mass Art.* Oxford: Clarendon Press, 1998.

Coastes, Paul. *Film at the Intersection of High and Mass Culture.* New York: Cambridge Univ. Press, 1994.

Cohen, Keith. "Eisenstein's Subversive Adaptation." In *The Classic American Novel and the Movies,* ed. Gerald Perry and Roger Shatzkin. New York: Frederick Ungar, 1977.

Collins, Jim, Hilary Radner, and Ava Preacher Collins, eds. *Film Theory Goes to the Movies.* New York: Routledge, 1993.

Cook, David A. *A History of Narrative Film.* New York: W.W. Norton, 1981.

Cooke, Lynne. "The Independent Group: British and American Pop Art, A 'Palimpcestuous'." In *Modern Art and Popular Culture: Readings in High & Low,* ed. Kirk Varnedoe and Adam Gopnik. New York: Harry N. Abrams, 1990.

Corliss, Richard. "Notes on a Screenwriter's Theory, 1973." In *Awake in the Dark:*

An Anthology of American Film Criticism, 1915 to the Present, ed. David Denby. New York: Vintage Books, 1977.

Couvares, Francis G., ed. *Movie Censorship and American Culture.* Washington: Smithsonian Institution Press, 1996.

Czitrom, Daniel. *Media and the American Mind: From Morse to McLuhan.* Chapel Hill: Univ. of North Carolina Press, 1982.

Danto, Arthur C. *After the End of Art: Contemporary Art and the Pale of History.* Princeton, N.J.: Princeton Univ. Press, 1997.

Davis, Robert E. *Response to Innovation: A Study of Popular Argument about Mass Media.* New York: Arno Press, 1976.

Denby, David, ed. *Film, 72/73: An Anthology by the National Society of Film Critics.* New York: Bobbs-Merrill, 1973.

————, ed. *Awake in the Dark: An Anthology of American Film Criticism, 1915 to the Present.* New York: Vintage Books, 1977.

Denney, Reuel. "The Discovery of the Popular Culture." In *American Perspectives: The National Self-Image in the Twentieth Century,* ed. Robert E. Spiller and Eric Larrabee. Cambridge: Harvard Univ. Press, 1961.

Dickstein, Morris. *Gates of Eden: American Culture in the Sixties.* New York: Basic Books, 1977.

Douglas, Ann. *Terrible Honesty: Mongrel Manhattan in the 1920s.* New York: Farrar, Straus, and Giroux, 1995.

Dreiser, Theodore. "The Real Sins of Hollywood." In *Authors on Film,* ed. Harry M. Geduld. Bloomington: Indiana University Press, 1972.

Dumenil, Lynn. *The Modern Temper: American Culture and Society in the 1920s.* New York: Hill and Wang, 1995.

Duncan, Carol. *Civilizing Rituals: Inside Public Art Museums.* London: Routledge, 1995.

Eisenstein, Sergei. *Notes of a Film Director.* Moscow: Foreign Language Publishing House, 1947.

Eksteins, Modris. *Rites of Spring: The Great War and the Birth of the Modern Age.* New York: Doubleday Books, 1989.

Elias, Robert H., ed. *Letters of Theodore Dreiser.* 2 vols. Philadelphia: Univ. of Pennsylvania Press, 1959.

Fass, Paula. *The Damned and the Beautiful: American Youth in the 1920s.* New York: Oxford Univ. Press, 1977.

Feldman, Charles Matthew. *The National Board of Censorship (Review) of Motion Pictures, 1909–1922.* New York: Arno Press, 1977.

Fine, Richard. *West of Eden: Writers in Hollywood, 1928–1940.* Washington: Smithsonian Institution Press, 1993.

Frank, Thomas. *The Conquest of Cool: Business Culture, Counterculture, and the Rise of Hip Consumerism.* Chicago: Univ. of Chicago Press, 1997.

Freeburg, Victor O. *The Art of Photoplay Making.* Reprint, New York: Arno Press, 1970.

Fox, Richard Wightman, and T.J. Jackson Lears, ed. *The Power of Culture: Critical Essays in American History.* Chicago: Univ. of Chicago Press, 1993.

Gabler, Neal. *Life the Movie: How Entertainment Conquered Reality.* New York: Alfred A. Knopf, 1998.

Gans, Herbert J. *Popular Culture and High Culture: An Analysis and Evaluation of Taste.* New York: Basic Books, 1974.

Geduld, Henry, ed. *Authors on Film.* Bloomington: Indiana Univ. Press, 1972.

Geertz, Clifford. *The Interpretation of Cultures.* New York: Basic Books, 1973.

Gelman, Barbara, ed. *Photoplay Treasury.* New York: Crown, 1972.

Giddings, Robert, Keith Selby, and Chris Wensley, eds. *Screening the Novel: The Theory and Practice of Literary Dramatization.* New York: St. Martin's, 1990.

Goodyear, A. Conger. *The Museum of Modern Art: The First Ten Years.* New York: Museum of Modern Art, 1943.

Gorman, Paul R. *Left Intellectuals and Popular Culture in Twentieth America.* Chapel Hill: Univ. of North Carolina Press, 1996.

Green, Martin. *New York 1913: The Armory Show and the Paterson Pageant Strike.* New York: Collier Books, 1988.

Griffith, James. *Adaptations as Imitations: Films from Novels.* Newark: Univ. of Delaware Press, 1997.

Grogg, Sam L., and John G. Nachbar, eds. *Movies as Artifacts.* Chicago: Nelson-Hall, 1982.

Hannon, William Morgan. *The Photodrama: Its Place Among the Fine Arts.* New Orleans: Ruskin Press, 1915.

Harris, Neil. *Cultural Excursions: Marketing Appetites and Cultural Tastes in Modern America.* Chicago: Univ. of Chicago Press, 1990.

Hawley, Ellis W. *The Great War and the Search for a Modern Order: A History of the American People and Their Institutions.* New York: St. Martin's, 1992.

Hickey, David. *Air Guitar: Essays on Art and Democracy.* Los Angeles: Art Issues Press, 1997.

Hickenlooper, George. *Reel Conversations: Candid Interviews with Film's Foremost Directors and Critics.* New York: Carol, 1991.

Hiller, Jim, ed. *Cahiers du Cinema: The 1950s—Neo-Realism, Hollywood, New Wave.* Cambridge, Mass.: Harvard Univ. Press, 1985.

Hoberman, J. *Vulgar Modernism: Writing on Movies and Other Media.* Philadelphia: Temple Univ. Press, 1994.

Jacobs, Lewis. *The Rise of the American Film.* New York: Teacher's College Press, 1969.

———, ed. *Introduction to the Art of the Movies.* New York: Noonday Press, 1960.

———, ed. *The Emergence of Film Art: The Evolution and Development of the Motion Picture as an Art, from 1900 to the Present.* 2nd ed. New York: W.W. Norton, 1979.

———, ed. *The Compound Cinema: The Film Writings of Harry Alan Potamkin.* New York: Teachers College Press, 1977.

Jacobs, Norman, ed. *Culture for the Millions? Mass Media in Modern Society.* Princeton, N.J.: D. Van Nostrand, 1959.

Jacoby, Russell. *The Last Intellectuals: American Culture in the Age of Academe.* New York: Noonday Press, 1989.

———. *The End of Utopia: Politics and Culture in an Age of Apathy.* New York: Basic Books, 1999.

Jowett, Garth. *Film: The Democratic Art.* Boston: Little, Brown, 1976.

Jumonville, Neil. *Critical Crossings: The New York Intellectuals in Postwar America.* Berkeley: Univ. of California Press, 1991.

Kael, Pauline. *I Lost It at the Movies.* Boston: Little, Brown, 1965.

———. *For Keeps: 30 Years at the Movies.* 2nd ed. New York: Plume, 1996.

Kammen, Michael. *The Lively Arts: Gilbert Seldes and the Transformation of Cultural Criticism in the United States.* New York: Oxford Univ. Press, 1996.

———. *American Culture, American Tastes: Social Change and the Twentieth Century.* New York: Alfred A. Knopf, 1999.

Kauffmann, Stanley. *A World on Film.* New York: Dell, 1966.

———. *Figures of Light: Film Criticism and Comment.* New York: Harper and Row, 1971.

———, ed. *American Film Criticism: From the Beginnings to Citizen Kane.* New York: Liveright, 1972.

Kazin, Alfred. *On Native Grounds: An Interpretation of Modern American Prose Literature.* Reprint, New York: Harcourt, Brace, 1995.

Knight, Arthur. *The Liveliest Art.* New York: Mentor Books, 1957.

Koszarski, Richard. *An Evenings Entertainment: The Age of the Silent Feature Picture, 1915–1928.* Berkeley: Univ. of California Press, 1990.

Kracauer, Siegfried. *From Caligari to Hitler: A Psychological History of the German Film.* Princeton, N.J.: Princeton Univ. Press, 1947.

Kramer, Hilton. *The Age of the Avant-Garde: An Art Chronicle of 1956–1972.* New York: Farrar, Straus, and Giroux, 1973.

Lasch, Christopher. *The New Radicalism in American, 1889–1963: The Intellectual as Social Type.* New York: Alfred A. Knopf, 1965.

Lev, Peter. *The Euro-American Cinema.* Austin: Univ. of Texas Press, 1993.

Levine, Lawrence. *Highbrow/Lowbrow: The Emergence of Cultural Hierarchy in America.* Cambridge: Harvard Univ. Press, 1988.

Lindsay, Vachel. *The Art of the Moving Picture.* Reprint, New York: Liveright, 1971.

———. *The Progress and Poetry of the Movies: A Second Book of Film Criticism.* Myron Lounsburg, ed. Reprint, Lanham, Md.: Scarecrow Press, 1995.

Lingeman, Richard. *Theodore Dreiser: An American Journey, 1908–1945.* New York: G.P. Putnam and Sons, 1990.

Lopate, Phillip. *Totally, Tenderly, Tragically: Essays and Criticism from a Lifelong Love Affair with the Movies.* New York: Anchor Books, 1998.

Lounsbury, Myron O. *The Origins of Film Criticism, 1909–1939*. New York: Arno Press, 1973.

Lynes, Russell. *The Tastemakers*. New York: Harper and Brothers, 1955.

———. *Good Old Modern: An Intimate Portrait of the Museum of Modern Art*. New York: Atheneum, 1975.

———. *The Lively Audience: A Social History of the Visual and Performing Arts in America, 1890–1950*. New York: Harper and Row, 1985.

Macdonald, Dwight. *Against the American Grain*. New York Random House, 1962.

———. *On Movies*. New York: Berkley Medallion Books, 1969.

Madoff, Steven Henry, ed. *Pop Art: A Critical History*. Berkeley: Univ. of California Press, 1997.

Manchel, Frank. *Film Study: An Analytical Bibliography*. 4 vols. London: Associate Press, 1990.

Mashun, Carol Anne. *Pop Art and the Critics*. Ann Arbor: Univ. of Michigan Press, 1987.

Mast, Gerald, ed. *Film Theory and Criticism*. New York: Oxford Univ. Press, 1985.

May, Henry F. *The End of American Innocence: A Study of the First Years of Our Own Time, 1912–1917*. New York: Alfred A. Knopf, 1959.

May, Lary. *Screening Out the Past: The Birth of Mass Culture and the Motion Picture Industry*. New York: Oxford Univ. Press, 1982.

McLuhan, Marshall. *The Medium is the Massage: An Inventory of Effects*. New York: Random House, 1967.

Mencken, H.L. *Prejudices*. New York: Alfred A. Knopf, 1927.

Montagu, Ivor. *With Eisenstein in Hollywood*. New York: International Publishers, 1969.

Mordden, Ethan. *Medium Cool: The Movies of the 1960s*. New York: Alfred A. Knopf, 1990.

Mukerji, Chandra and Michael Schudson, eds. *Rethinking Popular Culture: Contemporary Perspectives in Cultural Studies*. Berkeley: Univ. of California Press, 1991.

Münsterberg, Hugo. *The Photoplay: A Psychological Study*. 1916. Reprint, New York: Dover, 1970.

Murray, Edward. *The Cinematic Imagination: Writers and the Motion Picture*. New York: Frederick Ungar, 1972.

———. *Nine American Film Critics*. New York: Frederick Ungar, 1975.

Museum of Modern Art. *Art in Progress*. New York: Museum of Modern Art: 1944.

Nash, Roderick. *The Nervous Generation: American Thought, 1917–1930*. Chicago: Elephant Paperback, 1990.

Nathan, George Jean. *Art of the Night*. New York: Alfred A. Knopf, 1928.

Nowell-Smith, Geoffrey. "*La Notte*." In *Sight and Sound: A Fiftieth Anniversary Selection*. ed. David Wilson. London: Faber and Faber, 1982.

O'Neil, William. *Coming Apart: An Informal History of America in the 1960s.* New York: Quadrangle Books, 1971.

Panofsky, Erwin. *Transition.* Reprint, New York: Kraus, 1967.

Pells, Richard. *Radical Visions and American Dreams: Culture and Social Thought in the Depression Years.* Middletown: Wesleyan Univ. Press, 1973.

———. *Not Like Us: How Europeans Have Loved, Hated, and Transformed American Culture since World War II.* New York: Basic Books, 1997.

Perlman, William J., ed. *The Movies on Trial: The Views and Opinions of Outstanding Personalities Anent Screen Entertainment Past and Present.* New York: Macmillan, 1936.

Postman, Neil. *Amusing Ourselves to Death: Public Discourse in the Age of Show Business.* New York: Penguin Books, 1985.

Powdermaker, Hortense. *Hollywood: The Dream Factory.* Boston: Little, Brown, 1950.

Pye, Michael, and Lynda Miles. *The Movie Brats: How the Film Generation Took Over Hollywood.* New York: Holt, Rinehart, and Winston, 1979.

Remembering Iris Barry. New York: Museum of Modern Art, 1980.

Ramsey, Terry. *A Million and One Nights.* New York: Simon and Schuster, 1926.

Ray, Robert B. *A Certain Tendency of the Hollywood Cinema, 1930–1980.* Princeton, N.J.: Princeton Univ. Press, 1985.

Rosenberg, Bernard, and David Manning White, eds. *Mass Culture: The Popular Arts in America.* Glencoe, Ill.: Free Press, 1957.

Rosenberg, Harold. *The Tradition of the New.* 2nd ed. New York: McGraw Hill, 1965.

———. *The De-Definition of Art: Action Art to Pop to Earthworks.* New York: Horizon Press, 1972.

Rubin, Joan Shelley. *The Making of Middlebrow Culture.* Chapel Hill: Univ. of North Carolina Press, 1992.

Sarris, Andrew. "Notes on the Auteur Theory in 1962." In *Film Theory and Criticism,* ed. Gerald Mast. New York: Oxford University Press, 1985.

———. "Toward a Theory of Film History." In *Awake in the Dark: An Anthology of American Film Criticism, 1915 to the Present,* ed. David Denby. New York: Vintage Books, 1977.

Sayler, Oliver M. *Revolt in the Arts: A Survey of the Creation, Distribution and Appreciation of Art in America.* New York: Brentano's, 1930.

Schatz, Thomas. *The Genius of the System: Hollywood Filmmaking in the Studio Era.* New York: Henry Holt, 1988.

Schickel, Richard. *Intimate Strangers: The Culture of Celebrity.* New York, Fromm, 1986.

———, *Matinee Idols: Reflections on the Movies.* Chicago: Ivan R. Dee, 1999.

———, and John Simon, eds. *Film 67/68.* New York: Simon and Schuster, Inc., 1968.

Seabury, William M. *The Public and the Motion Picture Industry.* New York: Macmillan, 1926.

Seldes, Gilbert. *The Seven Lively Arts.* New York: Sagamore Press, 1924.

————. *An Hour with the Movies and the Talkies.* Philadelphia: J.B. Lippincott, 1929.

Sellin, Thorsten, ed. *Annals of the American Academy of Political and Social Science: The Motion Picture Industry.* Vol. 254, Nov. 1947.

Simon, John. *Movies into Film: Film Criticism, 1967–1970.* New York: Dial Press, 1971.

————. "Critical Credo." In *Awake in the Dark: An Anthology of American Film Criticism, 1915 to the Present,* ed. David Denby. New York: Vintage Books, 1977.

Sitney, P. Adams. *Film Culture Reader.* New York: Praeger Publishers, 1970.

Sklar, Robert. *Movie-Made America: A Cultural History of the Movies.* 2nd ed. New York: Vintage Books, 1994.

———— and Charles Musser, ed. *Resisting Images: Essays on Cinema and History.* Philadelphia: Temple Univ. Press, 1990.

Slide, Anthony. *Nitrate Won't Wait: Film Preservation in the United States.* Jefferson, N.C.: McFarland, 1992.

Sontag, Susan. *Against Interpretation.* New York: Dell, 1966.

Steel, Ronald. *Walter Lippmann and the American Century.* Boston: Little, Brown, 1980.

Steigarwald, David. *The Sixties and the End of Modern America.* New York: St. Martin's, 1995.

von Sternberg, Josef. *Fun in a Chinese Laundry.* New York: Macmillan, 1965.

Stewart, David C., ed. *Film Study in Higher Education.* Washington D.C.: American Council on Education, 1966.

Storey, John. *An Introductory Guide to Cultural Theory and Popular Culture.* Athens: Univ. of Georgia Press, 1993.

Stuart, Fredric. *The Effects of Television on the Motion Picture and Radio Industries.* New York: Arno Press, 1976.

Sussman, Warren I. *Culture as History: The Transformation of American Society in the Twentieth Century.* New York: Pantheon Books, 1984.

Swanberg, W.A. *Dreiser.* New York: Charles Scribner and Sons, 1965.

Talbot, Daniel, ed. *Film: An Anthology.* Berkeley: Univ. of California Press, 1967.

Taylor, Greg. *Artists in the Audience: Cults, Camp, and American Film Criticism.* Princeton, N.J.: Princeton Univ. Press, 1999.

Taylor, John Russell. "Letter: Critical Attitudes." In *Sight and Sound: A Fiftieth Anniversary Selection,* ed. David Wilson. London: Faber and Faber, 1982.

Taylor, Richard, ed. *S.M. Eisenstein: Selected Works, 1922–1934.* Vol. 1. London: BFI, 1988.

Toffler, Alvin. *The Culture Consumers: A Study of Art and Affluence in America.* New York: St. Martin's, 1964.

Trachtenberg, Alan. *The Incorporation of America: Culture and Society in the Gilded Age.* New York: Hill and Wang, 1982.

Twitchell, James B. *Carnival Culture: The Trashing of Taste in America.* New York: Columbia Univ. Press, 1992.

Tyler, Parker. *Three Faces of the Film.* New York: Thomas Yoseloff, 1960.

Varnedoe, Kirk, and Adam Gopnik, eds. *Modern Art and Popular Culture: Readings in High and Low.* New York: Harry N. Abrams, 1990.

Wagner, Geoffrey. *The Novel and The Cinema.* Rutherford: Fairleigh Dickinson Univ. Press, 1975.

Ware, Caroline. *Greenwich Village, 1920–1930: A Comment on American Civilization in the Post-War Years.* New York: Harper and Row, 1935.

Warshow, Robert. *The Immediate Experience.* Reprint, New York: Antheneum, 1975.

White, David Manning, ed. *Pop Culture in America.* Chicago: Quadrangle Books, 1970.

Whitfield, Stephen J. *The Culture of the Cold War.* 2nd ed. Baltimore: Johns Hopkins Univ. Press, 1996.

Wilson, David, ed. *Sight and Sound: A Fiftieth Anniversary Selection.* London: Farber and Farber, 1982.

Wolfe, Glen J. *Vachel Lindsay: The Poet as Film Theorist.* New York: Arno Press, 1973.

Wollen, Peter. "The Auteur Theory." In *Film Theory and Criticism,* ed. Gerald Mast. New York: Oxford Univ. Press, 1985.

Works Progress Administration. *The Film Index: The Film as Art.* New York: Museum of Modern Art and H.W. Wilson, 1941.

Articles

Ackerman, Carl W. "Pulitzer Prizes for the Cinema." *Cinema Arts* 1 (July 1937): pp. 15, 98.

Adams, Ward. "Heirlooms from Hollywood." *Country Life,* Mar. 1936, pp. 83, 93.

"Aesthetic vs. Moralistic Censorship." *Exceptional Photoplays,* June 1921, p. 8.

Alloway, Lawrence. "Critics in the Dark." *Encounter* 22 (Feb. 1964): pp. 50–55.

Alpert, Hollis. "The Big Change in Hollywood." *Saturday Review,* Dec. 21, 1957, pp. 9–11.

———. "So Deeply Obscure, So Widely Discussed." *New York Times Magazine,* Apr. 21, 1963, p. 68.

———. "One Man's Festival." *Saturday Review,* Oct. 5, 1963, pp. 18–19, 67–68.

———. "The Movies and the Critics." *Saturday Review,* Dec. 26, 1964, pp. 10–12, 55–56.

———. "Onward and Upward with the Institute." *Saturday Review,* June 24, 1967, p. 50.

———. "How Useful Are Film Festivals?" *Saturday Review,* July 8, 1967, p. 56

Anderson, Lindsay. "Stand Up! Stand Up!" *Sight and Sound* 26 (autumn 1956): pp. 63–69.

Anderson, Thom. "The Controversial Search for Value." *Saturday Review,* Dec. 26, 1964, pp. 18–19, 34.

Ansell, Gordon Brian. "Cinema for the Few." *Hollywood Quarterly* 2 (reprint, Berkeley: Univ. of California Press, 1946–47): pp. 179–83.

"Anything Goes: The Permissive Society." *Newsweek,* Nov. 13, 1967, pp. 74–78.

Armitage, Peter. "The Role of the Director." *Film,* Nov.-Dec. 1956, pp. 14–19.

———. "Free Criticism." *Film,* Mar.-Apr. 1961, pp. 8–10.

———. "The War of the Cults." *New York Film Bulletin* 2 (#12-14 1961): pp. 25–27.

Arnheim, Rudolph. "Who Is the Author of a Film?" *Film Culture,* Jan. 1958: pp. 11–13.

Astruc, Alexander. "What is Mise-en-Scene?" *Cahiers du Cinema in English* 1 (Jan. 1966): pp. 53–55.

Baker, Peter. "Focus on Festivals." *Films and Filming* 5 (July 1959): pp. 11, 30.

———. "Festival Fantasy." *Films and Filming* 7 (June 1961): p. 27.

———. "The Screen Answers Back." *Films and Filming* 8 (Apr. 1962): pp. 11, 45.

Bakshy, Alexander. "The Future of the Movies." *The Nation,* Oct. 10, 1928, pp. 360–61.

———. "The Talkies." *The Nation,* Feb. 20, 1929, pp. 236, 238.

———. "Dynamic Composition." *Experimental Cinema* 1 (Feb. 1930): pp. 2–3.

———. "Selling Sophistication." *The Nation,* Dec. 24, 1930, pp. 713–14.

———. "Emasculated Dreiser." *The Nation,* Sept. 2, 1931, p. 237.

Barbarow, George. "Anesthetic Film Criticism." *Hudson Review* 1 (autumn 1948): pp. 441–48.

Barr, Alfred. "Films and the Museum." *Museum of Modern Art Bulletin* 1 (Feb. 1934): p. 3.

Barrett, Wilton A. "The Work of the National Board of Review." *Annals of the American Academy of Political and Social Science* 128 (Nov. 1926): pp. 175–86.

Barry, Iris. "Hollywood Is Not America." *Sunday Review,* Mar. 11, 1934, pp. 8–9.

———. "The Founding of the Film Library." *Museum of Modern Art Bulletin* 3 (Nov. 1935): pp. 2–8.

———. "The Museum of Modern Art Film Library." *Sight and Sound* 5 (summer 1936): pp. 14–16.

———. "Works and Progress of the Film Library." *Museum of Modern Art Bulletin* 4 (Jan. 1937): pp. 2–12.

———. "Films." *Museum of Modern Art Bulletin* 5 (Apr.-May 1938): pp. 11–12.

———. "Film Library, 1935–1941." *Museum of Modern Art Bulletin* 8 (June-July 1941): pp. 3–13.

———. "Motion Pictures as a Field of Research." *College Art Journal* 4 (May 1945): p. 208.

———. "Why Wait for Posterity." *Hollywood Quarterly* 1 (Jan. 1946): pp. 131–37.

———. "The Film Library and How It Grew." *Film Quarterly* 22 (summer 1969): pp. 19–27.

Bauer, Leda. "The Movies Tackle Literature." *American Mercury*, July 1928, pp. 288–94.

———. "Movie Critics." *American Mercury*, Jan. 1929, pp. 71–74.

Baxter, Douglas L. "History of a New Art." *Scholastic*, Jan. 22, 1940, pp. 16–19T.

Bazin, André. "On the *Politique Des* Auteurs." *Cahiers du Cinema in English* 1 (Jan. 1966): pp. 8–18.

Behrman, S.N. "Movie Morals." *New Republic*, Aug. 25, 1917, pp. 100–1.

Beranger, Clara. "Motion Pictures as a Fine Art." *Theatre*, May 1919, pp. 300, 304.

Birkerts, Sven. "Cultural Hierarchies." *Partisan Review* 57 (spring 1990): pp. 317–21.

Block, Ralph. "The Movies *versus* Motion Pictures." *Century*, Oct. 1921, pp. 889–92.

———. "The Ghost of Art in the Movies." *New Republic*, May 14, 1924, pp. 310–12.

———. "Those Terrible Movies." *Theatre*, Feb. 1926, pp. 32, 52.

"The Birth of a New Art." *Independent*, Apr. 6, 1914, p. 8.

Blount, Jr., Roy. "Lustily Vigilant." *Atlantic Monthly*, Dec. 1994, pp. 131–43.

Boultenhouse, Charles. "The Camera as a God." *Film Culture*, summer 1963, pp. 20–22.

Bourne, Randolph S. "The Heart of the People." *New Republic*, July 3, 1915, p. 233.

Braun, Heywood. "Censoring the Censor." *Bookman*, May 1921, pp. 193–96.

Braver-Mann, Barnet G. "The Modern Spirit in Films." *Experimental Cinema* 1 (Feb. 1930): pp. 11–13.

———. "Josef von Sternberg." *Experimental Cinema* 5 (Feb. 1934): pp. 17–21.

Brustein, Robert. "The New Hollywood: Myth and Anti-Myth." *Film Quarterly* 12 (spring 1959): pp. 23–31.

Burt, Struthers. "God Rest You Merry Gentlemen." *Scribner's*, Aug. 1928, pp. 153–61.

Busch, Niven. "The Myth of the Movie Director." *Harper's*, Nov. 1946, pp. 452–56.

Bush, W. Stephen. "The Film of the Future." *Moving Picture World*, Sept. 5, 1908, pp. 172–73.

———. "Do Longer Films Make Better Shows?" *Moving Picture World*, Oct. 28, 1911, p. 275.

Callenbach, Ernest. "U.S. Film Journalism—A Survey." *Hollywood Quarterly* 5 (Reprint, Berkeley: Univ. of California Press, 1950–51): pp. 350–62.

———. "A New 'General Line'—for Critics." *Quarterly of Film, Radio, and Television* 9 (reprint, Berkeley: Univ. of California Press, 1954–55): pp. 374–79.

———. "Editor's Notebook." *Film Quarterly* 12 (spring 1959): pp. 2–3, 65.

———. "Editor's Notebook." *Film Quarterly* 13 (winter 1959): pp. 2–8.

———. "Editor's Notebook." *Film Quarterly* 13 (summer 1960): pp. 2–3.

———. "Editor's Notebook." *Film Quarterly* 14 (winter 1960): pp. 2–7.

———. "Editor's Notebook." *Film Quarterly* 14 (summer 1961): pp. 2–3.

———. "Turn On! Turn On!" *Film Quarterly* 15 (spring 1962), pp. 2–15.

———. "Looking Backward." *Film Quarterly* 22 (fall 1968): pp. 1–10.

———"Recent Film Writing: A Survey." *Film Quarterly* 24 (spring 1971): pp. 11–32.

Cameron, Ian A. "What's the Use?" *Film,* Mar.-Apr. 1961, pp. 10–11.

———. "All Together Now." *Film,* Sept.- Oct. 1969, pp. 12–13.

———, and Ian Jarvie. "Attack on Film Criticism." *Film,* Sept.-Oct. 1960, pp. 12–14.

———, V.F. Perkins, and Mark Shivas. "Oxford Opinion." *Film Quarterly* 14 (summer 1961): p. 64.

"Can Screen Writers Become Film Authors?" *Screen Writer* 3 (June 1947): pp. 34–38.

Carney, Raymond. "Writing in the Dark: Film Criticism Today." *Chicago Review* 34 (summer 1983), pp. 89–110.

Casty, Alan. "On Approaching the Film as Art." *Film Comment* 1 (summer 1963): pp. 28–34.

Catapano, Peter. "Creating 'Reel' Value: The Establishment of the MOMA'S Film Library, 1935–1937." *Film and History* 24 (Mar.-Apr. 1994): pp. 28–47.

Catling, Darrel. "Ourselves and Our Contemporaries." *Sight and Sound* 9 (spring 1940): pp. 16–17.

Cawelti, John. "Reviews." *American Quarterly* 20 (summer 1968): pp. 254–59.

———. "Notes Toward and Aesthetic of Popular Culture." *Journal of Popular Culture* 5 (fall 1971):pp. 255–68.

"Censorship and the Art of the Screen." *Exceptional Photoplays,* Nov. 1920, p. 6.

Chaplin, Charles. "Does the Public Know What It Wants?" *Ladies Home Journal,* Oct. 1923, pp. 40, 218.

———. "Can Art Be Popular?" *Ladies Home Journal,* Oct. 1924, pp. 34, 124.

Chayefsky, Paddy. "Art Films—Dedicated Insanity." *Saturday Review of Literature,* Dec. 21, 1957, pp. 16–17.

"A Checklist of World Film Periodicals." *Film Quarterly* 17 (winter 1963–64): pp. 49–50.

Chin, Daryl. "Festivals, Markets, Critics: Notes on the State of the Art Film." *Performing Arts Journal* 19 (winter 1997): pp. 61–75.

"Cinema as an International Art." *Time,* Sept. 20, 1963, pp. 78–82.

"Cinema of the New Generation." *Film Culture,* summer 1960: pp. 1–20.

"Cinema: The Film Maker as Ascendant Star." *Time,* July 4, 1969, p. 46.

"The Cinematography Craze." *Dial,* Feb. 16, 1914, pp. 129–31.

Clarke, Eric T. "The Special Feature for the Special Audience." *National Board of Review Magazine,* Mar. 1927, pp. 7–8.

——. "More Anent the Little Theatre." *National Board of Review Magazine,* Nov. 1927, p. 5.

Clayton, Bertram. "The Cinema and Its Censor." *Fortnightly,* Feb. 1921, pp. 222–28.

Cohen, Larry. "The New Audience: From Andy Hardy to Arlo Guthrie." *Saturday Review,* Dec. 27, 1969, p. 8.

Collins, Frederick. "Highbrow Hand-Me-Downs." *Saturday Evening Post,* Jan. 4, 1921, pp. 21, 93.

Corliss, Richard. "Richard Roud." *Film Comment* 25 (Mar.-Apr. 1989): pp. 78-79.

——. "70-Millimeter Nerves." *Film Comment* 23 (Sept.-Oct. 1987): 36–54.

"Correspondence and Controversy." *Film Quarterly* 17 (fall 1963): pp. 57–64.

Crichton, Kyle. "The View from the East." *Theatre Arts,* Aug. 1951, pp. 44, 83.

"The Critic." *Moving Picture World,* Jan. 15, 1910, p. 48.

"The Critic and the Box Office." *Sight and Sound* 14 (Apr. 1945): pp. 23–24.

"The Critical Issue: A Discussion Between Paul Rotha, Basil Wright, Lindsay Anderson, and Penelope Houston." *Sight and Sound* 27 (autumn 1958): pp. 271–75, 330.

Cross, Peter D. "Television—The End of Film?" *Sight and Sound* 17 (autumn 1948): pp. 131–32.

Crowther, Bosley. "It's the Fans Who Make the Films." *New York Times Magazine,* June 24, 1945, p. 30.

Culbert, Clifton. "An American Tragedy: Being a Chapter from 'Dreiser: A Critical Biography'." *Poet and the Critic* 1 (May 1930): pp. 29–36.

Dale, Alan. "Film Criticism in the Lay Press." *Moving Picture World,* May 20, 1911, p. 1.

"DeMille Foresees a Shakespeare for the Screen." *Current Opinion,* Sept. 1921, p. 318.

"A Democratic Art." *The Nation,* Aug. 28, 1913, p. 193.

Denby, David. "The Moviegoers." *New Yorker,* Apr. 6, 1998, pp. 94–101.

DiMaggio, Paul. *Sociological Review* 38 (Aug. 1990): pp. 608–12.

Dienstfrey, Harris. "Hitch Your Genre to a Star." *Film Culture,* fall 1964, pp. 35–37.

"Does the Public Know What It Wants?" *Theatre,* Aug. 1918, pp. 114–15.

Dreiser, Theodore. "Dreiser on Hollywood." *New Masses,* Jan. 1933, pp. 16–17.

——. "Letter to the Editors." *Experimental Cinema* 4 (Feb. 1933): p. 2.

————. "Myself and the Movies." *Esquire*, Oct. 1973, pp. 156, 382.

Durgnat, Raymond. "Who Really Makes the Movies? Where the Critics Go Wrong with the Auteur Theory." *Films and Filming* 11 (Apr. 1965): pp. 44–45.

Dyer, Peter John. "Counter Attack." *Film*, Nov.-Dec. 1960, pp. 8–9.

Eaton, Walter Prichard. "The Canned Drama." *American Magazine*, Sept. 1909, p. 499.

————. "Class-Consciousness and the 'Movies.'" *Atlantic Monthly*, Jan. 1915, pp. 48–56.

————. "The 'Art' of the Motion Picture." *Theatre*, Apr. 1917, pp. 218, 248.

"Editorial Statement." *Hollywood Quarterly* 1 (reprint, Berkeley: Univ. of California Press, 1945–46): p. 1.

Eisenstein, S. M. "An American Tragedy." *Close Up*, June 1933, pp. 109–24.

"Eisenstein and Hollywood." *New Republic*, Dec. 10, 1930, p. 103.

Espen, Hal. "Kael Talks." *New Yorker*, Mar. 21, 1994, pp. 134–43.

Evans, Montgomery. "The Movies and the Highbrows." *Bookman*, July 1928, pp. 533–37.

"Everybody Wants to Say It in Films." *Life*, Dec. 20, 1963, pp. 39–40.

"Editorial Statement." *Experimental Cinema* 4 (Feb. 1933): p. 1.

Fanning, Clara E. "Motion Pictures: A Brief for Debate." *Independent*, Mar. 5, 1917, pp. 426–27.

Farber, Manny. "Happiness Boys." *New Republic*, Feb. 28, 1944, p. 280.

————. "The Movie Art." *New Republic*, Oct. 26, 1942, pp. 546–47.

Farber, Stephen. "End of the Road?" *Film Quarterly*, winter 1969–1970, pp. 3–16.

————. "The Power of Movie Critics." *American Scholar*, summer 1976, pp. 419–23.

Farrell, James T. "The Language of Hollywood." *Saturday Review of Literature*, Aug. 5, 1944, pp. 29–32.

Ferguson, Otis. "Doldrum Weather." *New Republic*, Aug. 30, 1938, pp. 104–5.

"Film Archives." *Film Quarterly* 3 (summer 1935): pp. 220–22.

"Film Arts Em1-Em2." *Time*, Oct. 11, 1937, p. 36.

"Film Criticism in the Lay Press." *Moving Picture World*, May 20, 1911, p. 1113.

"Film Library of the New York Museum of Modern Art." *School and Society*, May 2, 1936, p. 591.

"Film Library of the New York Museum of Modern Art." *School and Society*, Apr. 16, 1938, p. 500.

"Film Museum." *Time*, July 1, 1935, p. 34.

"Films Reborn." *Literary Digest*, May 16, 1936, p. 23.

"Foreward." *Sight and Sound* 1 (spring 1932): pp. 1–4.

Fromm, Harold. "Cultural Power." *Georgia Review* 43 (spring 1989): pp. 179–88.

"The Front Page." *Sight and Sound* 26 (autumn 1956): p. 59.

Garis, Robert. "Art—Movie Style." *Commentary*, Aug. 1967, pp. 77–79.

Geruld, Katharine Fullerton. "The Lost Art of Motion-Pictures." *Century*, Aug. 1929, pp. 496–506.

Gilliatt, Penelope. "Only Films Are Truly Deep-Down Groovy." *New Yorker,* June 8, 1968, pp. 117–18.

Golden, Sylvia B. "The Best Talkie in Town." *Theatre,* May 1930, pp. 22, 60, 62.

Goldwyn, Samuel. "Television's Challenge to the Movies." *New York Times Magazine,* Mar. 26, 1950, pp. 17, 42.

Goodrich, Lloyd. "A Museum of Modern Art." *The Nation,* Dec. 4, 1929, pp. 664–65.

Gould, Symon. "The Little Theatre Movement in the Cinema." *National Board of Review Magazine,* Sept.-Oct. 1926, p. 4.

Griffith, D.W. "The Motion Picture To-day and To-morrow." *Theatre,* Oct. 1947, pp. 21, 58.

Griffith, Richard. "A Report on the Film Library." *Museum of Modern Art Bulletin* 24 (fall 1956): pp. 4–14.

"The Growing Fascination of the Film Play." *Current Opinion,* Sept. 1914, pp. 176–78.

Gunczy, Bettina. "The Bloodless Revolt." *National Board of Review Magazine,* May 1927, p. 3.

Guthrie, Tyrone. "Two Face Under One Hat." *Sight and Sound* 19 (Jan. 1950): pp. 22, 36.

Harris, Celia. "The Movies and the Elizabethan Theater." *Outlook,* Jan. 4, 1922, pp. 29–31.

Harrison, Louis Reeves. "Mr. Lowbrow." *Moving Picture World,* Oct. 7, 1911, p. 21.

———. "Playmaking." *Moving Picture World,* Oct. 21, 1911, p. 191.

———. "Mr. Critic." *Moving Picture World,* Oct. 28, 1911, p. 274.

———. "Over Their Heads." *Moving Picture World,* Nov. 11, 1911, p. 449.

———. "Both Entertaining and Educational." *Moving Picture World,* Sept. 7, 1912, p. 953.

———. "Too Deep." *Moving Picture World,* Oct. 4, 1913, p. 24.

———. "The Art of Criticism." *Moving Picture World,* Jan. 31, 1914, p. 521.

———. "Reviewing Photoplays." *Moving Picture World,* Dec. 19, 1914, p. 1652.

Hart, Henry. "NYC's First Film Festival: Appeared to Succeed with the Young but Disappoint the Adult." *Films in Review* 14 (Oct. 1963): pp. 449–50, 490.

Hatch, Robert. "Films." *The Nation,* Oct. 12, 1963, pp. 227–28.

Heckscher, August. "The Nation's Culture: A New Age for the Arts." *New York Times Magazine,* Sept. 23, 1962, pp. 15, 30–31.

Hine, Al. "Cinema 16." *Holiday,* Mar. 1954, pp. 26–27, 30.

Hitchens, Gordon. "The First New York Film Festival." *Film Comment* 1 (fall 1963): pp. 2–6.

Hodgins, Eric. "What's with the Movies?" *Life,* May 16, 1949, pp. 97–106.

"Hope of the Movies Seen in the Little Theater Movement." *Current Opinion,* Dec. 1921, pp. 762–63.

Hooker, Brian. "Shakspere [sic] and the Movies." *Century,* Dec. 1916, pp. 298–304.

Houseman, John. "Hollywood Faces the Fifties: The Lost Enthusiasm." Pt. 1. *Harper's,* Apr. 1950, pp. 50–59.

———. "Hollywood Faces the Fifties." Pt. 2. *Harper's,* May 1950, pp. 51–59.

Houston, Penelope. "Leading the Blind." *Sight and Sound* 18 (spring 1949): pp. 42–43.

———. "Hollywood in the Age of Television." *Sight and Sound* 26 (spring 1957): pp. 175–79.

———. "The Critical Question." *Sight and Sound* 29 (autumn 1960): pp. 160–65.

———. "Critic's Notebook." *Sight and Sound* 30 (spring 1961): pp. 62–66.

———. "Keeping Up with the Antonionis." *Sight and Sound* 33 (autumn 1964): pp. 163–68.

———. "Richard Roud." *Sight and Sound* 58 (winter 1988–89): pp. 103–4.

———, and Duncan Crow. "Into the Sixties." *Sight and Sound* 29 (winter 1959–60): pp. 4–8.

Hoveyda, Fereydoun. "*Les Taches du soleil.*" *Cahiers du Cinema* Aug. 1960, p. 37.

Howard, Jack. "Hollywood and Television—Year of Decision." *Quarterly of Film, Radio, and Television* 7 (summer 1953): pp. 359–69.

Howe, Irving. "The New York Intellectuals: A Chronicle and A Critique." *Commentary,* Oct. 1968, pp. 29-51.

Hubler, Richard G. "Opinion and the Motion Picture." *Screen Writer* 2 (Oct. 1946): pp. 25–28.

———. "A Pulitzer Prize for Motion Pictures." *Screen Writer* 2 (Jan. 1947): pp. 7–10.

Hursley, Frank. "An Evaluation of the *Screen Writer.*" *Screen Writer* 4 (June-July 1948): pp. 14–15, 22.

Hutchens, John. "L'Enfant Terrible: The Little Cinema Movement." *Theatre Arts Monthly,* Sept. 1929, pp. 694–97.

Ince, Thomas. "What Does the Public Want?" *Photoplay Magazine,* Jan. 1917, p. 66.

"Is It Art?" *National Board of Review Magazine,* Sept. 1927, p. 3.

"Is the Younger Generation in Peril?" *Literary Digest,* May 14, 1921, pp. 9–73.

Jackson, William Henry. "The Moving Picture 'World,'" *Moving Picture World,* June 4, 1910), pp. 931–32.

———. "The Moving Picture in Relation to the World." *Moving Picture World,* July 6, 1910), p. 135.

———. "The Value of Criticism." *Moving Picture World,* May 25, 1912, pp. 705–6.

Jacobs, Lea. "*An American Tragedy:* A Comparison of Film and Literary Censorship." *Quarterly Review of Film and Video* 15 (fall 1995): pp. 87–98.

Jacobs, Lewis. "Eisenstein." *Experimental Cinema* 3 (Feb. 1931): p. 4.

———. "The New Cinema: A Preface to Film Form." *Experimental Cinema* 1 (Feb. 1930): pp. 13–14.

Jackson, William Henry. "The Moving Picture 'World.'" *Moving Picture World,* June 4, 1910, p. 931.

Jameson, Charles. "The Endowed Photoplay." *Motion Picture Classic,* May 1919, pp. 26, 77.

Jarvie, Ian. "Preface to Film Criticism." *Film,* Sept.-Oct. 1960, pp. 13–14.

———. "Towards an Objective Film Criticism." *Film Quarterly* 14 (spring 1961): pp. 19–23.

———. "Comeback." *Film,* Mar.-Apr. 1961, p. 18.

Jean, Raymond. "Dialogue between the Movie-Going Public and a Witness for Jean Cocteau." *Film Quarterly* 10 (reprint, Berkeley: Univ. of California Press, 1955–56): pp. 160–66.

Johnson, Charles. "The Endowed Photoplay." *Motion Picture Classic,* May 1919, pp. 26, 77.

Johnson, Julian. "Close-Ups." *Photoplay Magazine,* July 1915, pp. 121–23.

———. "Aren't You Tired of Trash?" *Photoplay Magazine,* Oct. 1916, pp. 27, 63.

———. "I am the Motion Picture." *Photoplay Magazine,* Mar. 1917, p. 54.

———. "The Shadow Stage." *Photoplay Magazine,* Apr. 1917, pp. 75–77.

Josephson, Matthew. "Dreiser, Reluctant, in the Films." *New Republic,* Aug. 19, 1931, pp. 21–22.

Kael, Pauline. "Fantasies of the Art-House Audience." *Sight and Sound* 31 (winter 1961–62): pp. 4–9.

———. "Is there a Cure for Film Criticism? Or, Some Unhappy Thoughts on Siegfried Kracauer's *Theory of Film: The Redemption of Physical Reality.*" *Sight and Sound* 31 (spring 1962): pp. 56–64.

———. "Circles and Squares: Joys and Sarris." *Film Quarterly* 16 (spring 1963): pp. 12–26.

———. "Are the Movies Going to Pieces." *Atlantic,* Dec. 1964, pp. 61–66.

———. "It's Only a Movie." *Performing Arts Journal* 17 (May 1995): pp. 8–19.

Kanfer, Stefan. "The New Cinema: Violence . . . Sex . . . Art." *Time,* Dec. 8, 1967, pp. 66–75.

Kappler, Frank. "The Mixed Media—Communication that Puzzles, Excites, and Involves." *Life,* July 14, 1967, pp. 26–30.

Kauffmann, Stanley. "A Life in Reviews." *New Republic,* Dec. 1, 1958, pp. 18–19.

———. "An Intellectual and the Movies." *New Republic,* Jan. 22, 1962, pp. 16–17.

———. "End of an Inferiority Complex." *Theatre Arts,* Sept. 1962, pp. 67–70.

———. "After the Ball Was Over." *New Republic,* Oct. 5, 1963, pp. 33–36.

———. "Are We Doomed to Festivals?" *New Republic,* Oct. 2, 1965, pp. 30–32.

———. "A Lost Love?" *New Republic,* Sept. 8–15, 1997, p. 28.

Klawans, Stuart. "Mute and Glorious Miltons: On 'Cinematic Poetry' and Its Critics." *Parnassus* 22 (Jan.-Feb., 1997): pp. 78–96.

Knight, Arthur. "Art for Whose Sake?" *Journal for the Society of Cinematologists* 2 (1962): pp. 14–22.

———. "The Auteur Theory." *Saturday Review,* May 4, 1963, pp. 22.

Knight, Eric. "Moving Picture Goals." *Theatre Arts Monthly,* Jan. 1939, pp. 57–64.

Koch, Stephen. "The Cruel, Cruel Critics." *Saturday Review,* Dec. 26, 1970, pp. 12–15.

Kraft, Hy S. "Dreiser's War in Hollywood." *Screen Writer* 1 (Mar. 1946): pp. 9–13.

Krutch, Joseph Wood. "The Not So Hopeless Movies." *The Nation,* May 6, 1936, pp. 585–86.

Kuttner, Alfred. "Drama Comes Back from the Movies." *New Republic,* Aug. 14, 1915, pp. 51–52.

———. "Better Pictures." *Exceptional Photoplays,* Mar. 1921, p. 7.

———. "The Foreign Invasion." *Exceptional Photoplays,* Nov. 1921, pp. 1–2.

———. "Editorial Comment." *Exceptional Photoplays,* Mar.-Apr.-May, 1922, p. 9.

———. "Motion Pictures and the Photoplay." *Exceptional Photoplays,* Nov. 1922, p. 3.

———. "A Place for the Photoplay." *Exceptional Photoplays,* Dec. 1922, p. 3

———. "The Exceptional Photoplay." *Exceptional Photoplays,* Jan. 1923, p. 3

———. "Needed—One Free Screen on Broadway." *Exceptional Photoplays,* Feb. 1923, p. 3.

———. "A Question of Faith." *Exceptional Photoplays,* Oct.-Nov. 1923, p. 6.

———. "The Little Motion Picture Theatre." *National Board of Review Magazine,* May-June 1926, p. 3.

———. "Proof of the Pudding." *National Board of Review Magazine,* Nov. 1926, pp. 3–4.

———. "The Movies—Their Anatomy as an Entertainment." *National Board of Review Magazine,* May 1928, p. 4.

Lasky, Jesse. "Photoplays of Tomorrow." *Photoplay Magazine,* June 1915, pp. 101–2.

Lassally, Walter. "The Cynical Audience." *Sight and Sound* 26 (summer 1956): pp. 12–15.

"Lay Press and the Picture." *Moving Picture World,* Jan. 14, 1911, p. 69.

Laurot, Edouard de. "The Future of the New American Cinema." *Film Culture,* summer 1962, pp. 20–22.

Lears, T.J. Jackson. "Who Killed High Culture?" *Tikkun* 4 (Jan. 1989): pp. 70–74.

Lejeune, C.A. "On Not Being Committed." *Film and Filming,* June 1959, p. 9.

Leonard, Harold. "Hollywood." *Sight and Sound* 14 (July 1945): pp. 39–42.

———. "Recent American Film Writing." *Sight and Sound* 16 (summer 1947): pp. 73–75.

Leonard, Neil. "Theodore Dreiser and the Film." *Film Heritage* 2 (fall 1966): pp. 7–16.

Levinson, André. "The Nature of the Cinema." *Theatre Arts Monthly,* Sept. 1929, pp. 684–93.

Lindsay, Vachel. "Photoplay Progress." *New Republic,* Feb. 17, 1917, pp. 76–77.

———. "A Plea for the Art World." *Moving Picture World,* July 21, 1917, p. 368.

Lindgren, Ernest. "Nostalgia." *Sight and Sound* 9 (autumn 1940), pp. 49–51.

———. "Art of Our Age." *Sight and Sound* 19 (Apr. 1950): p. 89.

Lipsitz, George. "High Culture and Hierarchy." *American Quarterly,* Sept. 1991, pp. 518–24.

"The Literate Filmgoer." *Times Literary Supplement,* Apr. 30, 1964, p. 374.

Lounsbury, Myron O. "'Flashes of Lighting': The Moving Picture in the Progressive Era." *Journal of Popular Culture* 3 (spring 1970): pp. 769–97.

Lynes, Russell. "Flicks for the Fastidious." *Harper's,* June 1968, pp. 24–28.

Macdonald, Dwight. "Action on West Fifty-Third Street." Pt. 1. *New Yorker,* Dec. 12, 1953, pp. 49-82.

———. "Action on West Fifty-Third Street." Pt. 2. *New Yorker,* Dec. 19, 1953, pp. 35-72.

Macgowan, Kenneth. "Beyond the Screen." *Seven Arts* 1 (Dec. 1916): pp. 165-170.

———. "Cross-Roads of Screen and Stage." *Seven Arts* 1 (Apr. 1917): pp. 649-655.

———. "Keep the Lines Open." *Screen Writer* 1 (Feb. 1946): pp. 21-24.

Macklin, F. Anthony. "The Perils of Pauline's Criticism." *Film Heritage* 2 (fall 1966): pp. 1, 16–17.

MacMahon, Henry. "Big Shears—or Common Sense?" *Independent,* June 25, 1921, pp. 662, 679.

Madden, David. "The Necessity for an Aesthetics of Popular Culture." *Journal of Popular Culture* 7 (summer 1973): pp. 1–13.

Madsen, Axel. "Fission/Fusion/Fission." *Sight and Sound* 37 (summer 1968): pp. 124–26.

Magid, Marion. "Auteur! Auteur!" *Commentary,* Mar. 1964, pp. 70–74.

Mamoulian, Rouben. "The World's Latest Fine Art." *Cinema Arts* 1 (June 1937): pp. 15, 88.

Mankiewicz, Joseph L. "Film Author! Film Author!" *Screen Writer* 2 (May 1947): pp. 23–28.

Manvell, Roger. "Clearing the Air." *Hollywood Quarterly* 2 (reprint, Berkeley: Univ. of California Press, 1946-1947): pp. 174–78.

———. "A Forgotten Critic." *Sight and Sound* 18 (summer 1949): pp. 76–77.

Marchand, Roland. *Journal of American History* 76 (Sept. 1989): pp. 565–66.

Mayer, Arthur. "Are Moves 'Better than Ever?'" *Saturday Review of Literature,* June 17, 1950, pp. 34–38.

McBride, Joseph. "Mr. Macdonald, Mr. Kauffmann, and Miss Kael." *Film Heritage* 2 (summer 1967): pp. 26–34.

Mekas, Jonas. "Editorial." *Film Culture,* Jan. 1958: p. 1.

———. "A Call for a New Generation of Film Makers." *Film Culture,* Dec. 1959, pp. 1–3.

———. "Editorial." *Film Culture,* Jan. 1960, pp. 1–2.

———. "Notes on the New American Cinema." *Film Culture,* spring 1962, pp. 6–16.

Mellquist, Jerome. "Art of the People." *The Nation,* May 7, 1938, pp. 541–42.

Menand, Louis. "Finding it at the Movies." *New York Review of Books,* Mar. 23, 1995, pp. 10–17.

"The Modern Art Film Library Corporation." *School and Society,* July 6, 1935, p. 15.

Monaco, R.J. "You're Only as Young as They Think You Are." *Saturday Review,* Dec. 27, 1969, pp. 15–17.

"Morals and the Movies." *The Nation,* Apr. 20, 1921, p. 581.

Montagu, Ivor. "Birmingham Sparrow." *Sight and Sound* 37 (spring 1970): pp. 106–8.

"More Art." *National Board of Review Magazine,* Oct. 1927, p. 3.

"Movie vs. Kael." *Film Quarterly* 17 (fall 1963): pp. 1, 57–64.

"The Moving Picture and the Press." *Moving Picture World,* Mar. 8, 1913, p. 975.

"Moving Picture Shows as They Appeal to Our Critics—the Public." *Moving Picture World,* Jan. 4, 1908, pp. 4–5.

Munson, Lynne. "The New Museology." *National Interest,* spring 1997, pp. 60–70.

Noble, Peter. "A Survey of Film Periodical: Great Britain." Pt. 2. *Hollywood Quarterly* 3 (reprint, Berkeley: Univ. of California Press, 1947–48): pp. 140–51.

Oberholtzer, Ellis Paxson. "The Censor and the Movie 'Menace,'" *North American Review,* Nov. 1920, pp. 641–47.

O'Brien, Desmond. "Aspects of the Novelist." *Bookman,* Apr. 1933, pp. 7–8.

Pach, Walter. "Modern Art in Perspective." *The Nation,* Aug. 30, 1933, pp. 249–50.

Pardoe, F.E. "Film Critics and Criticism." *Sight and Sound* 14 (winter 1945–46): pp. 119–20.

Patterson, Frances Taylor. "Signs and Portents." *Exceptional Photoplays,* Apr. 1923, p. 4.

Patterson, Joseph Medill. "The Nickelodeons: The Poor Man's Elementary Course in the Drama." *Saturday Evening Post,* Nov. 23, 1907, pp. 10–11, 38.

"Pauline Kael: Abuser or Abused?" *Film Heritage* 2 (winter 1966–67): pp. 43–44.

Pearl, Jed. "A Quarter Century with Kael." *Yale Review* 81 (Apr. 1993): pp. 96–105.

"The Pearls of Pauline." *Time,* July 12, 1968, pp. 38–39.

Pearson, Ralph. "Why 'Modern'?" *New Republic,* Dec. 6, 1933, p. 104.

Pechter, William S. "Turn Off." *Film Quarterly* 15 (summer 1962): p. 62.

Peet, Creighton. "A Letter to Hollywood: In Reply to a Missive from a Producer." *Outlook and Independent*, Dec. 17, 1930, pp. 612–13, 632–37.

Pegge, C. Denis. "Another Forgotten Critic." *Sight and Sound* 18 (summer 1949): pp. 78–80.

Phelps, Donald. "Rosencrantz vs. Guildenstern." *Moviegoer* 1 (winter 1964): pp. 45–50.

Platt, David. "The New Cinema." *Experimental Cinema* 1 (Feb. 1930): 1–2.

———. "One Hour with Gilbert Seldes Is Too Much." *Experimental Cinema* 3 (Feb. 1931): pp. 19-20.

Podhoretz, John. "She Lost It at the Movies." *American Scholar*, winter 1989, pp. 117–22.

Potamkin, Harry Alan. "Novel into Film: A Case Study of Current Practice." *Close Up*, Dec. 1931, pp. 267–79.

Powell, Dilys. "The Importance of International Film Festivals." *Penguin Film Review* 3 (Aug. 1947): pp. 59–61.

Pratley, Gerald. "The Cult of the Unintelligible." *Hollywood Quarterly* 8 (spring 1954): pp. 302–6.

Quirk, James. "Art and Democracy." *Photoplay Magazine*, Apr. 1918, p. 19.

———. "The Fifth Estate." *Photoplay Magazine*, June 1918, p. 17.

———. "Realism v. Idealism." *Photoplay Magazine*, July 1918, pp. 75–76.

Rapf, Maurice. "Can Education Kill the Movies?" *Action* 2 (Sept.-Oct. 1967): pp. 10–11, 14–16.

Read, Herbert. "Towards a Film Aesthetic." *Cinema Quarterly* 1 (autumn 1932): pp. 7–11.

———. "The Poet and the Film." *Cinema Quarterly* 1 (summer 1933): pp. 197–202.

Reinhardt, Max. "Screen Visions." *National Board of Review Magazine*, Feb. 1928, p. 4.

"Replies to a Questionnaire." *Sight and Sound* 23 (Apr.-June 1953): pp. 99–103.

"Report from the Editors." *Hollywood Quarterly* 2 (reprint, Berkeley: Univ. of California Press, 1946–47): pp. 220–24.

Resnik, Harry. "A Seismic Moment in Cinematic History." *Saturday Review*, Apr. 4, 1970, pp. 23–28, 38.

"Return to Meaning." *Film Heritage* 2 (summer 1967): pp. 1–2, 36–39.

Richardson, Dorothy. "Talkies, Plays and Books." *Vanity Fair*, Aug. 1929, p. 56.

Robertson, William. "The World Likes American Films." *Sight and Sound* 17 (summer 1948): pp. 91–92.

Rosenfeld, Paul. "Bread Lines and a Museum." *The Nation*, Feb. 11, 1931, pp. 160–62.

Rosenheimer, Arthur Jr. "A Survey of Film Periodicals: The United States and England." Pt. 1. *Hollywood Quarterly* 2 (July 1947): pp. 338–52.

Roud, Richard. "Face to Face: James Agee." *Sight and Sound* 28 (spring 1959): pp. 98–100.

————. "Face to Face: André Bazin." *Sight and Sound* 28 (summer 1959): pp. 176–79.

————. "The French Line." *Sight and Sound* 29 (autumn 1960): pp. 167–71.

"Sanctuary for Film Art." *Literary Digest*, Jan. 11, 1936, p. 22.

Sankowski, Edward. "Art Museums, Autonomy, and Canons." *Monist*, Oct. 1993, pp. 535–55.

Sarris, Andrew. "The Director's Game." *Film Culture*, summer 1961, pp. 68–81.

————. "The High Forties Revisited." *Film Culture*, spring 1962: pp. 62–70.

————. "The American Cinema." *Film Culture*, spring 1963, pp. 1–51.

————. "The Autuer Theory and the Perils of Pauline." *Film Quarterly* 16 (summer 1963): pp. 26–33.

————. "Pop Go the Movies!" *Moviegoer* 2 (summer/fall 1964): pp. 24–34.

————. "The Farthest-Out Moviegoers." *Saturday Review,* Dec. 26, 1964, pp. 14–15.

————. "*Cahiers* in Context." *Cahiers du Cinema in English* 1 (Jan. 1966): pp. 5–18.

————. "Editor's Eyrie." *Cahiers du Cinema* 1 (1966), pp. 79-80.

————. "Notes on the Auteur Theory in 1970." *Film Comment*, 6 (fall 1970), pp. 7-9.

————. "Sarris vs. Kael: The Queen Bee of Film Criticism." *Village Voice*, July 2–8, 1980, pp. 1, 30–31, 70.

————. "Why the Foreign Film Has Lost Its Cachet," *New York Times*, May 2, 1999, pp. 15, 35.

Schickel, Richard. "A Way of Seeing a Picture." *New York Times Book Review,* Mar. 14, 1965, p. 6.

————. "The Movies are Now High Art." *New York Times Magazine*, Jan. 5, 1969, pp. 32–44.

————. "Movie Studies: Read All About It." *Harper's*, Mar. 1971, pp. 24–38.

————. "Cinema Paradiso." *Wilson Quarterly*, 23 (summer 1999), pp. 23–28.

Schillaci, Anthony. "Film as Environment." *Saturday Review,* Dec. 28, 1968, p. 8.

Schofield, Stanley. "They Built a Cathedral." *Sight and Sound* 14 (winter 1945–46): p. 129.

Schreiber, Flora Rheta. "New York—Cinema Capital." *Hollywood Quarterly* 7 (Reprint, Berkeley: Univ. of California Press, 1952–53): pp. 264–73.

Schlesinger. Arthur M. Jr. "The Plugged-In Generation." *Book Week,* Mar. 19, 1967, pp. 1–2.

Schuman, William. "The Idea: A Creative, Dynamic Force." *New York Times Magazine,* Sept. 23, 1962, pp. 1, 34–35, 38.

Seldes, Gilbert. "The Path of the Movies." *The Nation*, Apr. 29, 1925, pp. 498–99.

————. "'Art' in the Movies." *The Nation,* July 29, 1925, p. 148.

————. "A Letter to the International Film Art Guild." *New Republic,* Nov. 18, 1925, pp. 332–33.

———. "The Movies and the Masses." *New Republic,* June 8, 1927, pp. 61–62.

———. "The Movies Commit Suicide." *Harper's,* Nov. 1928, pp. 706–12.

———. "The Other Side of It." *Century,* July 1929, pp. 297–02.

———. "Talkies' Progress." *Harper's,* Nov. 1929, pp. 454–61.

———. "The Movies in Peril." *Scribner's,* Feb. 1935, pp. 81–86.

———. "Motion Pictures." *Scribner's,* Nov. 1937, pp. 63–64.

———. "The Impact of Television on Motion Pictures." *Film Culture,* Oct. 1957, pp. 3–6, 20.

Shaw, George Bernard and Archibald Henderson. "The Drama, the Theater, and the Films." *Harper's,* Sept. 1924, pp. 426–35.

Shaw, Robert. "New Horizons in Hollywood." *Public Opinion Quarterly* 10 (spring 1946): pp. 71–77.

Sheed, Wilfrid. "Cinema's Last Stand." *Commonweal,* Oct. 25, 1963, pp. 136, 138.

———. "The Good Word: Kael vs. Sarris vs. Simon." *New York Times Book Review,* Mar. 7, 1971, pp. 2, 42.

Sheldon, Rowland C. "Moving Pictures, Books, and Child Crime." *Bookman,* May 1921, pp. 242–44.

Sherwood, Herbert Francis. "Democracy and the Movies." *Bookman,* May 1918, pp. 235–39.

Sherwood, Robert E. "Renaissance in Hollywood." *American Mercury,* Apr. 1929, pp. 431–37.

"The Silent Stage." *Moving Picture World,* Feb. 20, 1909, p. 199.

Siska, William. "Movies and History." *Film Heritage* 4 (summer 1969): pp. 27–32.

Skinner, Otis. "The Motion Pictures Not an Art." *Ladies Home Journal,* May 1922, pp. 7, 89–90, 93.

Smith, Edward H. "Dreiser—After Twenty Years." *Bookman,* Mar. 1921, pp. 27–39.

Smythe, Dallas W., Parker B. Lusk, and Charles A. Lewis. "Portrait of an Art-Theater Audience." *Quarterly of Film, Radio, and Television* 8 (reprint, Berkeley: Univ. of California Press, 1953–54): pp. 29–50.

Sontag, Susan. "A Century of Cinema." *Parnassus* 22 (Jan.-Feb., 1997): pp. 23–28.

———. "The Decay of Cinema." *New York Times Magazine,* Feb. 25, 1996, p. 60.

Spearing, James O. "A Valuable Service." *Exceptional Photoplays,* Mar.-Apr.-May, 1922, pp. 1–2.

Staples, Donald E. "The Autuer Theory Reexamined." *Cinema Journal* 6 (1966–67): pp. 1–7.

———. "La Politique des Auteurs—The Theory and Its Influence on the Cinema." *Language and Style* 3 (fall 1970): pp. 303–11.

"Statement." *Experimental Cinema* 3 (Feb. 1931): p. 1.

Steel, Ronald. "Film Festival at the Concert Hall." *Christian Century,* Dec. 11, 1963, pp. 1150–54.

―――. "Film Scholars at the New York Film Festival." *Film Comment* 2 (fall 1964): pp. 41–43.

Steele, Robert. "Film Scholars at the New York Film Festival." *Film Comment* 2 (fall 1964): pp. 41–45.

Steiner, Shari. "Europe and America: A Question of Self-Image." *Saturday Review,* Dec. 27, 1969, pp. 18–20.

Stern, Seymour. "Hollywood." *Experimental Cinema* 2 (June 1930): p. 12.

Stewart, David C. "Movies on the Campus." *Saturday Review,* Feb. 20, 1965, pp. 82–83.

Strychacz, Thomas. "Dreiser's Suit Against Paramount: Authorship, Professionalism, and the Hollywood Film Industry." *Prospects* 18 (1993): pp. 187–203.

"There Is Nothing New Under the Sun—Not Even the 'Movies'." *Current Opinion,* Sept. 1915, pp. 172–73.

"Theodore Dreiser." *New Republic,* Apr. 22, 1931, p. 258.

"Theodore Dreiser Again." *Commonweal,* Apr. 22, 1931, pp. 677.

Thompson, Kenneth. "Criticism and Opinion." *Sight and Sound* 16 (summer 1947): pp. 71–72.

Toeplitz, Jerzy. "Film Scholarship: Present and Prospective." *Film Quarterly* 16 (spring 1963): pp. 27–36.

Twomey, John E. "Some Considerations on the Rise of the Art-Film Theater." *Hollywood Quarterly* 10 (reprint, Berkeley: Univ. of California Press, 1955–56): pp. 239–47.

"Tragicomedy of 'American Tragedy'." *Literary Digest,* Sept. 5, 1931, pp. 18–19.

Troy, William. "The Einstein Muddle." *The Nation,* July 19, 1933, pp. 83–84.

―――. "Infancy of an Art." *The Nation,* Jan. 29, 1936, p. 118.

―――. "The Film Library." *The Nation,* July 24, 1938, p. 112.

Truffaut, François. "A Certain Tendency of the French Cinema." *Cahiers du Cinema in English* 1 (Jan. 1966): pp. 31–41.

Van Doren, Mark. "Let the Movies Be Natural." *American Scholar,* autumn 1936, pp. 435–44.

Van Dyke, Williard. "The Role of the Museum of Modern Art in Motion Pictures." *Film Library Quarterly* 1 (winter 1967–68), pp. 36–38.

Vaughan, Dai, and Phillip Riley. "Letters from the Trenches." *Film,* Jan.-Feb. 1961, pp. 9–11.

Vidal, Gore. "Who Makes the Movies?" *New York Review of Books,* Nov. 25, 1976, pp. 35–39.

Vogel, Amos. "Film Do's and Don'ts." *Saturday Review,* Aug. 20, 1949, pp. 32–34.

―――. "Cinema 16: A Showcase for the Nonfiction Film." *Hollywood Quarterly* 4 (reprint, Berkeley: Univ. of California Press, 1949–50): pp. 420–22.

Wald, Malvin. "Who is the Film Author." *Cineaste* 2 (winter 1968–69): pp. 11–12.

Warner, Harry P. "Television and the Motion Picture Industry." *Hollywood Quarterly* 2 (reprint, Berkeley: Univ. of California Press, 1946–47): pp. 11–18.

Warshow, Paul. "Review of *The American Cinema: Directors and Directions, 1929–1968,* by Andrew Sarris." *Commentary,* Oct. 1969, pp. 89–94.

Wilson, Edmund. "Eisenstein in Hollywood." *New Republic,* Nov. 4, 1931, pp. 320–22.

Wilson, Norman. "The Spectator." *Cinema Quarterly* 1 (autumn 1932): pp. 3–5.

———. "Film Societies—The Next Phase." *Sight and Sound* 14 (July 1945): pp. 37–38.

Woolf, Virginia. "The Movies and Reality." *New Republic,* Aug. 4, 1926, pp. 308–10.

Worland, Rick, "Politics, Film Studies, and the Academy: A Commentary." *Journal of Film and Video* 46 (winter 1995): pp. 42–56.

Yerril, D.A. "On Film Critics." *Sight and Sound* 17 (summer 1948): pp. 98–99.

"Yes, There Is No Art in the Movies?" *Current Opinion,* Jan. 1924, pp. 73–74.

Young, Colin. "An American Film Institute: A Proposal." *Film Quarterly* 14 (summer 1961): pp. 37–50.

———. "A Special Report on the American Film Institute." *Film Society Newsletter,* Dec. 1964, pp. 5, 15–16.

Index